KITCHENER'S
MOB

PETER DOYLE AND CHRIS FOSTER

KITCHENER'S MOB

THE NEW ARMY TO THE SOMME

'Kitchener's Mob' they were called in the early days of
August 1914, when London hoardings were clamorous with
the first call for volunteers. The seasoned regulars of the
first British expeditionary force said it patronisingly, the
great British public hopefully, the world at large doubtfully.
'Kitchener's Mob', when there was but a scant sixty thousand
under arms with millions yet to come.

Private James Norman Hall, 9th (Service) Battalion, Royal Fusiliers

First published 2016

The History Press
The Mill, Brimscombe Port
Stroud, Gloucestershire, GL5 2QG
www.thehistorypress.co.uk

British Library Cataloguing in Publication Data.
A catalogue record for this book is available from the British Library.

ISBN 978 0 7509 6495 1

Typesetting and origination by The History Press
Printed in China

CONTENTS

Foreword by Professor Peter Simkins MBE, FRHistS   7

Acknowledgements   10

1   Men of the Moment   11

2   Kitchener's Men   54

3   Pals   91

4   Road to the Somme   162

5   End of an Experiment   198

Bibliography   206

Notes   213

Index   222

FOREWORD

The British Army in the Great War was not only the largest that this country has ever placed in the field but also the biggest single organisation created by the nation up to that time. In all, 5,704,416 served in its ranks between August 1914 and November 1918, of whom 4,970,902 – representing around 22 per cent of the male population of the United Kingdom – joined after the outbreak of war. Remarkably, 2,446,719 of those who enlisted between August 1914 and the end of 1915 were volunteers who responded to the successive appeals for recruits issued by Field Marshal Lord Kitchener, then the Secretary of State for War. The total of recruits secured by voluntary means in 1914–15 was actually higher than that obtained by conscription in 1916 and 1917 combined. Moreover, the number brought into the army by the compulsory system in 1918 was barely 30,000 more than the total of volunteers attested in just one month in September 1914.

Thanks to those impressive figures, Kitchener and the War Office were able to add five 'New Armies', comprising thirty divisions, to Britain's military strength; the organisation of each New Army being modelled upon the six infantry divisions of the original British Expeditionary Force (BEF) which had crossed the Channel in 1914. All but two of the New Army divisions would see action in France and Belgium at some stage in the conflict. Simultaneously, the Territorial Force (TF) – ostensibly intended for home defence – was allowed by Kitchener to raise fresh second- and third-line formations and undertake active service overseas. Seven of the fourteen second-line Territorial divisions thus produced would also go on to fight on the Western Front. Besides all the artillery, engineer, medical and other units required to complete every division, as many as 994 infantry battalions sprang into existence during Kitchener's tenure of office from August 1914 to June 1916. If one excludes the new Territorial battalions, 557 so-called 'Service' and 'Reserve' battalions were produced for the New Armies in this period.

This huge and rapid expansion of Britain's military forces in the midst of a major war – and achieved in spite of all the previous deficiencies in experience and preparation – represented a truly colossal act of national improvisation which gave the country its first ever mass citizen army. The problem was that, at the outset, there was no existing blueprint or appropriate plan for a corresponding mobilisation of Britain's industrial and manufacturing resources. As Peter Doyle and Chris Foster graphically illustrate in their valuable new study, many of the men of Kitchener's Army therefore suffered for some months – and particularly during the early phases of their training – from severe shortages of weapons, uniforms, equipment and accommodation.

In these circumstances, Kitchener and the War Office came to depend to an increasing degree on practical support from voluntary civilian organisations and ad hoc committees of leading local citizens throughout the British Isles. Such support manifested itself, above all, in the formation of the Pals battalions which were principally raised by local authorities, dignitaries and industrialists and were generally composed, at least in the beginning, of men who lived in a specific city or district, who shared a common social, occupational or geographical background, and who were attracted to enlist by the idea that they might be able to train and fight alongside their friends, neighbours or workmates. Ultimately 215, or 38 per cent, of the 557 Service and Reserve infantry battalions formed for the New Armies from August 1914 to June 1916 were locally raised by bodies other than the War Office.

There was nothing fundamentally new about the Pals concept in 1914, as many first-line Territorial and (before 1908) Volunteer rifle units had traditionally drawn whole companies of men from the same workplace or community. The chief difference was that in 1914, with the emergence of the Pals battalions, the idea was applied for the first time on a truly significant scale to the raising of units for active service abroad rather than home defence. Moreover, the birth of the Pals battalions in late August and September 1914 altered the patterns of enlistment, offering individual communities additional ways in which to express their patriotism by producing more new units with a clear local identity.

When the challenges of war fused with the peculiar combination of accelerating urbanisation, civic pride, lingering parochialism and local loyalties and rivalries that characterised early twentieth-century Britain, the mix proved irresistible and the Pals concept swiftly took hold, especially in industrial northern England. Peter Doyle and Chris Foster underline the fact that, in many respects, men joining Pals units were better off during the early weeks of their training than their counterparts in battalions recruited directly by the War Office, since the raisers of

Pals battalions were able to exploit the machinery of local government, and their knowledge of local manufacturers and conditions, to ensure the more efficient provision of uniforms, equipment, transport and accommodation.

Recent research has indicated that the losses suffered by the Pals battalions on the Somme in 1916 had more impact on social and occupational groups in particular towns and cities, rather than on people and families with a shared *residential* background. My own recent investigations into the performance of the New Armies on the Somme point to the fact that, in attacks against meaningful opposition, the Pals formations of the Fourth and Fifth New Armies had, in general, lower success rates in battle than the divisions raised directly by the War Office. This would seem to suggest that the social cohesion and community bonds of the Pals battalions did not necessarily guarantee operational success.

What is certain is that the unique localised character of the BEF of July 1916 did not survive the Somme. Mounting losses, the advent of compulsory military service and changes in the reserve and drafting system all meant that the replacement of casualties from a parent regiment or community was no longer assured, and the local identity of units was inevitably diluted as the war entered its third and fourth years. Even so, the courage and sacrifice of Kitchener's Army, on the Somme in particular, remains firmly lodged in the popular conception as a potent symbol of the perceived futility and waste of the First World War. I would argue, conversely, that the expansion of the army in 1914–15 laid the foundations for a force that eventually proved capable of waging a modern industrialised war on a continental scale and of beating the main enemy in the decisive theatre of operations – the Western Front.

Peter Doyle and Chris Foster, in this timely, scholarly and eminently readable new book, have splendidly captured and portrayed the very essence of those heady days of August and September 1914 when Kitchener's Army was being raised. As someone with a long established interest in Britain's New Armies, I am both flattered and delighted to be invited to contribute a foreword to this refreshing new study of the subject.

Professor Peter Simkins MBE, FRHistS
Author of *Kitchener's Army: The Raising of the New Armies, 1914–16*

ACKNOWLEDGEMENTS

We are grateful to all those who have assisted us in writing this book and their enthusiastic support of it – particularly to Jo De Vries, who was a keen advocate of the concept. We are indebted to Professor Peter Simkins, who kindly wrote our foreword, and to all those who responded to requests for help and assistance along the way, particularly: Alan Jeffreys of the Imperial War Museum, London, for access to collections in his care; Taff Gillingham, for assistance and advice on uniforms; Paul Reed, for advice and assistance; Keith Bartlett, of the Durham Pals Living History Group; Dr Bill Smith, for the supply of images and information on Tunstill's Men, Henry Bolton for access to his albums relating to these men, and Robert Smith for the image of the 'Kitchener's Man' armband; Kevin Thomas for the images of the insignia of the two Cardiff battalions; Neil Pearce for the picture of the Cardiff Pals fundraising badge; Stephen McGreal for the Bigland's Birkenhead Bantams badge; Julian Walker for obtaining copies of obscure publications; Dorrien Thomas for the loan of books on the Welsh Pals battalions; Mike Stockbridge for assistance with Pals sweetheart brooches; Francesca Fergusson for assistance transcribing soldiers' diaries; Beverley Whent for the gift of the Kitchener memorial card; and Rob Schäfer for advice on German views of Kitchener's men.

We are grateful also for all those authors who have plotted out the journey of the Pals battalions, and in particular Laurie Milner, who provided access to his collection of artefacts and ephemera, and the late Graham Maddocks.

Except where indicated, images are from our own collections, or were specially shot for this book. As always we reserve our greatest thanks for those who have supported us on our journey with love.

1

MEN OF THE MOMENT

'There's old Kitchener wants you,' he says, 'for your King and your Country need you,' says he. 'Them as goes now,' says he, 'will be bloomin' British heroes.'[1]

The Old Army was the nation in miniature. The New Army is the nation itself.[2]

With the outbreak of war and the appointment of Lord Kitchener as the man of the moment – Secretary of State for War – the raising of a mass army was of the greatest importance. Field Marshal Lord Kitchener of Khartoum (or simply, K of K) was seen universally as a hero.[3] At the age of 64 in 1914, he was a serious man of intent. He certainly struck an imposing figure. Looking as if he was born to wear a uniform, his military moustache enhanced his bearing. Equipped with steel blue eyes – though with a noticeable cast in the left one – his stern gaze would become internationally famous when the world erupted into war.

Trained as a military engineer, Herbert Kitchener was well suited to service overseas. From 1874 onwards, rising through the ranks, he worked on surveys in Palestine and Cyprus before arriving in Egypt in 1883 in time to witness the siege of Khartoum and the death of General Gordon. Within ten years Kitchener had worked his way through to command the Egyptian Army as its sirdar, fighting the 'Mad Mahdi' at the Battle of Omdurman in 1898 and avenging the death of General Gordon at Khartoum in 1895.

Man of the moment: Field Marshal Lord Kitchener.

A contemporary commentator serving with this earlier incarnation of Kitchener's Army described him thus:

> That morning I for the first time met the Sirdar – General Sir Herbert Kitchener ... His was a striking presence – every inch of him a soldier, above the average height of men, and with a face that told of an indomitable will and clear intellect. He was evidently a man of deeds rather than words.[4]

Though not a trained staff officer, here he would also demonstrate organisational skills – applied under his own rules – that would be of great value later.[5] In South Africa, as commander-in-chief from 1900, Kitchener showed his realistic determination to win at all costs. He removed the capability of the Boer armies to move unchecked across the veldt. After peace was signed in South Africa, the general served as commander-in-chief in India and was promoted to field marshal in 1909, returning to Egypt in 1911. In that fateful summer of 1914, Kitchener was at home in England. He would be called once more for his country's service.[6]

At the outbreak of war, the Liberal prime minister, Herbert Henry Asquith, was also the Secretary of State for War. He had taken this unusual step because of what amounted to a rebellion of officers in Ireland, men opposed to the introduction of Home Rule. The Curragh incident of 20 March 1914 had undermined the credibility of the War Office, when a pledge was given that in the face of rebellion the army would not commit to a battle against the paramilitary Ulster Volunteer Force (UVF) – raised to defend the rights of Protestant Ulstermen.

It had started with the commander-in-chief in Ireland, Sir Arthur Paget, sounding out his officers as to whether they would be prepared to face the UVF if they were to march on Dublin in defiance of the Home Rule Bill. With many dissenting voices, Paget had claimed that he was acting with the express permission of the Secretary of State for War, J.E.B. Seely, when he said that these men – many of whom had homes in Ulster – might be allowed to 'disappear' when action was to be taken against the UVF. With the officers of the 5th and 16th Lancers refusing to move against the Ulstermen, and with Brigadier General Sir Hubert Gough amongst them, there was serious concern that this amounted to a mutiny when Paget issued orders to the effect of 'duty as ordered – Active Operations in Ulster', on 20 March. His officers, and Gough, had all resigned before refusing to carry out the orders.

With serious cracks opening, the matter was smoothed over. The Secretary of State was forced to resign, as was the Chief of the General Staff (CIGS) Sir John French – a man who had issued a warning in 1913 that there might be resistance from some officers to facing the Ulstermen if called upon to do so.[7] Both had colluded with the 'mutineers', had softened their stance, and become embroiled in Irish politics. To prevent other such mishaps, Asquith took over the reins of the War Office on the brink of a war that would consume many of the men who had opposed Irish Home Rule – as well as those who supported it.

Yet, with war declared on 4 August 1914, leading the country and prosecuting a conflict with a determined enemy were just too much to ask of one man. Writing in his diary, Asquith recorded his views a day later:

August 5. I have taken an important decision to-day; to give up the War Office and install Kitchener there as an emergency man until the war comes to an end.[8]

This matter-of-fact statement was to have far-reaching ramifications. Kitchener was not a politician. He was not a man of many words and he was not a man to be trifled with. But he had other qualities required in wartime:

He was, however, a leader, in the sense of filling all those who served under him with deep confidence, through his brilliant intuition, his unrivalled capacity for improvisation and his immense force of character.[9]

Kitchener took up the commission in the spirit of doing his duty for his country, and was not impressed when he first arrived in Whitehall:

He entered his duties on August 6 ... his first appearance at the War Office. A specimen of his signature was required; pen and paper were put in front of him, but the pen refused to work. With a gesture of impatience the new Secretary of State flung it from him – 'What a War Office. Not a scrap of Army and not a pen that will write!'[10]

With the six Regular infantry divisions and one cavalry division of the British Expeditionary Force – a strike force capable of being deployed overseas created during the Haldane reforms – already being committed to the Western Front as part of Britain's support of the French in 1914, there was little left in reserve. There were Regulars posted across the globe on colonial service, and there were the volunteer, part-time Territorial Force battalions whose original destiny under the Haldane reforms was service at home.

For an experienced soldier who had seen the realities of war fighting against colonial rebellions the idea of facing a determined, highly trained and superbly organised army with such limited resources was anathema. The German Army was at the peak of its development and, as described by G.W. Steevens in 1897, a military machine with one intent – winning:

LORD KITCHENER.

Minister of War.　　　　Le Ministere pour la Guerre, Angleterre.

Kitchener as Secretary of State for War.

The cult of personality: Kitchener's famous Bassano photograph reproduced in ceramic, 1914.

The task facing the new Secretary of State was a huge one. Winston Churchill, Kitchener's opposite number as First Lord of the Admiralty, recorded his impressions of the man who would shape the army that would eventually bear his name:

> Lord Kitchener now came forward to the Cabinet, on almost the first occasion after he joined us, and in soldierly sentences proclaimed a series of inspiring and prophetic truths. Everyone expected that the war would be short; but wars took unexpected courses, and we must now prepare for a long struggle. Such a conflict could not be ended by sea power alone. It could only be ended only by great battles on the Continent. In these the British Empire must bear its part on a scale proportionate to its magnitude and power. We must be prepared to put armies of millions in the field and maintain them for several years. In no other way could we discharge our duty to our allies or to the world.[12]

As Kitchener's words sank in, so did the realisation of the nation's commitment. The new Secretary of State was one step ahead. He knew that there was no choice. He would start afresh and build an army of volunteers that would give him the raw material of the greatest army that Britain ever produced. Churchill continued:

> The German Army is the most perfectly adapted, perfectly running machine. Never can there have been a more signal triumph of organisation over complexity. The armies of other nations are not so completely organised. The German Army is the finest thing of its kind in the world; it is the finest thing in Germany of any kind. Briefly, the difference between the German and, for instance, the English armies is a simple one. The German Army is organised with a view to war, with the cold, hard, practical, business-like purpose of winning victories. And what should we ever do if 100,000 of this kind of army got loose in England?[11]

> He set himself to create the cadres of six, then of twelve, and ultimately twenty-four 'Kitchener Army' divisions, at the same time that the recruits were pouring in on him by the hundred thousand. That this vast feat of improvisation was accomplished must certainly rank among the wonders of the time.[13]

THE BIRTH OF KITCHENER'S ARMY

The story of the New Armies is the story of Britain's unreadiness for war and of her enormous energy when roused to battle.[14]

In 1914 the country soon became gripped with war fever. Patriotic songs became popular, and merchandise and advertising took on a war slant. Flags were flown and carried, and the atmosphere was one of uncertainty but excitement. The road to war had been a tortuous one, and with the idyll that was England in the summer of this momentous year, the build-up to war from an unfortunate affair in the Balkans must have been watched with trepidation.

After the assassination of the Archduke Franz Ferdinand on 28 June 1914, relationships on the continent had become tense. With the Austrian declaration of war upon Serbia (accused of being complicit in the Archduke's murder) a month later, and the mobilisation of Russia in support of its ally, the path for the German Empire was plain – it would have to put into action the Schlieffen Plan to ensure that a much dreaded long war on two fronts could be prevented.

With Germany, under Kaiser Wilhelm II, threatening British control of the high seas through his desire for a new navy, and Austria–Hungary under threat from the emerging and belligerent Balkan states in the late nineteenth and early twentieth centuries, there was growing uncertainty over the security of Europe. For Britain, traditionally isolated and aloof from continental neighbours, the development of the Entente Cordiale of 1904 settled many simmering and long-standing resentments over colonial possessions, hangovers from a century or so before.

Kitchener's Army enters the popular imagination. Here, on a trade card.

It marked the end of Britain's isolationism and the birth of the nation's involvement in mainland Europe. And with the Kaiser's increased interest in building the *Kaiserliche Marine* to threaten the power of the Royal Navy, there was added security in aligning with another major power – France. Having tidied up colonial issues with France, Britain did the same with Russia – France's ally since 1894 – as part of the Anglo-Russian Convention of 1907. From these steps was born the Triple Entente: all three nations bound together by intent to counterbalance the threat of the central European nations' Triple Alliance.

And with this, in 1914, came the response to the enactment of the Schlieffen Plan that would see Belgian neutrality and sovereignty ignored and bring Britain to the war. As the German armies swept through northern Europe, any suspected acts of 'terrorism' were dealt with severely, with summary executions and homes put to the torch, as the armies wheeled in an arc in their attempts to encircle Paris.

In the wake of these actions, the Allied propaganda machine moved into top gear. The crimes perpetrated by the Germans were given a new spin, and were presented as inhuman acts of savagery against the innocent. The British turned to this task with gusto, and posters, political cartoonists and leader writers all fell upon the ever more extreme 'horrors and atrocities' in an attempt to build up national indignation and bolster recruitment.[15]

Yet, despite this outpouring of bile, recruitment in the early part of the war had been steady – but unspectacular. The fact was, there had been a decline in recruitment to the British Army in the pre-war period; so much so that it had been a point of concern for some years. The reforms brought in by Haldane in 1906–08 had been intended to create a clear structure for the army that would

guarantee a recruitment base tied to a regional depot, and there had never yet been the need for compulsion to join the army. But increasingly there was a growing shortfall in the number of men signing on for service with the Colours.

Shifting to a continental model of compulsion and national service was one option – but one that went against the grain. From medieval times the armies of the British Isles had been volunteers, raised by monarchs and feudal leaders. Though compelled to serve at times of emergency, gathered in local militias or trained bands they were individual in spirit and appearance. It was Oliver Cromwell's New Model Army of May 1645 that sowed the seeds of the modern Regular army. Though formally disbanded during the restoration of Charles II, many of its regiments would be taken into the king's service. And over time, new corps would be added to the military roster at times of national emergency. Kitchener's Army would fall into this category.

The British Army proper was born following the unification of the English and Scottish Crowns in 1707. During the century that followed the unification, this new army was deployed across the world. The victories of the Duke of Marlborough over the French in the early eighteenth century, far-flung campaigns in four continents in the latter part of that century and the pivotal battles of the Napoleonic War in the early part of the nineteenth century culminating in the victory at Waterloo in 1815, were all to gild the achievements of British regiments.

The Victorian wars that followed would bring mixed fortunes: the Crimea, which exposed weaknesses in army logistics; the Victorian 'small wars' against a variety of foes; and, at the close of the

Propaganda: British representation of the German Iron Cross, here awarded for the spread of German 'Kultur'.

The Highlanders withstand
a cavalry charge at
Waterloo, 1815.

The Gordon Highlanders in
Afghanistan, 1897.

nineteenth century, the Second Boer War, fought against a determined, irregular, but well-equipped force. These campaigns would nevertheless contribute battle honours that would be husbanded with pride.

The regimental system so pivotal to the British Army was developed in the latter part of the seventeenth century.[16] Then, the regiment was a working business, raised and led by its colonel and attracting monies from the state. Regiments originally bore the colonel's name, but in the mid part of the eighteenth century, by Royal Warrant the arms and insignia of the colonels were removed, their names struck from titles and a new system of numbered regiments of foot (the infantry), and horse (the cavalry) was instigated. A further dramatic change was the programme of reforms brought by Lord Cardwell, Secretary of State for War in 1868–70 (and continued by Hugh C.E. Childers, who became the Secretary of State in 1880 when the Liberals returned to power), which created the county regiments and installed shorter service periods for soldiers.

Before the reforms there were 109 Regular infantry regiments. Afterwards, those regiments numbered from twenty-five onwards were paired, producing sixty-one in total, each with two Regular battalions allied with a county or region, and each given a home depot. Militia and Volunteer battalions (VBs), part-time units with a long history of service, were also linked to these county regiments.

It was Haldane's reforms of 1906–08 that announced the birth of the Territorial Force. With Haldane, each infantry regiment typically gained, in addition to its Regular battalions, a Special Reserve battalion, its sole purpose to gather recruits for the Regular battalions. There were also, variously,

either two or four Territorial battalions, born of the Volunteer battalions raised in 1859, responding to threats from the continent. Like the VBs, the Territorial battalions were locally raised and under the control of county Territorial associations, who managed recruitment through drill halls in different parts of each county.

Irish regiments (as the whole of Ireland was then part of the United Kingdom) were never to have Territorial battalions. The intention was that the part-time Territorials would be used for home defence in times of conflict, with the bulk of the available Regulars deployed as part of the Expeditionary Force. Although with the outbreak of the Great War in 1914, most would volunteer for

THE CONNAUGHT RANGERS
88TH & 94TH FOOT

The Connaught Rangers – created by amalgamation.

overseas service. In addition there was the yeomanry (cavalry), together with units of the support arms and services, all taking up their roles in the Territorial divisions.

Maintaining the level of recruitment required to sustain the system of Regulars and Territorials in peacetime was a tall order – particularly when that recruitment was a matter of adding men who had come forward voluntarily to the ranks. The deep-seated principle of voluntary enlistment still applied, as commentator W.G. Clifford noted at the time:

> In our Army, as in every other, the first need is men to fill the ranks. These we obtain by voluntary enlistment, and in normal times some thirty thousand men are required every year for the Regular Army alone. It is well to point out that we can never raise these men by any form of compulsion. No matter what may be done for home defence, the professional soldier raised to serve anywhere in peace or war must be a volunteer.[17]

With the crisis developing on the continent of Europe, the possibility of maintaining this level of recruitment was increasingly uppermost in the minds of MPs, especially as it was looking increasingly likely that Britain would be sucked into the growing conflict. Two weeks after the assassination of Franz Ferdinand on the streets of Sarajevo, the military correspondent of *The Times* signalled the possibility that the current system was likely to fail. On 13 July 1914, the newspaper carried a major article with a serious message: 'The Failure of Recruiting. A Serious Situation. The Need for Drastic Reform.'[18]

What were the numbers required to keep the establishment fully staffed? With Haldane's army reforms it was carefully calculated that 37,710 men per year would be needed to support the whole military edifice of Regulars and Territorials, all voluntary and all without wartime imperatives. Of this, 22,008 were for the infantry alone.[19] Yet the figures were not encouraging. From 1908, enlistments had been falling annually, reaching 5,000–6,000 per year with a deficit of 25,000 overall (more, given that the government had revised its figures down in 1914).

Yet the government was still opposed to conscription, and mass compulsion would be a difficult path to follow – surely there was plenty of time available to attempt the raising of a citizen army? To make good the pre-war deficit, and to add sufficient men to the ranks to prosecute a war on the continent, with all that entailed, there would need to be a significant step up.

Kitchener's approach was clear. Impatient, imperious, and insistent, the field marshal got straight to the heart of the matter. There would be no time for the ponderous mechanisms of the Territorial county associations to take their part in building up sufficient men to fight the cause. The role of the associations was specific and county focused, each 'composed of influential men in each county whose business it is to receive and expend the money allotted by government to the Territorial Forces in the county, and generally to encourage and assist in their raising and maintenance'.[20]

In any case, though the Territorials had once been perceived as a second-line expeditionary force for service overseas, Haldane had fudged this in his 1907 bill, by announcing the creation of the force, and the 'Saturday Night Soldiers' were destined to be part-timers with no obligation to serve outside of the home countries.

The military expectations for these men were low, based simply on the time that was available to train them, as noted in a 1915 book on the British Army:

> The Territorial recruit now enlists for four years, and becomes liable to make himself efficient under a penalty of £4. To do this, he has, in the Infantry, to do twenty drills before the Annual Camp – which he must attend for at least eight days – twenty days' drill after, and a recruit's course on musketry. This is in his first year. After that his training is limited to ten drills, camp, and annual musketry course. This cannot make a soldier of any man.[21]

Perhaps wary of this county-based and part-time arrangement, Kitchener struck right at the heart of the matter. He steered away from the recruiting and organisational machinery of the Territorial Associations – instead of divisions of soldiers imbued with the Territorial spirit, he would create new battalions to be appended as new units of the Regular army.[22] In so doing, the new soldiers would not be employed under special conditions; they would have to see the war out, and be willing to be sent wherever the army required them to go.

In seemingly ignoring the Territorials, the Secretary of State put himself in the way of criticism. But Kitchener also recognised their value, as discussed by Victor Germains in 1930:

R.F.A. Camp Tidworth Park' Salisbury Plain. (7)

Territorial Royal Field Artillery camp in the pre-war period.

It has been suggested that he could have raised his New Armies more 'scientifically' ... It has been suggested that owing to his long residence abroad he knew little of the Territorial Force and underrated and despised it. [But] his general attitude to the Volunteer movement was much more sympathetic than that of the average Regular officer, for he had commanded Volunteer units in South Africa and appreciated their value.[23]

He knew that for all its value, 'it had been devised as a Home Service army, and could not be transformed into a Foreign Service army by a mere stroke of the pen', and that 'a Territorial unit cannot train itself and expand simultaneously'.[24] No, Kitchener knew that if Britain was to be able to take on one of the major continental powers, it would have to create an army that would be capable of doing the job, with numbers to match: 'a nation in arms'. Putting intolerable strains on the Territorial Force just would not cut it.

As noted by historian David French, this would be one of Kitchener's finest hours:

The raising of the New Armies was one of the most important and far-reaching decisions taken by the British throughout the war. Kitchener's advocacy of raising a continental-scale force must remain his major claim to fame. It ensured that by 1916 Britain was able to assume a major share of fighting on the Western Front.[25]

Without delay, sanction was sought for the raising of an additional 500,000 men at Kitchener's first engagement in the Cabinet; and the opening of recruitment for the first 100,000 – which became known as the 'First Hundred Thousand', or even simply 'K1' – was announced as a front-page advertisement in the press on 8 August 1914.[26]

AUGUST 8TH, 1914.

Your King and Country Need You.

A CALL TO ARMS.

An addition of 100,000 men to his Majesty's Regular Army is immediately necessary in the present grave National Emergency.

Lord Kitchener is confident that this appeal will be at once responded to by all those who have the safety of our Empire at heart.

TERMS OF SERVICE.

General Service for a period of 3 years or until the war is concluded.

Age of Enlistment between 19 and 30.

HOW TO JOIN.

Full information can be obtained at any Post Office in the Kingdom or at any Military depot.

GOD SAVE THE KING!

The 'Call to Arms', 8 August 1914.

The appeal went straight to the heart of the situation: 'A Call To Arms! Your King and Country Need You.' A stark advertisement appeared in all the newspapers. It was carried prominently in *The Times* – as well as all major regional papers – on Saturday 8 August 1914:[27]

YOUR KING AND COUNTRY NEED YOU
A CALL TO ARMS
An addition of 100,000 men to His Majesty's Regular Army is immediately necessary in the present grave National Emergency.
Lord Kitchener is confident that this appeal will be at once responded to by all those who have the safety of our Empire at heart.
TERMS OF SERVICE
General Service for a period of 3 years or until the war is concluded. Age of Enlistment between 19 and 30.
HOW TO JOIN
Full information can be obtained at any Post Office in the Kingdom or at any Military depot.
GOD SAVE THE KING![28]

Kitchener's brusque approach was precipitous; but he knew what was needed for the task in hand, and he set about doing it in a manner that, according to Victor Germains, was 'peculiarly British':

No other country in the world would have set itself to raise these armies in quite the same fashion or have displayed so little foresight before the crisis was upon us or so much foresight when the emergency was to hand.[29]

Kitchener's call made a direct connection with the men of Britain, asking them to join their country's army and enlist with the Regulars. At this stage in the war, it was young men who were required, aged between the ages of 19 and 30. They had to be fit, with a height minimum of 5ft 3in and a chest expansion of at least 34in. These statistics would change as the need for yet more men grew exponentially. All were asked to serve for the duration of the war; they would be paid the traditional 1 shilling a day for their trouble – plus allowances for wives and dependants. This shilling was symbolic, as noted by Thomas O'Toole in 1916:

It doesn't matter who he was before,
Or what his parents fancied for his name;
Once he's pocketed the shilling
And a uniform he's filling
We call him 'Tommy Atkins' just the same.[30]

It would be little enough, but for those without work it was something and for those in work it was some consolation. Men joined for all sorts of reasons. Some for patriotism, some for adventure, some to 'do the right thing'. As considered by Victor Germains, there were others too, who escaped the drudgery of their everyday lives and joined with assumed names so they could not be found: 'The motives which led men to take up arms were many: patriotism, want of employment, ambition, personal courage, love of adventure, the sheer impulse of going with the crowd.'[31]

And then there were the schoolboys, young lads who concealed their true ages and sought the opportunity to become a man, to live a man's life and to take on adventure. They all added to the potent mix of the First Hundred Thousand. On the day the Call to Arms was announced, *The Times* reported on recruiting progress:

RECRUITING IN LONDON. STEADY STREAM OF APPLICANTS. Lord Kitchener's call to arms, states the War Office, has met with such success that it has been found necessary to open several new recruiting agencies both in London and in the large towns in the north.

An hour spent in the recruiting station at headquarters, Great Scotland Yard was as inspiring as it was instructive. Ever since Tuesday there has been a steady stream of men anxious to enlist in the various branches of the service. Yesterday the crowd of applicants was so large and so persistent that mounted police were necessary to hold them in check, and the gates were only opened to admit six at a time. Inside the process of sorting and 'weeding out' was carried out with great dispatch. There was no cheering and little excitement, but there was an undercurrent of enthusiasm, and the disappointment of those who failed to pass one or other of the tests was palpable.[32]

In his contemporary account, *Kitchener's Army and the Territorial Forces*,[33] the writer and journalist Edgar Wallace – himself an old soldier who had reported on the British actions in the Boer War – described these early days:

A few days after the announcement had been made in Parliament that the British Army was to be so enormously increased, there appeared on every public vehicle in London a neat placard to supplement the official posters which at that time were covering the windows of post offices and public buildings and were occupying large spaces in the columns of the daily Press. You saw this appeal in long blue and red strips fastened to the wind-screens of the taxi-cabs; you saw it on a larger scale plastered to the sides of the motor-buses.[34]

Buses, trams and recruiting offices – wherever there was an opportunity, the recruiting posters were pasted to give the maximum effect. In some cases, these documents were brutally direct. Philip Gibbs, a vocal critic of the war in the early 1920s, certainly viewed them this way:

The New Army was called into being by Lord Kitchener and his advisors, who adopted modern advertising methods to stir the sluggish imagination of the masses, so that every wall in London and great cities, every fence in rural places, was placarded with picture-posters.

'… What did *you* do in the Great War, Daddy? … What will your best girl say if you're not in khaki?'

Those were vulgar appeals which, no doubt, stirred many simple souls, and so were good enough. It would have been better to let the people know more of the truth of what was happening in France and Flanders …[35]

Late in August, most of these posters were the output of the Parliamentary Recruiting Committee (PRC), a cross-party body whose sole aim was to direct men to the Colours.[36] From this group, MPs and peers saw their opportunity to influence the public directly through this medium. Basil Williams described the scene:

The hoardings of the kingdom were covered with the posters issued by the Parliamentary Recruiting Committee, some designed by great artists, some frankly sentimental, some broadly humorous to catch the passing smile and arrest the attention of men not yet certain where their duty lay ... Altogether it has been reckoned that in this campaign ... over 54,000,000 posters, leaflets and other publications were issued; while 12,000 meetings were held and over 20,000 speeches delivered.[37]

On top of the PRC output there were other posters, including perhaps the most famous of them all, illustrating Kitchener's icy stare and accusingly pointing finger, which were privately produced and issued to aid the campaign.[38]

Taken together, the poster campaign was an assault on the senses. Arthur Guy Empey fell under its spell:

Recruiting posters were everywhere. The one that impressed me most was a life-size picture of Lord Kitchener with his finger pointing directly at me, under the caption of 'Your King and Country Need You'. No matter which way I turned, the accusing finger followed me.[39]

This level of direct engagement would take time to develop, and with the PRC only coming into existence at the end of August, there was a lot of ground to make up if recruitment to the proposed New Armies was to be effective, and if the pre-war

Recruitment posters became the norm in 1914.

deficit was to be made good.[40] There appeared to be a lag time, as if it was taking time to awaken people to the seriousness of the situation. Men were coming to join, but not in immense numbers – yet. The recruiting returns actually showed that from Tuesday 4 August to Saturday 8 August, just prior to Kitchener's call, nationally some 8,193 men joined the Colours.[41] At this rate it would take some time for Kitchener's ambition to come to fruition.

Writing in 1915, Edgar Wallace was at pains to explain why this might have been:

The average young man of Britain was wont to cheer enthusiastically stories of British heroism. He himself was immensely patriotic and honestly desired to serve his country as best he could. That he did not enlist was not due to his lack of patriotism, not to his failure to appreciate the extraordinary demands which were being made on his country, but just from sheer failure to understand that he himself could be of any service in the ranks of the Army.[42]

'Recruiting for Kitchener's Army', a board game from 1914.

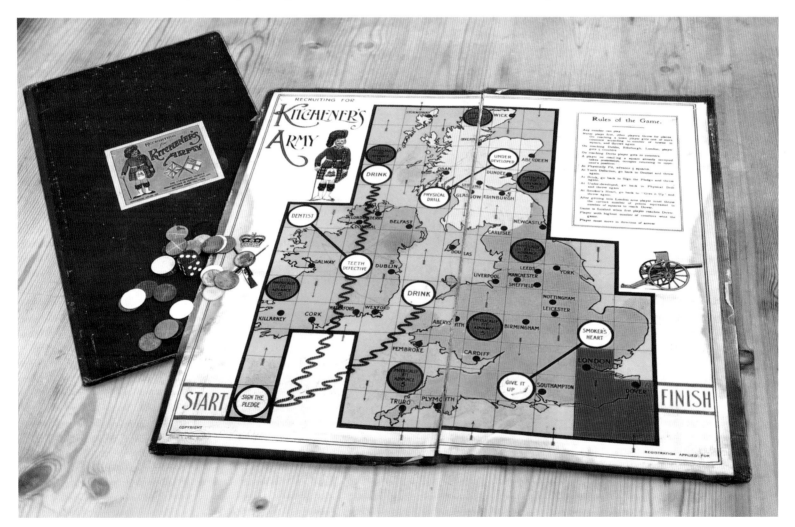

Recruiting office decked in posters, 1914.

Recruiting tramcars were a common sight in many cities; this is Leeds.

Opposite: 'Lend your strong right arm', a Parliamentary Recruiting Committee (PRC) poster.

The Kitchener poster — one of its variants. None of them were official PRC issues.

WHY AREN'T YOU IN KHAKI? YOU'LL BE WANTED. ENLIST AT ONCE.

PUBLISHED BY THE PARLIAMENTARY RECRUITING COMMITTEE, LONDON. POSTER No. 62.   PRINTED BY JAS. TRUSCOTT & SON, LTD., SUFFOLK LANE, LONDON, E.G.

Quite possibly this came down to a misunderstanding about the nature of the modern soldier. Rudyard Kipling had done much to propagate the idea of the British soldier as a rough diamond in the late nineteenth century, and this was perhaps at odds with the expectations of the 'commercial classes' who would come to supply a larger proportion of the citizen army that Kitchener was hoping to create. Captain Atteridge, a contemporary commentator, was clear that Kipling's view was incorrect in 1915:

> Mr Rudyard Kipling's pictures of the hard-drinking, rough-tongued Tommy Atkins are now out of date. The British soldier is an educated man with a good record, doing his work seriously, and finding in and around the military quarters where he is stationed ample opportunity for honest social recreation in his spare time.[43]

While Atteridge's picture was somewhat overly rosy, it was more indicative of the character of the coming army and of the men who overcame any inhibitions to join.

Recruitment soon fell into a predictable pattern. Many fewer men joined on a Sunday. Perhaps surrounded by their family, or given that, for Christians at least, this was the Sabbath, the decision to join the army was in abeyance. For the remainder of 1914, Mondays would be the busiest recruiting day of the week; though just why this is the case is obscure.[44] Perhaps men's consciences were sharpest on returning to work. Perhaps, away from their families, they made life-changing decisions as they passed recruiting offices, or they responded to compulsion – not from the government, but rather from the pointing fingers and sly words expressed as a man in civilian clothes passed by. 'Why aren't *you* in khaki?'[45] Perhaps they were escaping the overcrowded houses of pre-war Britain. Or simply, perhaps, it was the chance to escape the drudge of work, the reality of everyone's every day.

In any case, for every week in 1914 the pattern of the Monday recruiting spike falling away to a Sunday low was repeated. If it was to deliver a citizen army, some fillip was needed to push on recruitment to a new height. By Sunday 23 August, the day the British Expeditionary Force first met the German Army in battle on the continent of Europe, some 104,510 men had joined the Colours.[46] With the standing deficit of around 25,000 men for the Regular army, this left approximately 80,000 to be housed, equipped and trained. With an infantry division at this stage of the war consisting of four brigades, each amounting to around 4,000 men (consisting in turn of four battalions of around 1,000 men), this had the potential to supply five divisions – and not counting the manpower of the support services.

It was fortunate, then, that recruitment took a sharp upwards turn in the wake of the retreat from Mons. The initial engagement of the BEF had tested the Germans, but the weight of their advance in enacting the Schlieffen Plan was too much. With the French armies in retreat, the BEF had no choice but to retire. 'Thrilling' stories of plucky soldiers filled the newspapers on Saturday 29 August:

MONS AND AFTER

A thrilling story of the fighting in the trenches at Mons has been told me by five British soldiers who escaped through the German lines and reached Ostend to-day after many adventures. I met them here, and returned with them to England. They were in private clothes, ragged, weary, and un-washed. They looked like tramps, but I discovered that they were British soldiers who had walked all the way from Warmes, the British hospital station, about five miles south-west of Mons.[47]

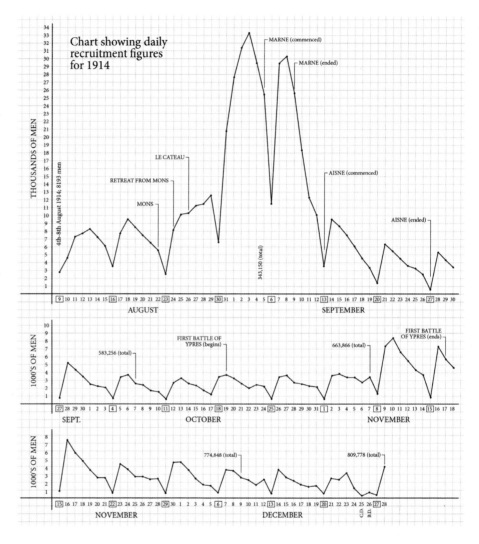

Chart showing daily recruitment figures for 1914

Recruiting statistics for 1914. Recruitment lows fell on Sundays.

Opposite: 'Why aren't you in Khaki?' – PRC poster from 1914.

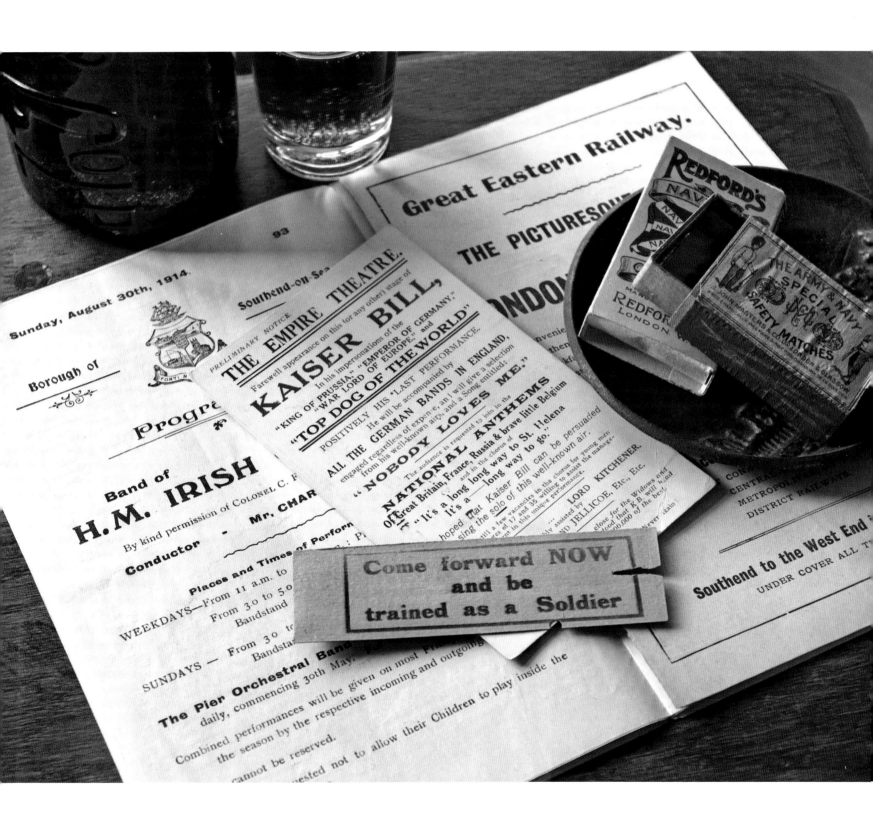

The British public lapped this up. After the customary Sunday dip, the effect on recruiting was immediate – some 20,909 joined on Monday 31 August; 27,914 on the Tuesday; 31,947 on the Wednesday; and 33,204 on Thursday 3 September.[48] These figures were unprecedented. Britons had responded to the call at the time when the army most needed them, in the face of the crushing odds presented by the 'German steamroller'. Even in 1915 this effect was evident to Edgar Wallace:

On that Sunday, there was one question asked: where are the French? Wherever they were, or whatever they were doing (and we know now how they were occupied), it was obvious they were not in a position at that moment to help this retiring British Army, battling from Mons to Mauberge, from Mauberge to Le Cateau, and fighting every inch of its way to Paris.

Monday morning took the great army of young men by train, by 'bus, by tram-car … to their offices and business in the city. At every few yards they were confronted with the simple statement that their King and Country needed them. Then, perhaps, the inspiration came in a flash that it was *they themselves to whom this appeal was being made!*[49]

Whatever the reason, the effect was dramatic. Recruiting offices were now flooded with volunteers, with three times the average daily rate of enlistment – a rate that would continue until mid September, when it once more reverted to the familiar pattern. And the PRC kept up the momentum with rousing speeches, public meetings and an output of posters and patriotic literature that would reach 13 million leaflets and 1 million posters by the end of January 1915.[50]

Opposite: Men were assaulted on all sides by the recruiting message.

The queue at a recruiting office, 1914.

Civilians and army retirees were drafted in to assist the recruitment effort.

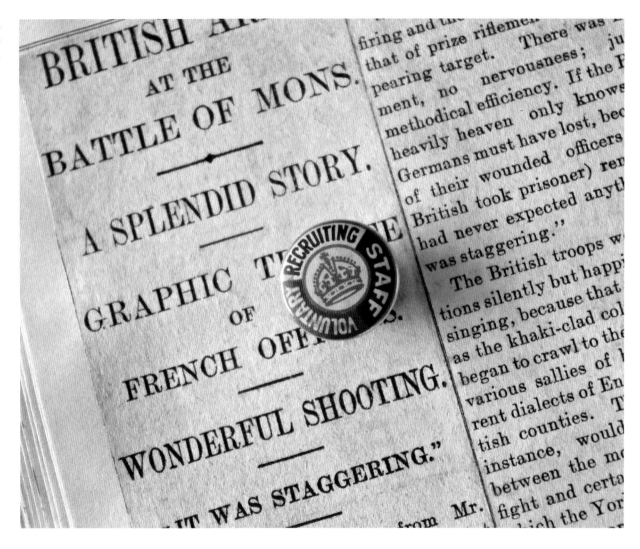

The swell at recruiting offices was such that there were lines of men snaking around the corner. In order to process the crush of would-be soldiers, new offices had to be opened and civilian personnel and retired officers were drafted in. In Glasgow, the officer commanding No. 2 District, Hamilton, advertised for experienced recruiters:

RECRUITING
RETIRED OFFICERS –
The services of Retired Officers are wanted at once for duty as paid Assistant Recruiting Officers.
PENSIONER RECRUITERS –
Retired Non-Commissioned Officers are required at once for duty as Pensioner Recruiters.[51]

Old soldiers and senior civilians – all would be drafted in. Wherever there was enthusiasm for recruitment, there was the chance to gather new recruits to the fold. And as Edgar Wallace noted, the government had to be there to receive them:

> The Government established offices, not only in the principal centres of all the great towns of England, but in the outlying suburbs and in the villages and market towns which were accessible to would-be recruits.[52]

The pattern of recruiting in the early days was cyclical – with fallow days as well as feast. The flow had certainly increased after Mons, and the flow became a crush. 'Kitchener's Mob', with James Norman Hall one of its number, was on the increase:

> 'A Mob' is genuinely descriptive of the array of would-be soldiers which crowded the long parade ground at Hounslow Barracks during that memorable last week in August. We herded together like so many sheep. We had lost our individuality, and it was to be months before we regained it in a new aspect, a collective individuality of which we became increasingly proud.[53]

With the queues building at the recruiting offices, there developed a familiar routine. On arrival, recruits would be asked their age – with 19 being the nominal minimum. It is well known that there were to be very many underage soldiers; the army would later insist that such boys were taken in good faith, having 'lied about their age', and would release them only in exceptional circumstances. Nevertheless, underage soldiers were admitted if they could 'demonstrate' that they were older than they really were. Very many boy soldiers, such as Ernest Parker, would join in this way.[54]

> On the night of 1 September 1914, when I enlisted in Kitchener's Army, the war was barely a month old and my birthday was just approaching. I was far from being the youngest recruit, for in the queue was a boy of fifteen. I had to line up again to give my age as nineteen before I was finally accepted.[55]

The recruitment process then followed a standard pattern. Would-be soldiers were given a brief medical that assessed physical development and general fitness, based around the height (at first,

Taking details at a recruiting office.

above 5ft 3in) and chest measurements (34in maximum expansion), the condition of the soldiers' teeth (to handle the almost unbreakable ration biscuit) and their eyesight (to be able to sight his rifle effectively).

In some cases, the medical was peremptory. As Edgar Wallace put it, 'The machinery of the peacetime recruiting office was not designed to pass thousands of men in a day.'[56] The recruit, he continued:

Formed one of the long queue outside the chief recruiting office, shuffling forward at a snail's pace as the queue moved up, and as the men, in parties of six and seven, were released to the medical inspection room … In a few moments the would-be recruit is standing erect in nature's uniform. The examination is brief but thorough. Heart and lungs are tested by stethoscope and by judicious tapping. His chest is measured and his exact weight recorded. The recruit hops across the bare room, first on one leg and then on the other. His teeth are inspected, and then comes the crucial test of eyesight … A quick examination follows for varicose veins and other infirmities, and then with a curt nod he is dismissed to his clothing. The Medical Officer signs the attestation form.[57]

There were many categories of fitness and, at this stage in the war, grades would be given that would define a soldier's capability for general service overseas, or lower grades that would tie a man to home service, or garrison service.[58] Often he would be rejected on grounds of fitness, physical development or defect.

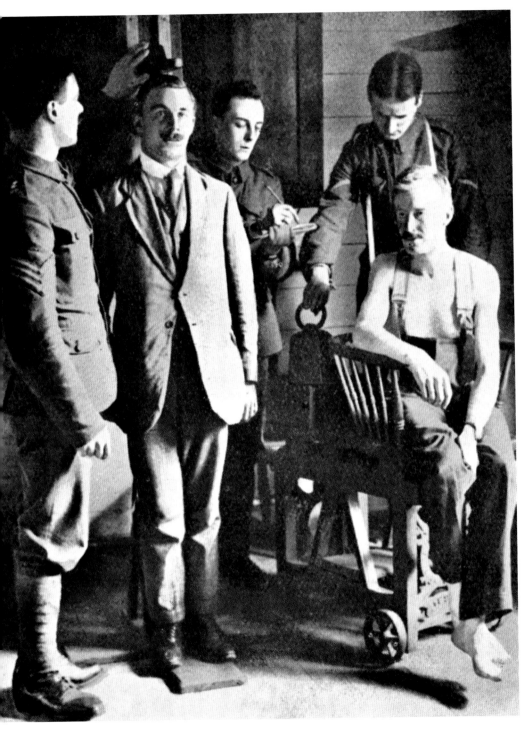

The medical.

MEN OF THE MOMENT

Not every recruiting line would be an edifying sight. James Norman Hall was particularly surprised:

My first impression of the men with whom I was to live for three years, or the duration of the war, was anything but favourable. The newspapers had been asserting that the new army was being recruited from the flower of England's manhood. The throng at the Horse Guards Parade resembled an army of the unemployed, and I thought it likely that most of them were misfits, out-of-works, the kind of men who join the army because they can do nothing else. I soon learned, however, that the general out-at-elbows appearance was due to another cause.[59]

However, Hall soon realised that the men in that line were indifferently dressed in old clothes – rather than subject their best suits to the rigours of military service. They would need training to whip them into shape. 'There was good stuff in the ranks, the material from which real soldiers are made; but it had not yet been rounded into shape. We were still nothing more than a homogenous assembly of individuals.'[60]

Those who 'made the grade' would be called upon to attest, a process that involved the swearing of an oath of allegiance to the king. Swearing in was carried out by the recruiting officer, each recruit holding a New Testament in his right hand. The oath was an oath of allegiance to the Crown, and to the officers designated by the Crown. It was a solemn undertaking. As the *Manual of Military Law* put it, 'The enlistment of the soldier is a species of contract between the Sovereign

and the soldier, and under the ordinary principles of law cannot be altered without the consent from both parties.'[61]

That contract would be sealed by formal oath:

I swear to serve His Majesty the King, his heirs and successors and the generals and officers set over me by His Majesty the King, his heirs and successors, so help me God.[62]

Recruits would then sign their attestation forms in duplicate. The purpose of attestation, applied since the formal army began, was a means of making sure that the potential soldier knew what he was getting himself into, and to prevent claims of entrapment.[63] Signing their forms, they would receive the King's Shilling, the symbolic issue of the first day's pay for what was to be a long stint in the army, and was a practice instigated as a means of sealing 'a bargain'.[64] The issue of the shilling, and the repeat of the oath of allegiance to the Crown, would bind the Great War recruit to service for 'three years or the duration of the war'.

With so many men joining the army as private soldiers, more officers would be required to command them, and there would be a severe shortfall. Regular officers and non-commissioned officers (NCOs) would provide the backbone for the new battalions that were raised following Kitchener's call. But, with the demands of Regular units to be met, manpower resources were tight.

Ex-Regular NCOs, men who had retired but were still active, were asked to re-enlist – up to the age of 50. As Victor Germains noted, Kitchener was clear from the outset that at the core of each New Army battalion had to be experience:

Volunteers attesting.

Almost the first act of Kitchener as Secretary of State for War was to telegraph orders for each battalion of the Expeditionary Force to leave behind three officers and fifteen NCOs to form a nucleus for a fresh battalion, and for other units of the Expeditionary Force to leave behind proportionate cadres.[65]

Other sources were men on the reserve lists – usually just retired from service, but including more senior men 'dug out' of retirement – together with 500 men on leave from the Indian Army, who were 'detained' from returning to their regiments. Direct recruitment from public schools and universities was also tried, but as many had joined the ranks as private soldiers it would take some time to persuade them that they might have the skills to command.

Two days after Lord Kitchener issued his first Call to Arms, seeking 100,000 men – on 10 August 1914 – the government advertised widely in the press for junior officers:

TEMPORARY COMMISSIONS IN HIS
MAJESTY'S ARMY
2,000 Junior Officers (unmarried) are
immediately required in consequence of the
increase in the Regular Army
TERMS OF SERVICE
To serve with the Regular army until the war
is concluded. Age 17 to 30.
An allowance of £20 will be made for
uniform and £5 15s for equipment
HOW TO OBTAIN HIS MAJESTY'S
COMMISSION
Cadets or ex-Cadets of the
University Training Corps or Members
of a University should apply to their
Commanding Officers or to the authorities
of their University. Other Young Men of
good general education should apply in
person to the Officer commanding the
nearest Depot. Full information can be
obtained by written application to the
Secretary, War Office.
GOD SAVE THE KING[66]

The Officer Training Corps (OTC) had been developed under Haldane to provide a trained reserve of men for just such an eventuality, with senior (university) and junior (public school) branches. The intention was to tackle the inadequacy of the supply of trained officers, as had been experienced in previous conflicts – particularly the Boer War.[67]

The government's advertisement was successful – very successful – but those who were impatient to join the Colours found other routes, a factor identified by the first chronicle of the University & Public Schools Brigade:

The public school class now saw the particular form of its duty in the national emergency more plainly before it, and the 2,000 vacancies were very quickly filled from this source. So great, in fact, was the flood of applications for the limited number of commissions available that it soon became apparent that applicants not immediately successful would probably have to wait a long time before they could hope to obtain commissions.[68]

Those men would ultimately join as private soldiers in Kitchener's Army – in the first instance at least.

THE FIRST HUNDRED THOUSAND – K1

Kitchener's first call for 100,000 men to swell the ranks in 1914 – the First Hundred Thousand – had achieved its aim within two weeks. These men were quickly dispersed amongst Regular army regiments across the country – creating new Service battalions in turn. Captain Atteridge explained their purpose:

Besides the regiments of the Regular Army, the Special Reserve and the Territorial Army, which were all in existence before the war, hundreds of new regiments [sic] have been formed out of the recruits who came forward in hundreds and thousands when in the first days of the war the King called for enlistments on a large scale. As the call was sent out by Lord Kitchener, as Secretary of State for War, it became the fashion to speak of these new levies as 'Kitchener's Army,' but they are really the newest part of the King's army.[69]

Kitchener's Army – its diversity is expressed in one of Jessie Pope's patriotic verses.

THE K.A. BOYS.

Dr-rud—dr-rud—dr-rud—dr-rud—
Kitchener's Army marching round
Through Bristol City to Durdham Down,
Men in motley, so to speak,
Been in training about a week,
Swinging easy, toe and heel,
Game and gay, and keen as steel.

Dr-rud—dr-rud—dr-rud—dr-rud—
Norfolk jackets, city suits,
Some in shoes and some in boots ;
Clerk and sportsman, tough and nut,
Reach-me-downs, and Bond-street cut ;
Typical kit of every kind,
To show the life they've left behind.

Dr-rud—Dr-rud—Dr-rud—Dr-rud—
Marching by at an easy pace,
The great adventure in every face,
Raw if you like. but full of grit,
Snatching the chance to do their bit.
Oh, I want to cheer and I want to cry
When Kitchener's Boys go marching by.

JESSIE POPE.

Opposite: Private Humphrey Mason's cap badge carved in the chalk of Salisbury Plain. Mason was a Kitchener volunteer in the 6th Oxfordshire & Buckinghamshire Light Infantry.

In those counties where recruiting was strongest traditionally, it followed that there would be the greatest chance of adding new Service battalions. With Haldane's reforms creating the two Regular battalions of each county regiment (leaving a third, Special Reserve, battalion to handle day-to-day recruits), there were either two or four further Territorial battalions. The Kitchener units were thus normally numbered onwards from either the 6th or 8th (Service) Battalions, in an ever expanding line of numbered formations. It was Army Order 324 that made this announcement, published on 21 August 1914.[70] The order read:

The new battalions will be raised as additional battalions of the regiments of Infantry of the Line and will be given numbers following consecutively on the existing battalions of their regiments. They will be further distinguished by the word Service after the number.[71]

None would have special or individual titles to distinguish them. Perhaps because of this, they sat in the shadow of the local Pals battalions of later raising. But very quickly, these men took on the trappings of their home regiment and were imbued with the traditions and adopted the honours of the host regiment. To some men serving with the Territorials, this must have been a slight. Territorial battalions were barred from claiming the historical honours won by the Regulars over some 200 years of history. In their caps, badges would have empty scrolls and erased honour bars. This was not the case for Kitchener's men.[72]

Private Mason, of the 6th (Service) Battalion Oxfordshire & Buckinghamshire Light Infantry (K2), made a point of carving his new cap badge – admittedly one that bore no honours of any sort – into a piece of chalk and sending it home. He had become the regiment – despite the fact that he was clad in the spectacularly unsoldierly, shoddy blue uniform that typified these early volunteers.

Yet with Kitchener's no-nonsense approach, it could so easily have been different; with numbers of men the priority there was no room for romanticism. As far as he was concerned, the New Army needed nothing more than to serve in battalions that were numbered in a simple fashion from one onwards; but for Lieutenant General Sir Arthur Codringham, Kitchener's military secretary, the fact that the new soldiers would have no military traditions to

draw upon was a negative. Despite his own views, Kitchener gave in to his secretary – to him it was simply the men that mattered, nothing more. For the fostering of *esprit de corps*, it was as well that the general got his way.[73]

Though recruitment had been steady, if not spectacular, there were enough men to add at least a single new battalion to most infantry regiments and to fill the ranks of the service organisations that would support them. It was all well and good to have new fighting infantrymen, but it would be less effective if those infantrymen were not supported by artillerymen, engineers, medics and the somewhat less glamorous Army Service Corps.

These essential arms and services had had their own Regular and Territorial units in the pre-war period and it was obviously essential that Kitchener's Army equivalents were raised to support them. In many ways the volunteers for the essential arms and services are the real forgotten men of Kitchener's Army. For example, the strength of the Royal Engineers (RE) in August 1914 was 25,090. A year later there were 126,165 men on establishment.[74]

This rapid expansion was very necessary. Each of the proposed infantry divisions would require a field company of trained engineers to tackle the myriad problems of the coming battlefields, and in addition to the field companies, the RE was expected to be expert in logistical issues as diverse as water supply, fortress construction, searchlight provision, tunnelling and mining, field survey, bridging, hutments and so on. To carry out these important tasks the corps would require a huge influx of men.

Fortunately, there was no shortage of recruits in 1914, not least because these specialist units carried a much higher daily wage than the average soldier. But given the specialist nature of the corps, the new men would need a significant amount of training before they would be fit to take to the field and achieve 'the rank and pay of the sapper'.

The officer in command of a new RE field company, the 82nd, assigned to the 19th Division (K2), recounts a story typical of these early days:

I was furnished with a nominal roll of 200 men, and instructed to have them ready to march to the station en route for Bulford Camp ... No uniform or equipment of any sort had been issued, so that the men had only to put together their small possessions, which were collected by lorry and taken direct to the station. On our departure, I was the only officer and the only one individual in uniform, but I marched off proudly at the head of this gallant, ill-clad, almost ragged, ten score of young men who were to become, in due course and after many tribulations, a field company R.E. trained and equipped for war.[75]

A similar tale would be told for other specialists – the gunners of the Royal Field Artillery, the transport men of the Army Service Corps, the medics of the Royal Army Medical Corps. Assembling, training and equipping Kitchener's Mob was a huge undertaking.

Together, the First Hundred Thousand – of the 500,000 men projected – were sufficient to form six new divisions, originally numbered 8th to 13th, following on from the Regular divisions, but in the end becoming 9th to 14th – as the 8th was taken by Regular battalions, being formed into a new Regular division.

Royal Engineers – Kitchener's Army men in Chatham, 1914.

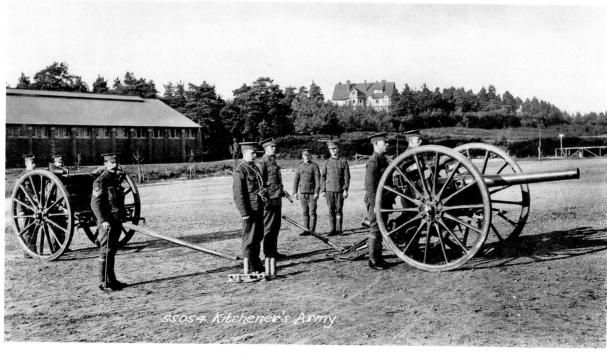

Royal Artillery – Kitchener's Army men with obsolete-calibre weapons, 1914.

Each new division was named with some indication of the geographical origin of its constituent battalions: 9th (Scottish) Division, formed in Scotland, but to be trained at Aldershot under General Sir H.L. Smith-Dorrien; the 10th (Irish), raised in Dublin and the Curragh under General Sir Bryan Mahon; 11th (Northern) Division to be based in Grantham, the 12th (Eastern) at Colchester, 13th (Western) at Salisbury Plain; while the 14th (Light) Division was formed of battalions garnered from light infantry and rifle regiments, and was also to be based at Aldershot.[76]

Each of the component battalions was built piecemeal. As recruits enlisted in penny packets, so they were added to the strength and transferred to the relevant home depot.[77] Where recruitment was most successful, this led to a logjam – as in the depot of the Cameron Highlanders in September:

> During this period we had great difficulties to contend with. We had to house and feed all recruits; they came in so fast that it was impossible for us to deal with them the same day. It sometimes happened too that although we had practically cleared the barracks one evening there would be 400 recruits on parade the following morning, these having come in in the night.[78]

The first of the new Service battalions to reach full strength was the 11th (Service) Battalion of the King's (Liverpool) Regiment, on 25 August 1914.[79] On the same day, Kitchener gave his maiden speech in the House of Lords. He stressed that, as a soldier, his term of service would match that of his own soldiers:

> My occupation of the post of Secretary of State for War is a temporary one. The terms of my service are the same as those under which some of the finest portions of our manhood, now so willingly stepping forward to join the Colours, are engaging – that is to say, for the war, or, if it lasts longer than three years, then for three years. It has been asked why the latter limit has been fixed. It is because should this disastrous war be prolonged – and no one can foretell with any certainty its duration – then after three years' war there will be others fresh and fully prepared to take our places and see this matter through.[80]

And it was clear also that his soldiers, newly raised, would take up the challenge of the 'Empires with whom we are at war', who had 'called to the Colours almost their entire male population'. He continued:

> The principle which we on our part shall observe is this – that while their maximum force undergoes a constant diminution, the reinforcements we prepare shall steadily and increasingly flow out until we have an Army in the field which, in numbers not less than in quality, will not be unworthy of the power and responsibilities of the British Empire.[81]

The new battalions were all nucleated around the cadre of experienced men derived from Regular units that had already seen action in some cases, commanded by the officer in charge of the depot, and this was central to Kitchener's concept of his developing battalions. If nothing else, these experienced soldiers were to provide stiffening to the understandably raw troops as they arrived.

The First Hundred Thousand, published in 1915, which told the story of the recruitment and training of a typical K1 battalion.

Finding uniforms and equipment for these men was more of a challenge, but Kitchener's drive to fill his New Armies was such that these matters were to be dealt with as they arose. It was right to get volunteers while it was still possible – and while the BEF in France was still doing its level best to hold back the tide of the German armies. New recruit James Norman Hall took comfort from the crush of men in the same circumstances:

We derived what comfort we could from the knowledge that we were but one of many battalions of Kitchener's First Hundred Thousand equipped in this makeshift fashion … Supplies came in driblets. Each night, when parades for the day were over, there was a rush for the orderly room bulletin board, which was scanned eagerly for news of an early issue of clothing. As likely as not we were disappointed, but occasionally jaded hopes revived.[82]

Arguably the most famous men of the First Hundred Thousand, or K1, were those who were caricatured in Second Lieutenant John Hay Beith's famous 1915 book, *The First Hundred Thousand*, written under the pseudonym of Ian Hay.[83] Light in tone and fictionalised, the book takes as its inspiration Beith's own unit, the 10th (Service) Battalion Argyll & Sutherland Highlanders, raised in Stirling in August 1914. Beith recognised the scratch nature of the first volunteers in his poem, 'K1':[84]

We do not deem ourselves A1
We have no past: we cut no dash:
Nor hope, when launched against the Hun,
To raise a more than moderate splash.

But yesterday, we said farewell
To plough; to pit; to dock; to mill.
For glory? Drop it! Why? Oh well—
To have a slap at Kaiser Bill.

Beith's account was highly regarded and went into multiple editions – no doubt because of the way it captured the spirit of the day, and of the men who joined the battalion and would ultimately serve in the 9th (Scottish) Division in France. It describes the heady nature of the early phase of the war, after recruitment and during training, through the medium of fictional everyman characters – a device that was popular at the time:

And so the drill goes on. All over the drab, dusty, gritty parade ground, under the warm September sun, similar squads are being pounded into shape. They have no uniforms yet: even their instructors wear bowler hats or cloth caps. Some of the faces under the brims of these hats are not too prosperous. The junior officers are drilling squads too. They are a little shaky in what an actor would call their 'patter', and they are inclined to lay stress on the wrong syllables; but they move their squads about somehow.[85]

Major John Ewing, of the 6th King's Own Scottish Borderers, would echo Beith's description in his history of the 9th (Scottish) Division. The 9th was the most senior of the Kitchener's Army divisions, of which Beith's battalion was a component part.

It was to the officers that the soldiers turned, and it was to the senior and experienced NCOs that these men looked in turn:

The training was on lines identical with those of the old army and a similar syllabus was carried out with satisfactory results. The hardest lot fell to the young recently commissioned officers; they went through exactly the same routine as the men but were also obliged to spend their spare time learning their particular duties as officers.[86]

The recruitment of the second 100,000 tranche of Kitchener's men – the Second Hundred Thousand – was announced on 28 August. This was timely, as the news from France, with the retreat from Mons, was sufficiently alarming to cause the recognisable hike in the numbers of men already discussed. Men were taking themselves to the recruiting offices that were springing up across the nation.

Recruits were now joining from across a range of social classes, hardly a feature of the average pre-war battalion. This was at odds with the First Hundred Thousand, who were, more often than not, 'of the same class as the average run of Regular recruit', many of them ex-soldiers.[87]

The next day, a new set of divisions was drawn up; there was no time to waste. As historian of Kitchener's Army, Peter Simkins, records:

It was now becoming imperative for the Army Council to proceed with considerable haste, for men were pouring into the regimental depots from recruiting offices at a much faster rate than the depleted depot staffs could process them and post them to the training centres or Special Reserve battalions.[88]

The pressure was building on the depots.

THE SECOND HUNDRED THOUSAND – K2

Army Order 382 sanctioned the formation of the next six divisions of the Second New Army, or K2, in early September, to be formed from the new battalions. As before, the press carried advertisements on their front pages to try to fill the vacant places:

YOUR KING AND COUNTRY NEED YOU
ANOTHER 100,000 MEN WANTED

Lord Kitchener is much gratified with the response already made to the appeal for additional men for His Majesty's Regular Army. In the grave national emergency that now confronts the Empire he asks with renewed confidence that another 100,000 men come forward.[89]

The K2 divisions that were formed following this announcement were created in the same tidy geographical format as K1, again with a 'light division', and all to be numbered 15th to 20th divisions. This would not be repeated again.

The 6th Oxfordshire & Buckinghamshire Light Infantry was a Service battalion raised in Oxford in September. It was destined to serve with the 60th Brigade, a component of the 20th (Light) Division. Father and son, Benjamin and Humphrey Mason, joined the battalion in 1914. Benjamin was 44, and Humphrey was 19 years old. The younger Mason's reasons for joining were soundly based on the propaganda output: 'Then the first war broke out and the early news of the invaders terrorising the women made me feel that must not happen here so I decided to enlist.'[90]

The two men were to serve together with the battalion in the autumn and winter of 1914–15. Yet they were not the only father and son to join; there was another duo in the same battalion. In common with most battalions of K2, they experienced the shortages of uniform and equipment, clad first in their own clothes, and then, from November, Kitchener blue.

With K1 being first in line, in some cases resources were more limited for the next hundred thousand. This was particularly the case when it came to officers and NCOs. In battalions of the 15th (Scottish) Division there was in many cases only one Regular officer per battalion – hardly the kernel of knowledge required to ensure efficiency – and senior officers were often 'dug outs', or retired men. As recorded by Victor Germains, shortages in uniforms were as common as they were in other divisions and battalions of the Second Kitchener's Army:

The first consignment of uniform arrived at the end of September and was a weird and wonderful collection of relics of ancient days – scarlet tunics dating from 1893. These were to be worn with blue serge trousers; a few pairs of tartan trews [trousers] were eagerly snapped up by the NCOs.[91]

The same was true of equipment:

Odds and ends of equipment dribbled along: early in October the first batch of D.P. [Drill Purpose] rifles; shortly afterwards 100 modern rifles per battalion ... Then came a batch of the old buff leather equipment, waist belts, scabbards and bayonets. Brodrick hats, dating from 1902, turned up and 'a curious collection of civilian boots'.[92]

The 6th (Service) Battalion, Oxfordshire & Buckinghamshire Light Infantry. Ben Mason is in the cap (second from left), his son, Humphrey, is to his right (second row).

The shortages seen in K2 were to be magnified even further in the third of Kitchener's armies, K3.

THE THIRD HUNDRED THOUSAND – K3

While the original intention was to raise 200,000 of the first 500,000 men to be recruited for the New Army, the crush was such that this half a million had been almost achieved by 10 September, and sanction for the raising of a further 500,000 was sought the next day.[93] Kitchener was confident, and two more sets of divisions, for K3 and K4, were planned.

For the Third New Army – K3 – recruited on 13 September under Army Order 388, the system was varied. Gone were the regional descriptors, for this had been all well and good when a steady supply of men could be relied upon from across the United Kingdom, but it was much easier to recruit in the more populous industrial centres of England than it was in the more rural parts, including much of Ireland (some had resorted to recruiting men to Irish battalions by 'poaching' in northern English cities).[94] Victor Germains identified that the Highlands of Scotland, too, were challenged:

> Those fine Highland regiments, The Black Watch and Gordon Highlanders, recruiting from a large but sparsely peopled area which must already provide recruits for two Regular and one Special Reserve battalion, besides four Territorial battalions, could not provide more than three battalions each to the New Armies and it was doubtful that they would be able to maintain these.[95]

Opposite: Corporal Benjamin Mason (left), and his son Private Humphrey Mason (right), 6th (S) Battalion, Oxford & Buckinghamshire Light Infantry.

An original 'Kitchener's Man' armband.

Opposite: Tunstill's Men were given an armband and packet of 'comforts' as they left for the training camp.

This meant that it was less possible to construct dedicated regional divisions, and the titles were dropped. The recruitment of K3 was concurrent in some ways with the growth of the concept of locally raised battalions under the auspices of concerned and well-connected citizens. This, in part, contributed to the fact that in some more sparsely populated regions it was difficult to get recruits through the depots – and this meant that the last 200,000 men would be formed of these Pals battalions.[96]

Dr Harry Gilbert Tunstill, C.C. Otterburn, Bell Busk. Captain, 10th D.W.(W.R.Reg't) In Command of his Company in France. In Sep 1914 he raised a Craven Legion of 100 men, & enlisted himself as a Private but rose to the rank of Captain in Nov. 1914.

Captain Harry Gilbert Tunstill, originator of Tunstill's Men.

As before, the K3 battalions were not rewarded with the attribute of a special or unusual title; each remained undistinguished as a simple, numbered Service battalion. But it is also true that some of the battalions of the first few hundred thousand men of Kitchener's Army can be identified as regional in scope and context, and one of the most notable of these was the company-sized unit known as Tunstill's Men, or Tunstill's Legion.

In the Yorkshire Dales region of Craven in 1915, Harry Gilbert Tunstill was a land agent and county council representative for the Settle district. An imposing 6ft and aged 33, the Dalesman was quite a respected man locally. Returning from a trip to Russia on 20 August 1914, Tunstill had become wound up with patriotic fervour, having seen passions running high in this Allied country. Aware of Kitchener's Call to Arms, Tunstill was one of many who took responsibility for raising men to serve in the New Army.

He took it upon himself to raise 100 men, a tenth of a battalion, for service in Kitchener's Army. A number of local meetings ensued and, following the recruitment drive of late August, there was

Tunstill's Men from Upper Wharfedale: William Burley and Walter Limmer both died of wounds, in September 1915 and September 1918 respectively. Ben Beaumont, transferred to the Regular 2nd Suffolk Regiment, was killed in action during Third Ypres in 1917.

"THE UPPER WHARFEDALE Cº, WEST RIDING REGIMENT."
W. PINMAN.   W. LIMMER.   A. STUBES. W. OLDFIELD! R. HARPER.   T. S. WORSLEY."
         B. BEAUMONT.   C. J. KELLY.   W. BURLEY.   W. ELEY.

no shortage of men who were available to attest to the Colours. In the aftermath of meetings held between 7 and 18 September 1914, some eighty-seven men had enlisted.[97] These men paraded on 19 September, distinguished only by their civilian clothes and a distinctive armband or brassard that identified each one as 'Kitchener's Man'.

This was unique. In this way each man was visibly identified with the great man himself and individually as a volunteer who had answered the call on his own conscience. It was as if there was a personal bond made between each Dalesman and the nation's hero and war leader. It was a historic contract that would not be broken by the strains of the months to come.

Arriving at the station, local people made sure the new recruits would not leave empty-handed.

They received 'comforts, clothing and fruits'.[98] Leaving with great pomp and circumstance, accompanied by a brass band and the sounding of fog signals, they boarded a train at the Dales town of Settle on 19 September, bound for Halifax and ultimately for their training camp near Aldershot. Here, they would go on to train with a home battalion, forming A Company, 10th (Service) Battalion, Duke of Wellington's (West Riding) Regiment – a component part of the Third Hundred Thousand, the Third Kitchener's Army or K3, and marking the move from civilian clothes to Kitchener blue.

Tunstill would be offered a commission on 28 September. His desire was that he would serve with the local men he had raised and he accompanied them, with the rest of the battalion, to their training camp in Frensham.

Tunstill's Men, and his patriotic fervour to raise them, are a microcosm of Kitchener's Army as a whole – and of the prodigious recruiting efforts to come.

Tunstill's Men formed part of the 10th (Service) Battalion, Duke of Wellington's Regiment (West Riding). Initially in civilian clothes, then Kitchener blue, they would be issued with khaki before moving overseas.

KITCHENER'S MEN

The task the government set itself was formidable … It was in the first place to take 500,000 raw men from the streets, from the clubs, from the fields, from the villages, towns and cities of Great Britain, and not only to train them in the art of war in the shortest space of time that it is possible to train soldiers, but also to prepare the equipment, the arms, and the munitions and stores of war.[1]

The first men in Kitchener's Army met with challenges. Though recruitment in early August had been modest, with the turn of the tide flowing against the British Expeditionary Force in France in late August things changed. There was now a realisation that it was no longer acceptable to expect others to carry out their patriotic duties for them. With the dawn of the retreat from Mons came the growth of the army. Could the army gather them in, equip them, train them and ready them for the fray? The prime minister recorded his views:

There is no doubt from what K reports that French's [Field Marshal Sir John French, commander of the BEF] troops, always fighting and always retiring, have been a good deal battered … Recruiting is now going on at such a tremendous rate – 30,000 men a day – that it will soon become impossible to digest the new material and provide it with clothing and arms.[2]

If der KITCHENER'S Men haf gone by, den I kan kom out.

One of the many propaganda cards from 1914–15 that portrayed the Germans as buffoons.

'On Parade' – Kitchener's men in their own clothes with blankets worn *en banderole.*

And so it was. The men of Kitchener's Army faced shortages. With the Regular Army and Territorial Force soldiers coming first, many would have to drill in their own clothes, be shod with their own boots and wear their own hats, come rain or come shine. The War Office itself noted the limitations of its supply chain:

> War reserves of clothing at the outbreak of war served for little more than the fitting out and upkeep for a few weeks of the original Expeditionary Force of six divisions and a cavalry division. During normal times the manufacture of clothing had been practically confined to a few firms, the requirements being small and insufficient to attract a wide field of production.[3]

And at a time when white feathers – for cowardice – were distributed by 'earnest young things' to any man not in uniform, there was a pressing need to mark the man as a willing volunteer. Armbands, hastily contrived, were worn with tweed jackets and impossibly large caps, while men drilled with canes and improvised wooden weapons. This phenomenon would be repeated when the local 'Pals' battalions were raised.

One of the many types of badge worn to counter the threat of the white feather, distributed by women to men in civilian clothes in 1914–15.

KITCHENER BLUE

The difficulties in clothing the recruits were very great. The available stocks in the country were soon exhausted; and the machinery and the supply of dyes, cloth, leather, etc., for the manufacture of new stocks could not be improvised.[4]

With khaki serge cloth in such short supply and civilian clothes becoming threadbare, replacements were sought. In place of khaki, there was what became known as 'Kitchener blue', the origins of which were hinted at by Basil Williams in 1917:

Mere expedients had, therefore to be resorted to in order to clothe the men during the first rush of recruits. A supply of 500,000 suits of blue serge uniform was obtained, this material being the only colour procurable in sufficient quantities, and these uniforms were delivered at a rate of 10,000 suits per day.[5]

The resulting uniform, created in haste to clothe a mass army, was almost universally shapeless and was worn with a cap that defied all attempts at smartness. The first brand of 'blues' was reputedly derived from unwanted uniforms – from the Post Office and the tramways department. Despite this assertion, there is no direct evidence that it was made up of existing uniforms rather than simply from bolts of uniform cloth.[6] Certainly, actual Post Office uniforms of the day had a completely different cut, were open necked and piped in red. This was a new development.

'Kitchener blue' in camp.

Uniform for Lord Kitchener's Army.

'Kitchener blue', reported to the trade in an article in *Tailor & Cutter*, November 1914.

The 'Kitchener blue' uniform was most likely to have been developed to be simple, and therefore most capable of being reproduced rapidly, which would explain its poverty of style. The uniform was intended to do just that – to present a uniform image – but there is no doubt it was universally despised. *Tailor & Cutter* was quick to comment on its workhouse-like cut:

[The uniform] is made of blue serge with black buttons. The cap is finished with red braid and two brass buttons ... this is not at all liked, the first men to wear it being mistaken for the inmates of an industrial home. We suppose some little latitude must be allowed for these emergency arrangements, the attempt evidently being to produce something extremely simple which could be made up at small cost. It is satisfactory to know that this outfit will only be used during the preliminary training, and as soon as the men go on active service they will be dressed in the regulation khaki uniforms.[7]

In a series of articles written for *The Daily Telegraph* in 1914, author Rudyard Kipling described a typical format of the blues when he observed some 'North Country' Kitchener men:

They were clad in a blue garb that disguised all contours ... When the New Army gets all its new uniform, it will gaze upon itself like a new Narcissus. But the present kit is indescribable. That is why, English fashion, it has been made honourable by its wearers; and our world in the years to come will look back with reverence as well as affection on those blue slops and that epileptic cap.[8]

Accompanying the cap was a blue jacket with closed collars, five horn buttons and two pocket flaps on the jacket skirt (whether there were actually pockets there is equivocal).[11] Contemporary photographs show the jacket flaring outwards from the waist and there are no darts or pleats to enhance the look and fit. There were also no shoulder straps, and therefore no viable means of attaching insignia.

In some battalions, the uniform was smartened by the addition of such embellishments – which at least helped to build up that essential attention to detail and 'bull' that was held to be so important in developing discipline. Obtaining buttons, shoulder titles and other items of brassware often fell upon the wiles of the commander himself, the plan being to set his men apart from the others – and to help fill their long days of training. As Kipling noted:

> One far-seeing commandant who had special facilities has possessed himself of brass buttons, thousands of 'em, which he has added to his men's outfit for the moral effect of (a) having something to clean, and (b) of keeping it so.[12]

The first of the Kitchener blue. A simple uniform, with simple buttons and what Kipling described as 'an epileptic cap'.

Impractical and shapeless it might have been, but at least it was a uniform – of sorts. The 'epileptic cap' was actually a simple blue 'Austrian', or field service, cap which was variously perched or plonked on the head depending on the character of the recruit. Blue was its colour, though some versions were piped in red.[9] This colour variation – deemed by some to be 'Foreign' – caused some confusion amongst the ranks of the University & Public Schools (UPS) battalions. 'What is the name of the UPS man who, on meeting in Town some of the New Army in their blue uniforms and forage caps with red piping, began to talk to them in Flemish, under the impression they were Belgians?'[10]

The absence of shoulder straps meant that the uniform itself was devoid of a place to display the mostly curved brass titles that distinguished battalions and regiments on the service dress. Cast in abbreviated form, these titles were sometimes worn incongruously on their collars.[13] In other cases, armbands, brassards and unofficial badges were all worn with Kitchener blue. Trousers were of simple cut, narrow in the leg and, more often than not in this first issue, they were worn without puttees. The quality of these uniforms was a point of some contention.

Some officers provided men
with brass buttons to replace
the horn ones supplied.

Even the supply of blues was sometimes variable, as was the issue of boots. Pre-war red tunics were also commonly issued, and must have presented a startling vision of the ragtag army of Kitchener's men. The author, A. Neil Lyons, known for his character studies in town and country before the war, described the phenomenon in a fictional northern battalion from Wigan, in a county then known for its almost universal wearing of stout, wooden-soled clogs:

In two or three weeks' time the clogs had disappeared, having been superseded by leather boots and puttees ... you kept on accumulating clothes. When you set out to perform those marches which you could not (in theory) accomplish, you looked like some kind of zebra – blue cap, brown jacket, blue trousers, brown puttees, or blue puttees, brown trousers, blue jacket, and brown 'Brodrick' cap. With a checkered overcoat, worn *en banderole*, across your shoulder.[14]

This hotchpotch approach can be seen in many photographs of men drilling in fields and parks, variously equipped and attired in civilian jackets and large caps. James Norman Hall experienced the supply problems first-hand when he joined

Royal Engineers in Kitchener blue. The Austrian cap is replaced by peaked caps with some men, and the title 'RE' is prominent on their collars.

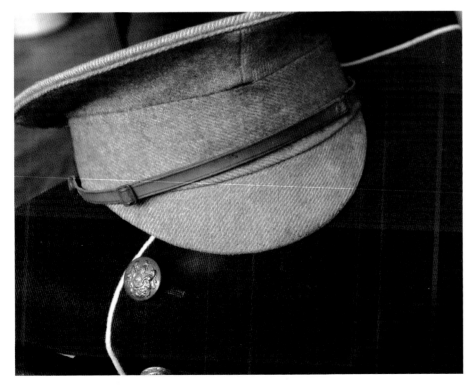

In some cases, red full dress tunics were issued, often with blue trousers and whatever caps were available.

the 9th (Service) Battalion, Royal Fusiliers (part of K1) in 1914:

> Although we were recruited immediately after the outbreak of war, less than half of our number had been provided with uniforms. Many still wore their old civilian clothing. Others were dressed in canvas fatigue suits, or the worn out uniforms of policemen and tramcar conductors. Every old-clothes shop on Petticoat Lane must have contributed its allotment of cast-off apparel.[15]

In many cases, Kitchener's Mob was equipped piece by piece, leading to a motley appearance when gathered in front of huts and tents, or upon parade grounds. Hall continued:

> Supplies came in driblets. Each night, when parades for the day were over, there was a rush for the orderly room bulletin board, which was scanned eagerly for news of an early issue of clothing. As likely as not we were disappointed, but occasionally jaded hopes revived.[16]

The supply of boots was similarly a challenge. The British shoe and boot industry was much admired, and there was conflict between not only supplying boots for the Regular Army, and through contractors for the Territorial Force, but also fulfilling large contracts for allies such as France. The number of boots required annually to satisfy the army's peacetime establishment was 245,000 pairs, all supplied from twenty-five firms in Northamptonshire.[17] With the rapid expansion of the army, this was clearly inadequate, and the supply had to be

Kitchener's men in red tunics at camp.

expanded rapidly, sourced much wider than the firms of one English county. *The Boot & Shoe Retailer*, the magazine of the boot trades, was not slow in defending the industry which, it felt, could easily handle the increased pressure the raising of the New Army brought with it.[18]

The impact of intensive training was telling on the boots themselves, however:

The tremendous amount of energy which the new army is putting into its preparations for the field, including many hours a day of heavy marching, is having its effect upon sole leather, and we hear from a correspondent who visited Aldershot that a large proportion of the boots issued when war broke out are already sadly in need of repair.[19]

Indifferently dressed in awkward and ill-fitting suits and boots of variable quality, there was nevertheless a pride in knowing that this style of dress set these men apart from others. 'We derived what comfort we could from the knowledge that we were but one of many battalions of Kitchener's First Hundred Thousand equipped in this makeshift fashion.'[20]

If the first men to join Kitchener's Army – the men of the First, Second and Third New Armies – faced being garbed indifferently, it was a different story altogether once local dignitaries and regional pride started to play its part. With the supply of khaki serge cloth still an issue, blue serge remained the most viable option – though full-page advertisements in the trade journal, *Tailor & Cutter*, screamed 'KHAKI' in 2in block letters, suggesting that the sought-after cloth was available to those willing to look for it.[21]

The supply of boots, as with
all equipment, was a challenge
for Kichener's Army.

Other battalions – with friends in high places – ignored the blues altogether. As discussed by Basil Williams, for some the shame of wearing such shapeless garb was too strong and it was having a negative effect on morale: 'The early enthusiasm of many recruits was considerably damped [*sic*] by being obliged to march and drill in public, attired in all sorts of garments, some in khaki, some in blue, some in civilian clothes of varying hues and cuts.'[23]

This would not happen with the first of the Pals battalions – the Liverpool City battalions – under the patronage of the 'King of Lancashire' himself, Lord Derby. His brother, Brigadier General F.C. Stanley, described the lengths taken to supply his own brigade of 'Pals':

Mrs Stanley [Lord Derby's sister-in-law] … was wired to in the early morning of the first day of recruiting, telling her that she was to arrange, by hook or by crook, to contract for the clothing of at least a thousand men. This appears a tall order, but within a very few hours she was able to wire back that the contract had been fixed up for clothing the men in khaki in a few weeks. This was much appreciated later by those serving in our City Battalions, because they were able to go about clothed in khaki, instead of having to go about in that terrible blue uniform, which was worn by most of the locally raised battalions, and which looked awful.[24]

Superseding the awful blue uniform was something that was much more in line with the smart service dress worn by the Regulars and Territorials. Known as 'Jackets, Emergency Pattern', these uniforms had brass buttons, patch pockets, darts at the collar to improve fit, and all the other refinements of the standard pattern of uniform which had been worn, with some modifications, continuously since 1902.[22] With civic pride at stake, the battalions of such cities as Manchester and Birmingham were clothed in smart blue service dress and matching caps from at least early 1915 – dispensing with the dreadful and impractical Austrian-style cap.

In wool towns like Bradford, it was a matter of pride that uniforms were to be made up to the sealed pattern in the best-quality blue serge wool. Both types of emergency Kitchener blue uniforms would eventually find their way to British prisoners of war in Germany.

Other battalions would take it to be their duty not to circumvent the procedures and bypass the supply line, putting strain on the creaking system by seeking out their own sources and jumping the queue. For the Welsh Army Corps, raised late in 1914 to fulfil a dream of the Chancellor of the Exchequer,

David Lloyd George, for a uniquely Welsh army to fight the German threat, there would be another option. The committee charged with considering all aspects of the raising of the corps also considered the supply of a uniquely Welsh uniform, too:

> The Committee conceived the idea of clothing as many of the troops as possible in uniforms of native homespun ('Brethyn Llwyd'), and succeeded in stimulating the manufacturers of the cloth to produce it in greater quantities than had ever before been manufactured in so short a time.[25]

Some thirteen Welsh woollen mills were in action producing the cloth, predominantly in South Wales.[26] No surviving examples of this uniform exist, and even its colour is disputed – despite the fact that 'brethyn llwyd' simply means 'grey cloth'. Samples varied from greenish to grey cloth, while the Cardiff-based Western Mail noted, 'Now that the Welsh battalions are to be clad in brethyn llwyd Cymru a correspondent suggests they should be named the Welsh Greys.'[27]

The insistence on the use of this material did little to assist in the supply of adequate uniforms, however, as the mills simply could not keep up with demand. Though it was a brave attempt to create a national uniform, it was a challenge to supply even one battalion, never mind a whole army corps.[28] As such, Welsh soldiers, like their English, Irish and Scottish comrades, were more invariably clad in Kitchener blue before adopting the khaki that they all finally wore before leaving for France. Brethyn llwyd, hard-wearing as it was, was relegated to the status of an emergency uniform equipping reservists.[29] It had been a bold experiment.

EQUIPPING THE SOLDIER

In that most important factor, the material of war, the failure to produce supplies on a scale adequate for even the small forces envisaged by the experts at the War Office in the days preceding August 4th, 1914, was the more serious in that facilities were lacking for their rapid manufacture.[30]

With quartermasters having difficulties supplying the uniform needs of a greatly expanded army, it is not surprising that they were faced with an even bigger crisis when it came to military equipment – and this crisis went much deeper than just the personal equipment of an individual soldier.

The individual Regular infantryman's loadbearing equipment set was the innovative Pattern 1908 Web Infantry Equipment. The official guide to this set praised its versatility, its balance, its flexibility and its lack of constricting chest straps.[31] Part of the success of this equipment set lay with its greatest innovations. Designed by an infantry officer in 1906, it was a complete system. Its thick, woven cotton strapping had many advantages over leather. Leather was difficult to keep clean, was cumbersome and liable to stretching when wet – characteristics not ideal in military equipment. Not so for webbing – the cotton used in constructing it was specially waterproofed, the effect being 'to render the material practically impervious to the weather, which might otherwise have tended to make it hard or cause it to stretch and shrink'.[32]

To prevent fraying, the webbing straps were finished with riveted brass ends that also allowed the component pieces to be easily fitted together – but which also provided the army with something else for its soldiers to polish until gleaming. Corresponding to these straps were tongueless buckles, finished in heavy gauge brass. The full set consisted of belt, cross-straps, left and right cartridge carriers (designed to carry 150 rounds in ten pouches), water bottle, bayonet frog and entrenching tool. In addition, there was a small haversack and large pack, with cross-straps to keep the pack in place. It was all perfectly balanced – whether the cartridge carriers were full or not (previous equipment sets had the disadvantage of pulling up the belt and creating imbalance). Another advantage of the system was that it was directly fastened together, and could be removed as a whole, providing the opportunity to take the equipment off on the march.

But not all British soldiers could be equipped with 1908 webbing in 1914. Once again, supplying so many men was a major issue, as noted by the War Office just after the war:

The standard pattern of infantry equipment was the '1908 Web Equipment'. Prior to mobilisation, all our annual requirements could only be supplied by the two firms possessing the machinery capable of making the material. Subsequent to mobilisation, a certain number of additional firms began to learn the process, but no firm except these two possessed or could obtain the special machinery required for certain portions of the equipment.[33]

The significant expansion of Kitchener's Army left the military authorities with a huge shortfall in equipment stocks, leaving Kitchener's men with a typical motley arrangement of equipment items. Though the New Army could aspire to webbing equipment, it would have to make do. The Mills Equipment Company and M. Wright & Sons, the only two companies capable of producing webbing, were seriously overstretched – they simply could not meet the demand placed upon them to supply Regular, Territorial and Service battalions with sufficient webbing equipment sets.

With men seeking some form of military equipment to train with, at least before the universal issue of equipment sets, photographs illustrate the miscellaneous collection of belts, pouches and straps used. Elements of obsolete equipment sets were in use – whatever would do the job. There were

An older recruit in first pattern 'Kitchener blue'. He wears an earlier pattern leather belt, issued with the 1888 Slade Wallace equipment set.

Kitchener's men equipped with the pipe-clayed 1888 Slade Wallace equipment, and Magazine Lee–Enfield (MLE or 'Long Lee') rifles.

impossibly large pouches belonging to the Valise Equipment Pattern 1882, or the belt and straps of the Pattern 1888 (Slade Wallace) Equipment – anything that created a military impression, even if they were unsuited for modern warfare.[34]

If supply of the standard 1908 sets was limited, then an alternative would be needed. If the heavy woven fabric was scarce, then a similar set could be manufactured from leather – a material which, despite its many deficiencies, was still freely available. As such, the War Office commissioned a set of equipment in leather that was based upon the basic format of the webbing, but which was quicker to manufacture and easier to source from overseas manufacturers. Though leather was in demand for boots (with allegations of 'adulteration', the packing of inferior leather with chemicals, greases and other products to improve its bulk),[35] it was also available to be used for equipment.

The Infantry Equipment, Pattern 1914 was the result of the New Army's desperate need for

equipment, and was based on the 1908 set. Though intended only as an emergency measure, it would be worn throughout the war and would become as much associated with the New Army as Kitchener blue was in 1914. Officially introduced on 30 August 1914, the official orders state that 'the equipment, except for the pack and haversack, is made of pliable hide leather, stained as near as possible to the colour of service dress'.[36]

Large orders were placed, but the first sets of the equipment were not available until months after the soldiers concerned had received their uniforms – not an ideal situation in a completely novice army. Nevertheless, the Pattern 1914 equipment set was serviceable, though less efficient at distributing weight than the original webbing, and was issued most commonly to Service battalions.

In some cases, the leather equipment was discarded in favour of webbing salvaged from the battlefield. A particular case, when new men arrived at Regular battalions equipped with the

Kitchener's men in a Service battalion of the Somerset Light Infantry, wearing later pattern 'Kitchener blue' tunics cut in the style of standard service dress, khaki caps and a motley set of equipment.

A Kitchener volunteer in first pattern 'Kitchener blue', equipped with leather leggings and a cartridge case and belt from the obsolete Valise Equipment, Pattern 1882.

The equipment sets were produced in Britain and in the United States, with varying quality, made from brown marbled leather and, in some cases, dyed green. In all, some 1 million sets of equipment were manufactured.[38] Although it used webbing for the haversack and large pack, the Pattern 1914 equipment employed leather for the waist belt, cross-straps, ammunition pouches, entrenching tool holder, bayonet frog, water bottle cradle and entrenching tool carrier. The two ammunition pouches were designed to take a cotton bandolier, each holding fifty cartridges in five-round chargers, with an additional ten rounds in a pocket, The pouches took 120 rounds in all. Ungainly and unbalanced, these bulky leather pouches pulled down on the belt and were consequently uncomfortable to wear on the march.

Part-set of Infantry Equipment, Pattern 1914 with belt, ammunition pouches and bayonet frog.

As described in the official manual, the essence of having the equipment well fitted was to ensure that the straps and buckles were as tight as possible, but with front-line use, and with constant dampness, achieving this aim was often nigh on impossible.[39] Whichever pattern of equipment was carried, although the weight of the soldier's individual equipment varied through the war, around 60lb was not unusual – a challenge for some of the city workers who had joined Kitchener's Army in a flush of enthusiasm.

Opposite: In the quarter-masters' store – Infantry Equipment, Pattern 1914, ammunition pouches and entrenching tool covers.

leather set, was observed by Regular officer Sydney Rogerson:

When the regiment had landed in France in November 1914, every man had naturally been equipped with webbing, but of recent months the new reinforcement drafts had arrived with the unsightly leather belts and cartridge pouches such as were issued to Kitchener's Army … Efforts were constantly being made to discard the leather, for not only was it clumsy, unsightly, and difficult to fit, especially when wet, but it was held to be the badge of the new arrival or temporary soldier.[37]

An actual assessment of the weight carried by the average soldier was given in the officers' *Field Service Pocket Book*.[40] 'Non-mounted, Non-Highland soldiers' would carry just a bit less than Highland soldiers. With their distinctive dress and weighty woollen kilt, Highlanders carried just that bit more than soldiers from England, Wales, Ireland, or even the Scottish lowlands:

"FULL MARCHING ORDER"
WHAT YOUR KIT FEELS LIKE
AFTER TEN MILES !

Above left: In the quarter-masters' store – Infantry Equipment, Pattern 1914, water bottles.

Above right: Donald McGill's take on the growing level of equipment issued to the average soldier.

Total weight carried	lb	oz
A. Clothing worn (non-Highlander)	14	11
A. Clothing worn (Highlander)	18	12⅜
B. Arms	10	8½
C. Ammunition	9	0
D. Tools	2	9¼
E. Accoutrements	8	4¼
F. Articles in Pack	10	1¾
G. Rations and water	5	13½
Totals		
Normal weight carried by a non-Highland private	61	0¼
Normal weight carried by a Highland private[41]	65	1⅜

As usual, Captain Atteridge gave a clear indication, for anyone who wanted to read it, of the nature of the equipment that would have to be carried by the average soldier in 1915:

The soldier has to carry his weapons, a supply of ammunition, food, and water, and a heavy load in his pack, made up of all that he must have on active service, including a change of clothes, an extra pair of boots, and the greatcoat and waterproof ground-sheet which will make his bed if he has to sleep in open air. In all he has to carry a load of over sixty pounds' weight. The trained soldier must be able to march fifteen or twenty miles

The men of a Service battalion of the Royal Fusiliers equipped with Pattern 1914 equipment and SMLE (Short, Magazine, Lee–Enfield) rifles, *c.* 1916.

carrying this weight, and he must be fit to do a mile 'at the double', that is, with the quick-running step, without being out of breath and helpless at the end of it.[42]

On the Somme on 1 July 1916, every one of Kitchener's men – officers included – would have to carry a load similar to this when wearing 'battle order' in their assault on the German front line. There would also be additional ammunition, Mills bombs, food and other kit, amounting to a weight of some 66lb. For the official historian this meant that, for the assault troops, it was 'difficult to get out of a trench, impossible to move much quicker than a slow walk, or to rise and lie down quickly'.[43] It would become a cause célèbre.

Supplying equipment sets was one thing; making sure that soldiers were equipped with an appropriate modern weapon was another. The principal weapon of the British soldier from 1904 had been the Short, Magazine, Lee–Enfield rifle, or SMLE. The SMLE was based on its predecessor, the Magazine Lee–Enfield (MLE), or 'Long Lee', which was first introduced in 1895. The MLE was around 5in longer than the SMLE.[44] To make sure the SMLE-equipped infantryman would not be 'out-reached' by an enemy with a longer rifle, the shorter bayonet of the MLE was replaced with a long 'sword' bayonet for the SMLE.

The MLE was the first British service rifle to be equipped with a ten-round magazine and was famed for its bolt action, which cocked the striker

when the bolt was closed. This was a swift action, important in battle, meaning that the weapon could be cocked and fired rapidly. The charger system allowed for five rounds to be loaded at a time, the magazine holding ten altogether. The high-capacity magazine and efficient bolt action meant that in the right hands the rifle had an impressive rate of fire. Well-trained soldiers could fire around fifteen aimed bullets a minute with the SMLE – but it was unlikely that the majority of Kitchener's recruits would be able to emulate this ideal in the limited amount of training time available to them.

However, in 1914, stocks of the admired SMLE were few and far between. As with uniforms and equipment sets, total peacetime output was just sufficient to supply the peacetime army – some 795,000 serviceable rifles for an army of 725,000 men.[45] Even with a slight surplus, and this taking into account the older Long Lee rifles, there was a shortfall that would not cover the requirements of even K1. The historian of the 20th (Light) Division (K2) recorded an undoubtedly typical situation in September 1914 which went beyond the supply of rifles:

> Throughout the period of training … there was the greatest difficulty in getting clothing and equipment. No uniform was available until November, when a suit of emergency blue pattern was issued to each man. A certain number of old rifles for drill purposes became available about the same time. There were so few S.M.L.E. rifles in some battalions that only one or two companies could fire at a time, and even then each detail after firing had to hand over the rifles to another detail

SMLE rifles – the magazine could take ten rounds.

waiting to fire. The artillery at first had only enough harness for one six-horse team in each brigade. The shortage of saddles was made good to a certain extent by private gifts. Each brigade had two 90-mm and two 15-pr guns, but these had no sights. Wooden sights and wooden guns were improvised to carry out battery gun drill. It was not until February that one 18-pr gun was issued to each battery.[46]

For most men of Kitchener's Army, getting their full allocation of kit often meant a long wait. This was certainly the case for Private James Norman Hall, of the 9th (Service) Battalion, Royal Fusiliers:

One Sunday morning in May we assembled on the barrack square at Aldershot for the last time. Every man was in full marching order. His rifle was the 'Short Lee Enfield Mark IV [*sic*],' his bayonet, the long single-edged

Opposite: SMLE rifles in the armourer's shop.

MLE rifles – known as 'Long Lees' – in the armourer's shop.

blade in general use throughout the British Army. In addition to his arms he carried 120 rounds of '.303' calibre ammunition, an intrenching-tool, water-bottle, haversack, containing both emergency and the day's rations, and his pack, strapped to shoulders and waist in such a way that the weight of it was equally distributed. His pack contained the following articles: a greatcoat, a woollen shirt, two or three pairs of socks, a change of underclothing, a 'housewife' – the soldiers' sewing kit – a towel, a cake of soap, and a 'hold-all', in which were a knife, fork, spoon, razor, shaving brush, toothbrush, and comb. All of these were useful and sometimes essential articles, particularly the toothbrush, which Tommy regarded as the best little instrument for cleaning the mechanism of a rifle ever invented. Strapped on top of the pack was the blanket roll wrapped in a waterproof ground sheet; and hanging beneath it, the canteen [water bottle], in its khaki-cloth cover. Each man wore an identification disc on a cord around his neck. It was stamped with his name, regimental number, regiment, and religion. A first-aid dressing, consisting of an antiseptic gauze pad and bandage and a small vial of iodine, sewn in the lining of his tunic, completed the equipment.[47]

And so it was that Kitchener's soldier was equipped for war: in a piecemeal fashion, often with equipment that was pressed into use, or that was rushed into production to fulfil the needs of the growing mass of new soldiers. It would take some time for the supply issues to be resolved.

The indifferent supply of suitable rifles was clearly an issue as the successive New Armies were raised, as described by Captain Basil Williams writing in 1918:

The first and second armies, containing the earliest recruits, did comparatively well, since by January 1915, the first new army had about 400 Service rifles per battalion, and the second about 100; and by March they were beginning to be fully armed. But the third and later-formed armies were much worse off.[48]

The supply of sets of 1914 equipment would similarly be challenging.[49] Ultimately, though, with supply problems finally ironed out, the New Armies would make their crossing to France and other battlefronts ready for war, arguably with the best rifle of the conflict and with an equipment set that, though not the ideal, would serve them well throughout the conflict.

TRAINING

When the recruits were marched off from the recruiting stations or depots to the division to which they were assigned their first impression was that they were just units in a mere mob of men. They and their fellow-soldiers were mostly in civilian dress; no rifles or equipment were at first available; and the accommodation available for them was not in all cases sufficient.[50]

The strains that had been felt by the army in supplying the influx of new men with uniforms and equipment were magnified when it came to housing the recruits. With the Haldane reforms came a focus on a regimental depot located regionally in order to act as a centre for recruitment. Regiments that proudly carried the name of their county usually had a depot and barracks located within a prominent county town. It was from here that the two Regular battalions found in most regiments served in turn during peacetime, replacing each other overseas in turn in order to take on Imperial duties, garrisoning the outposts of Empire. Also in peacetime it was to the third, Special Reserve, battalion that recruits reported before they were posted to the Regular battalions. These men would be housed in the regimental barracks, often located in old buildings – purpose-built, if austere – before going on to their Regular postings.

With Kitchener's Call to Arms in 1914, camps were set up across the country to house the vast influx of new recruits, though the first men to join invariably lived at home. The new camps would vary considerably from villages of bell tents to timber-constructed huts. Basil Williams described the situation:

Our housing accommodations, throughout the autumn and winter of 1914–15, when England was in such urgent need of shelter for her rapidly increasing armies, were also of makeshift order. We slept in leaky tents or in hastily constructed wooden shelters, many of which were afterwards condemned by the medical inspectors.[51]

While the new camps were being built, tented accommodation was provided – adequate for a two-week Territorial field camp, but hardly the

One of the many tented camps occupied by Kitchener's Army on Salisbury Plain, here, at Frensham Common.

Kitchener's Army, Frensham Common, Oct, 1914.

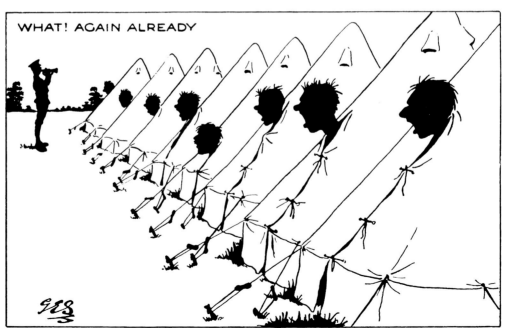

WHAT! AGAIN ALREADY

Photochrom's 'Camp Silhouette Series' depicted life in the camps in 1914–15. The early call of reveille came as a shock to some of the recruits.

PHOTOCHROM COPYRIGHT

CAMP SILHOUETTE No.7

perfect setting to train an amateur army to the peak of military effectiveness.

The camps spread across the country, and were located to ensure that they were close enough to the points of major accumulation of soldiers (garrisons and depots), that there was suitable access, suitable ground for building and training, and, from the soldiers' perspective, suitable access to local facilities – not always the case, at least in James Norman Hall's view:

Camps were sited in the wrong places and buildings erected only to be condemned.

Tons of food were purchased overseas, transported across thousands of miles of ocean, only to be thrown in refuse barrels. The Government was robbed by avaricious hotel-keepers who made and were granted absurd claims for damages done to their property by billeted troops. But with vast new armies, recruited overnight, it is not strange that there should be mismanagement and friction at first.[52]

By mid 1915 most of the tented accommodation had been replaced with wooden huts, and

Hut building. The standard design was produced by the Royal Engineers. Here, men of the University & Public Schools Brigade take a hand in construction.

The interior of a typical Kitchener's Army hut. Well organised, the simple beds are trestles and planks, with paillasses rolled up. Pattern 1914 equipment hangs from hooks.

A YMCA hut in a camp in Britain. Such huts provided a welcome respite from training for Kitchener's soldiers. Here, men in khaki – and some still in Kitchener blue (right) – pose for a photograph with YMCA workers, c. 1914–15.

conditions improved. The redoubtable corps of Royal Engineers shouldered much of the burden for not only supplying detailed plans for each hutted camp, but also surveying and assessing the suitability of the ground where each camp was to be built.[53]

Salisbury Plain was an obvious site for development, with many camps here, but others would be at Cannock Chase in Staffordshire, Clipstone in Nottinghamshire and Kinmel Park in north Wales. There were many others, as the great crush of men arrived to take up their places. Each camp had as its basis a typical sleeping hut measuring 60ft long and 20ft wide, with an average height of 10ft. This provided accommodation for thirty men, and forty huts provided the accommodation for a battalion. Some 800,000 men were accommodated this way in 1914.[54]

In addition, there were all manner of other huts on camp to enable it to function properly – not forgetting the soldiers' canteens provided by the Young Men's Christian Association (YMCA). Paid for through charitable means, they provided a place for relaxation on site. Nevertheless, soldiers accommodated in these camps regularly wrote home describing their monotony, the banality of the experience and aspects of the training. It became the usual lot of Kitchener's Mob in 1914–15.[55]

For the locally raised Pals battalions, however, with local committees left to their own devices, finding suitable initial accommodation was a challenge – especially as the raising committees would have to fund this before the War Office officially took the new battalions on. As reported in the Manchester press, Lord Kitchener made sure that local raisers were fully aware of this fact:

Lord Kitchener hopes that those large cities and private companies which are now raising complete battalions will be able to make arrangements in connection with county associations to find training grounds and housing or tentage, and to clothe and feed the men on a contract scale fixed by the War Office until they can be taken over by the military authorities.[56]

DOWN IN OUR KINMEL PARK CAMP.

To the tune of "Back Home in Tennessee."

I'm so lonely, oh, so lonely,
  In our Blinking Camp,
I'm like a bloomin' tramp,
  Not worth a penny stamp.
Father, Mother, Sister, Brother,
  All are waiting me,
I'm getting thinner, miss my dinner
  And my Sunday's tea.
CHORUS :
Down in our Blinking camp,
  We're always on the ramp,
That's where we cop the cramp,
  Through sleeping in the damp,
All we can hear there each day,
  Is Left . . . Right, . . . march away,
Sergeants calling, Lance-jacks bawling
  "Get out On Parade."
We go to bed at night,
  It is a glorious sight,
The earwigs on the floor,
  Double-up and then Form Fours,
Then when daylight is dawning,
  You can hear our Sergeant yawnin'
Show-a-leg there, Show-a-leg there,
  Down in our Kinmel Camp.

Postcards bemoaning life in the camps were very popular. This one is from Kinmel Park Camp, near Abergele, which was built specifically for training Kitchener's Army.

With authorities required to accommodate their own men locally, some lateral thought was required. Disused buildings were targeted, as was the case for the first of the Pals, in Liverpool, as described by their commanding officer:

> The housing problem was a decidedly difficult one ... we had to work out our own salvation. Arrangements had already been made, when we should only get about a battalion, to put them in the watch factory at Prescot. It was not ideal ... but it was a palace compared with many places we have had to put up with since.[57]

But the creation of an efficient soldier did not rely solely upon the issue of uniform and the provision of suitable accommodation. If the army was to mould the civilians of Kitchener's Army into efficient fighting men there would have to be a full programme of training that was intended to create a fit body and calmness under fire. Introducing some form of military training for the raw recruits was a challenge, nevertheless. The historian of the Royal Fusiliers explained the situation:

> For the first year of the war large numbers of recruits for the regiment arrived at the depot, were given a few hours of squad drill and, if time allowed, a little elementary musketry. They were then sent off in batches as soon as the various battalions could receive them. At times the nucleus of a whole battalion was despatched in one day.[58]

Local Pals battalions were housed, fed and clothed by the committees who raised them. Finding suitable space was often a struggle. In Liverpool, the Pals were housed initially in a disused watch factory (closed in 1910) at Prescot, on the outskirts of Liverpool.

—AND THEN WE HAVE ALL THE REST OF THE DAY TO OURSELVES!

I'M NOT HALF PICKING UP SINCE I JOINED THE ARMY!

"WELL, I'VE DONE MY BIT IF I NEVER SEE A GERMAN!"

The main job of the army instructors was to create a fit, efficient fighting force attuned to discipline and steady under fire, as the manuals in 1914 stated: 'The object to be aimed at in the training of the infantry soldier is to make him, mentally and physically, a better man than his adversary on the field of battle.'[59]

First things first, the fitness of the new recruits was an issue that had to be tackled – particularly as much of Britain's new citizen army hailed from cities, the industrial centres and powerhouses of the British Empire. Edgar Wallace explained:

The broad doorway of the chief recruiting office was the gate to a land of strange and tragic adventure and it was with a light heart and a high hope that the young men of Great Britain passed through ... it was likewise seen in every great town and every small town throughout the kingdom. Birmingham, Manchester, Newcastle, Cardiff – all the great industrial and manufacturing towns.[60]

For most, such training was a new, challenging experience – the basis for the transition from civilian to soldier, and the foundation of his new life as a man serving in the front line facing a determined foe. Captain A.H. Atteridge, in his role as interpreter of the army for a wider public, expressed it thus in 1915:

Above: Camp routine as depicted by Donald McGill, part of the 'Recruits' series, published in 1914 by Inter-Art Company. Training involved trench digging and other aspects of pioneer work.

'Raw Recruits', from Photochrom's 'Camp Silhouette' series.

Swedish drill, from Photochrom's 'Camp Silhouette' series.

Once the idea of training a soldier was to try and make a machine of him. He used to be told that his business was not to think, but to do what he was told and let other people do the thinking for him. But our drill books of today lay it down that the object of training must be to bring out all that is best in the man. To develop a soldierly spirit, to appeal to his sense of honour, and to make him proud to bear toil and privation, and danger cheerfully; to cultivate his power of thinking for himself, to teach him self-confidence, and train him not only to obey orders, but to think and act for himself, even when he has no officer near him; to lead him to trust his commander and his comrades, to make him proud of the regiment he belongs to, and his privileges as a citizen of a great Empire, and a soldier serving his King and country. Body and mind are both trained together.[61]

It was the manual *Infantry Training (4 – Company Organisation)* that set out the training course syllabus which, it was hoped, would see the transition of the recruit to trained soldier. There were eleven components to this:

1   The development of a soldierly spirit
2   Instruction in barrack and camp duties
3   Physical training
4   Infantry training
5   Marching and running
6   Musketry instruction
7   Movements at night
8   Guards and outposts
9   Duties of soldier in the field
10 Use of entrenching equipment
11 Bayonet fighting

Recruits engaging in fitness training in 1914.

The average recruit might expect to receive training in all of these on his journey to becoming a soldier – a journey expected to last some six months.

The army was clear, even in wartime, that the development of 'soldierly spirit' was a crucial part of training. Though there was pressure to fill the ranks, 'good character' was still an essential condition of enlistment in the British Army. In 1914, the essence of this character and of soldierly spirit was boiled down to the statement: 'The ideal which inspires a man is that of willing self-sacrifice for the welfare of the State and the good of his fellow citizens. To this ideal, should occasion arise, the soldier must be faithful unto death.'[62]

These high ideals were to be further developed, it was hoped, through training and particularly through the development of discipline and initiative, and through the use of ceremonial parades,

inspections and pride in the regiment. For Captain Basil Williams, an officer of the Royal Field Artillery, the value of these was all too apparent, although only after the many matters of military supply had been resolved:

Before the hosts of raw recruits were converted into the armies which have given a good account of themselves in France, the Dardanelles, Egypt and Mesopotamia they had to be housed, fed, clothed, armed, equipped, distributed into units and taught drill, discipline and the technical skill needed of modern soldiers; in a word, animated with *esprit de corps* and the true military spirit.[63]

The prescribed diet of training that would achieve this was grounded in a simple regime of physical training based on the Swedish drill system of 'physical jerks'. Such activity, together with long runs and route marches in full equipment, was essential to bring the Kitchener's men into line with the standard of the Regulars. Gymnastics, drill, competitive sports and running formed a large part of the army's drive to develop the recruit into a fighting man. The relevant manual, first published in 1908, stated its objectives:

> The object of physical training is the production of a state of health and general physical fitness in order that the body may be enabled to withstand the strains of daily life and to perform the work required of it without injury to the system.[64]

Swedish drill, in effect a system of military-style gymnastics, had been invented by Pehr Henrik Ling in the late nineteenth century. Described in detail in the *Manual of Physical Training*, each recruit

Recruits engaging in Swedish drill fitness training in 1914.

was set on a path to fitness by progression through tables of development in order that he could meet a set of simple requirements: 'A soldier should be well-disciplined, a good marcher, intelligent, smart, active and quick, able to surmount obstacles in the field and capable of withstanding all the strains and hardships of active service.'[65]

Fitness was accompanied by lectures and a syllabus of training. Private James Norman Hall experienced it first-hand with the 9th (Service) Battalion, Royal Fusiliers:

> Our vigorous training continued from week to week in all weathers, even the most inclement. Reveille sounded at daybreak. For an hour before breakfast we did Swedish drill, a system of gymnastics which brought the lazy and disused muscle into play. Two hours daily we were instructed in the description and recognition of targets, the use of cover, but chiefly the use of our rifles.[66]

Alongside fitness, the army was keen to inculcate discipline and precision in drill, and this formed a major part of the training of all new recruits, with *Infantry Training* being the basis of all wisdom.[67]

A new soldier had to learn how to operate in the many different units available to him, from battalions to squads. As the manual put it: 'The general principle to be observed is first to give the individual a thorough knowledge of his duties and then to teach him to act in combination with his comrades.'[69] Squad drill without arms introduced the basics: standing at ease and to attention, saluting and marching at different rates. The official manual described that, for the average soldier, military instruction included proper care and use of his principal weapon, the Short, Magazine, Lee–Enfield (SMLE) rifle, and the means to use it in action: 'Musketry training is to render the individual soldier proficient in the use of small arms, to make him acquainted with the capabilities of the weapon with which he is armed, and to give him confidence in its power and accuracy.'[69]

But for Kitchener's New Army, valuable weapons such as the SMLE were in short supply, and trainees would have to make do with wooden stand-ins while learning how to carry out manoeuvres with appropriate military bearing.

As discussed, in August 1914 the whole stock of serviceable rifles stood at a little less than 800,000, and just over half of these were the SMLE – with most of these weapons already issued, there was a reserve of no more than 10 per cent. With the two main manufacturers (the Royal Small Arms Factory at Enfield, and the Birmingham Small Arms Company) already committed, the War Office brought in two other companies to supply the SMLE (Vickers and the Standard Small Arms Company) and filled the gap with rifles from other countries. Ross rifles from Canada and Japanese Arisaka rifles were used in training by Kitchener's Army, alongside the obsolete Long Lee–Enfield.

Accompanied by lectures on the theory of rifle firing, the recruit was taken through his paces to learn the fundamentals before progressing to actually firing his weapon. Aiming practice – learning how to line the back and foresights accurately – was first, before progressing to firing practice. Arranged in groups of seven men, the instructor first explained the finer points of trigger pressing, before proceeding to actually shooting the

Musketry training. Here recruits are trained using SMLE rifles.

weapon. James Norman Hall recorded his impressions of the training:

> We fired the recruit's, and later, the trained soldier's course in musketry on the rifle ranges at Hythe and Aldershot, gradually improving our technique, until we were able to fire with some accuracy, fifteen rounds a minute. When we had achieved this difficult feat, we ceased to be recruits.[70]

Marching was also an essential part of a soldier's training: 'The chief work of the infantry soldier is marching ... In preparing for a campaign or series of marches, care must be taken that only fit men form part of the columns.'[71] Learning how to march was an important part of the physical development of the average soldier. Hall continued:

Recruits in the Gloucestershire Regiment marching in *c.* 1914, equipped with the earlier Pattern 1903 Bandolier Equipment and SMLE rifle.

After musketry practice, the remainder of the day was given to extended order, company, and battalion drill. Twice weekly we route-marched from ten to fifteen miles; and at night, after the parades for the day were finished, boxing and wrestling contests, arranged and encouraged by our officers, kept the red blood pounding through our bodies until 'lights out' sounded at nine o'clock.[72]

The diaries of Private Humphrey Mason, a Kitchener volunteer with the 6th (Service) Battalion Oxfordshire & Buckinghamshire Light Infantry (K2), give a good indication of the diet of training he received over two months in April 1914 and 1915. His daily entries make reference to physical training, route marching, battalion and company drill, tactical training and musketry.

Yet it was bayonet fighting that was the culmination of the recruit's formal training, and it involved learning the cold, unvarnished truth that a charge at the enemy will bring the soldier face to face with a man he would have to kill. Lance Corporal Norman Roberts, one of Tunstill's Men serving with the 10th (Service) Battalion Duke of Wellington's Regiment (K3), recorded his experiences of the training regime in a letter to the *Craven Herald* newspaper:

An Army Gymnastic Service instructor and squad in 1914; bayonet training was the last part of the training sequence.

Recruits receiving bayonet instruction. The last component of this was the assault – charging sacks like these suspended from wooden frames.

We are having it very rough. It is 'drill, parade, drill' and so on all day long. I have hardly any time for letter writing we are so rushed. The NCOs have been doing bayonet drill this afternoon; quite hard work and very businesslike. This is a marine instructor here and he nearly frightened us all to death; we dared not move our eyes.[73]

The 'spirit of the bayonet' was in some ways central to the concept of the infantryman. Training in the bayonet was a psychological tool; if a man could be trained to use the bayonet, he could also be trained to kill his opponent. Killing was expected to be at close quarters, at a range of around 2ft, 'when troops are struggling corps á corps in trenches or darkness'.[74] The final component of bayonet training was the assault. The reality of charging home with the bayonet, even into a lifeless sack hung from a wooden gallows, must have struck home to the average citizen soldier in 1914–15.

3

PALS

Lord Derby ... had asked for a thousand men to turn from the ranks of Liverpool commerce and join the ranks of His Majesty's army. The young men of Liverpool responded magnificently – not one, but three, thousand came forward.[1]

The retreat from Mons in August 1914 had proven to be the necessary fillip to recruiting in late August, persuading those yet to join that there was a significant threat to Britain, if its Expeditionary Force was being pushed back to the Channel ports. Although the increased recruitment brought problems with it – particularly in the supply of uniforms and equipment, and the ability of the War Office to support the training of the men and housing recruits – Kitchener pressed ahead. As usual, he was sufficiently clear that if the recruits were forthcoming, they should not be turned away.

Towards the end of August, prominent citizens were taking on the role of recruiting agents. Local committees were formed, led by lord mayors, people of influence and senior municipal officers, with the intention of gaining as many recruits as possible to fill the ranks of Kitchener's New Army. Taking the lead from the Parliamentary Recruiting Committee, politicians used to operating in wards and constituencies applied themselves to the task of gathering recruits. In Southampton, for example, an unholy alliance of 'Unionist and Liberal

YOUR COUNTRY NEEDS YOU

FALL IN!

What will you lack, sonny, what will you lack
    When the girls line up the street,
Shouting their love to the lads come back
    From the foe they rushed to beat?
Will you send a strangled cheer to the sky
    And grin till your cheeks are red?
But what will you lack when your mate goes by
    With a girl who cuts you dead?

Where will you look, sonny, where will you look
    When your children yet to be
Clamour to learn of the part you took
    In the war that kept men free?
Will you say it was nought to you if France
    Stood up to her foe or bunked? [glance
But where will you look when they give the
    That tells you they know you funked?

How will you fare, sonny, how will you fare
    In the far-off winter night,
When you sit by the fire in an old man's chair
    And your neighbours talk of the fight?
Will you slink away, as it were from a blow,
    Your old head shamed and bent?
Or say—I was not with the first to go,
    But I went, thank God, I went.

Why do they call, sonny, why do they call
    For men who are brave and strong?
Is it nought to you if your country fall,
    And Right is smashed by Wrong?
Is it football still and the picture show,
    The pub and the betting odds,
When your brothers stand to the tyrant's blow,
    And Britain's call is God's?

HAROLD BEGBIE.

Reproduced from the London "Daily Chronicle."

'Where will you look when they give the glance that tells you they know you funked?' The pressure on men who had not joined in 1914–15 was intense.

A staged photograph illustrating a recruitment line in 1914; the demographic of these lines had certainly changed by late August 1914.

"THE COOKS" 10TH BATTN RF

The 10th Royal Fusiliers – the Stockbrokers' Battalion – was arguably the first of the Pals battalions. Here battalion cooks are in action.

leaders' applied themselves to stimulating recruiting by 'making a thorough canvass of the wards and clubs of the town'.[2] How this was received was not reported.

Others would even go so far as to attempt to influence recruits by using the press to simply appeal to their pockets – tempting for some in straightened circumstances:

Lord Aberconway has offered a bounty of £5 for every recruit belonging to local families who enlists in Lord Kitchener's army between now and the end of September, from all parishes in the Vale of Conway, in which his estates are situated.[3]

Those engaging in recruitment were not only men, but included some influential women. As a whole, their interventions were to shape the latter stages of the recruitment drive and were, in the words of Peter Simkins, 'to develop the unique character of the New Army'. He calculated that some 38 per cent of all the Service battalions raised were created by this route.[4]

Arguably the Pals concept was born following a request that the City of London should raise a whole battalion of 'stockbrokers' in a letter from the Director of Recruiting, on 12 August 1914. The regimental history of what would be its host, the Royal Fusiliers (City of London Regiment), identifies that the origins of the Pals lay in the City of London, and in the gentlemen's clubs of Pall Mall:

The 10th (Stockbrokers) Battalion was raised at the direct suggestion of Sir Henry Rawlinson, then Director of Recruiting, by Major the Hon. R. White. In a letter to the latter at the Traveller's Club, Sir Henry stated his belief that there were 'many city employees who would be willing to enlist if they were assured that they would serve with their friends'.[5]

There was an obvious implication: by 'friends', Rawlinson surely meant 'men of the same social class'. It was highly successful:

Recruiting began on the 21st [August], when 210 men presented themselves. The following day the battalion was 425 strong; it was 900 on the 24th, 1,300 on the 25th and 1,600 on the 27th ... Parading in all sorts of clothing from silk hats and morning coats to caps and Norfolk jackets, the battalion was inspected on the 29th by Lord Roberts in Temple Gardens.[6]

The Stockbrokers were to form part of Kitchener's Second Army (K2), and in so doing lost their distinctive title.

If such men were to be persuaded to join the ranks of an infantry battalion, then they would need some assurance that they would not feel out of place when standing in the ranks next to navvies and dock workers – a feature that immediately set apart the Pals battalions from the men of the First Hundred Thousand who had joined in the initial recruiting boom. Early on the recruits were predictable, drawn mostly from the working classes – according to the first chronicler of Kitchener's Army, Edgar Wallace, writing in 1915:

A great throng surged into New Scotland Yard; enormously long queues filled with the youth of the City made their way to the recruiting office ... But large as the crowd was, it was, generally speaking, made up of that class which the rank and file of the Army had always been formed, with here and there a sprinkling of a better type of man.[7]

'A better type of man' – Wallace recognised that the effect on recruiting of the British Expeditionary Force's retreat from Mons in late August was dramatic, forcing up numbers but also changing the very demographic of recruitment:

New faces appeared in the recruiting queue, a new type of recruit began to elbow its way to the front, first in a trickling stream and then in a whole volume ... making for the new emergency recruiting stations which were being opened all over town. A new tone came to the tents, a new intonation, a suggestion of Public School and University.[8]

Men joining these queues and attesting in the recruiting offices were passed to the regimental depot and the Special Reserve battalion, there to be processed and passed on to their permanent battalion. While it was common for some men to join in groups and serve together – as did George Tunstill's Men, who joined in Skipton and formed a company of the 10th (Service) Battalion, Duke of Wellington's Regiment – the mix in these early days of Kitchener's Army was more homogenous.

The proliferation of the Pals concept was in large part due to the action of Lord Derby, who, like Rawlinson, considered that the large number of working men serving in battalions might be off-putting to those whose workplace was the stock exchange, or works drafting office. Lord Derby was a hugely influential figure in Lancashire, and his intervention was to have a dramatic effect in the north-western industrial powerhouses of Liverpool and Manchester. Lord Derby also raised the notion that men of the 'commercial classes' might wish to serve their country in a battalion of their comrades – their pals – in a letter to the Liverpool morning paper, the *Daily Post* (and repeated in the *Liverpool Echo* that evening) on 27 August 1914:

> It has been suggested to me that there are many men, such as clerks and others engaged in commercial business, who wish to serve their country and would be willing to enlist in the battalion of Kitchener's New Army if they felt assured that they would be able to serve with their friends and not be put in a battalion with unknown men as their companions. Lord Kitchener has sanctioned my endeavouring to raise a battalion that would be composed entirely of the classes mentioned, and in which a man could be certain that he would be amongst friends.[9]

Once again the implication was that middle-class men would not be forced to serve alongside men they would neither know nor understand – men of 'lower social strata'. At a recruitment meeting in early September in Burnley, Lieutenant A.C. Robinson, a Territorial officer with the Lancashire Fusiliers, reflected that the Territorial Force was suffering for this very reason:

He said that he recognised that a great number of young men would like to offer their services and yet did not want to separate. It had to be recognised that there were classes – cliques if they liked – and in Liverpool, Manchester, etc, there had been started 'pals' battalions of men of the same class and known to each other, and who were offering their services *en bloc*.[10]

That was certainly the case in Liverpool, and the Liverpool Pals was the result. In his history of the 89th Brigade, Lord Derby's brother, F.C. Stanley, recounted the tale of the raising of the Pals, drawing upon the reports under dramatic headlines in the Liverpool press on 31 August 1914:

Lord Derby – originator of the Liverpool Pals. The success of the Pals was soon repeated across Britain.

'PALS' FIRST BATTALION COMPLETE
Full Number Obtained in an Hour
STIRRING SCENES
Great Rally of Liverpool's Young
Business Men
'No Undesirables'[11]

'No undesirables' – Lord Derby's appeal had achieved its aim. Men came forward to serve with those they felt most comfortable with. The report continued:

The First Battalion of Liverpool 'Pals' for Lord Kitchener's New Army, composed of young men engaged in commercial and business offices in the city, has been raised. The requisite number of men, 1,030, was obtained in one hour at St George's Hall today. The rush to join was so great that the lists had to be closed for the rest of the day.[12]

The response was overwhelming. By Tuesday 31 August some 1,200 men had volunteered, and the city was well on its way to filling its second city battalion. Lord Derby was thus the first to coin the phrase 'Pals battalion', which was to become a watchword for the devastating losses felt by some local communities after the Somme in 1916.

Four battalions were raised in total: 17th–20th (Service) Battalions, King's Liverpool Regiment (1st–4th City). This was enough to form a whole brigade, the 89th, which was a significant component of the 30th Division. All would wear the crest of the Stanley family, by royal assent.[13] Lord Derby responded directly to the king's privilege:

The Pals march through central Liverpool.

Civis Britannicus Sum. A badge worn by a Liverpool Pal that echoed the Roman dictum, *civis Romanus sum* – 'I am a Roman citizen'. The wearer implies he earns the right to claim his citizenship through service with the Pals.

Right: A fully equipped soldier of the Liverpool Pals. The Pals did not wear the despised Kitchener blue. He is equipped with Pattern 1914 leather equipment, Long Lee rifle and the shorter Pattern 1903 bayonet.

Far right: A soldier in the Liverpool Pals, wearing the special '3rd City Batn, The King's' shoulder title (see p.108).

The Liverpool Pals parade to receive their silver badges from Lord Derby.

Lord Derby, in accordance with the privilege that he had claimed, presented all the men who had joined up with one of these badges in silver. This was to be given only to those who had enlisted at that time, and was to be a mark that they were one of the 'originals'.[14]

Hallmarked, these silver badges were designed by Birmingham silversmiths Elkington & Company, and were destined to be transformed into brooches for wear by mothers, wives and sweethearts – they would be replaced by sturdy brass examples for wearing in the cap.[15]

Lord Derby's example would be followed by Lord Lonsdale, who was set on raising his own battalion of men from Cumberland. Lonsdale was relentless in

his pursuit of recruits, infamously issuing a striking and direct recruiting poster, garishly striped with his racing colours of red, yellow and white:[16]

ARE YOU A MAN OR ARE YOU A MOUSE?
Are you a man who will for ever be handed down to posterity as a Gallant patriot?
Or
Are you to be handed down to posterity as a Rotter and a Coward?[17]

Lonsdale announced the raising of his own battalion, with him as chairman of the executive committee, to the press in late September,[18] and recruitment from Cumberland and Westmorland continued throughout September and October.

Above left: The silver cap badge (left) given by Lord Derby to all the original Liverpool Pals. It depicted the Stanley crest of eagle and child with the motto, *Sans Charger* ('without change'). As in this case, most of these badges were transformed into brooches with brass ('gilding metal'; right) or bronze versions worn by the soldiers themselves.

Above right: Sweetheart brooches, usually representations of cap badges like this one of a Liverpool Pal, were commonly given to loved ones as gifts by soldiers.

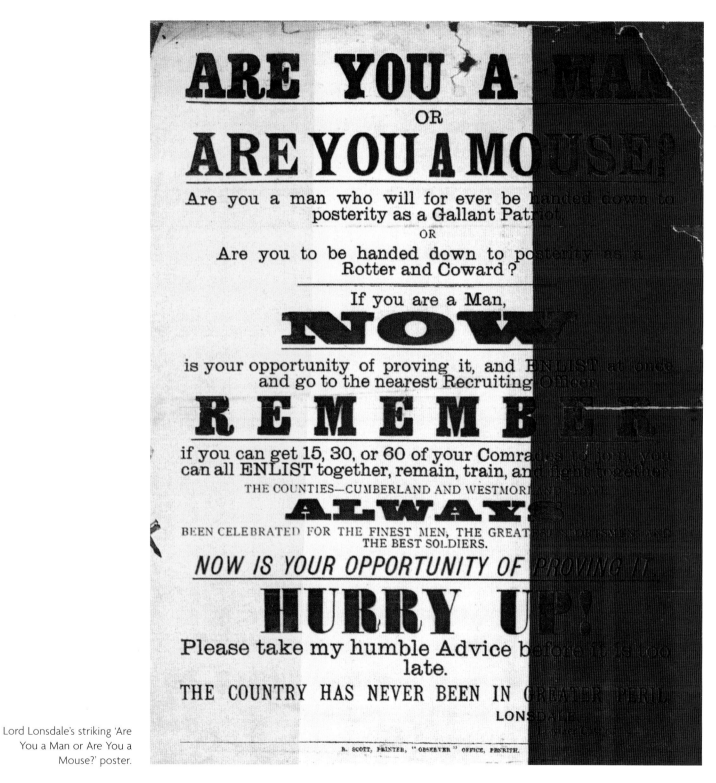

Lord Lonsdale's striking 'Are You a Man or Are You a Mouse?' poster.

Lonsdale also had a view – reported in the local press – as to what his soldiers would be wearing:

At a meeting of the Cumberland and Westmorland Joint Territorial Associations, under the chairmanship of Lord Lonsdale, it has been decided to raise a new regiment [sic] for Lord Kitchener's Army. The unit will be known as the Lonsdale Battalion of the Border Regiment, and will have an establishment of 1,000 men, composed of farmers' sons and professional men. The uniform will be grey serge, not khaki.[19]

Whether the possibility of confusion with German *feldgrau* (field grey) was entertained, is not recorded. Taking Lord Lonsdale's name, the Lonsdale Battalion would also take the earl's own coat of arms as its cap badge – just as the Liverpool Pals had done with Lord Derby – and Lonsdale would issue silver versions of it, badges that again were mostly destined to see life as sweetheart brooches.

Lord Derby's initiative, and Liverpool's example, would help drive the Pals idea. And Kitchener was not in a position to refuse such positive assistance. Kitchener's sanction was avidly sought. Captain Basil Williams described the intensity of activity in 1914:

The War Office, faced with difficulties for which it was not and could not have been prepared, showed no hesitation in accepting the offers of business-like civilians to supply the dearth of expert recruiters. Energetic Members of Parliament armed with a scrap of Lord Kitchener's handwriting rushed forth North, South, East and West of the Kingdom to take the responsibility of doing unheard-of things quite contrary to the regulations.[20]

Energetic individuals took it upon themselves to create a mechanism suited to recruitment, and in so doing, largely exceeded their authority. Williams continued with his caricature:

In one city of the Midlands the local Member of Parliament within twenty-four hours changed the recruiting office from a poky back street to the town hall, engaged eight civilian doctors to help one overworked medical officer to examine recruits, [and] printed locally the sacred Army Forms for recruits, with their seventeen elaborate questions.[21]

Lord Lonsdale's *dragon passant* crest formed the basis for the Lonsdale Battalion's (Border Regiment) cap badge – this is an officer's bronzed version.

The first recruits to the Lonsdale Battalion received a silver version of their cap badge from Lord Lonsdale. Too precious to be worn in action, many were transformed into sweetheart brooches.

With the concept in the air – and with other cities and towns experiencing a great feeling of civic pride – there was an avalanche of Pals battalions. Manchester was not far behind Liverpool; but then, Lord Derby was equally well known there and there was a strong element of rivalry between the two north-western cities.

There had already been a suggestion that Manchester might find recruits amongst the city's warehouses and offices on 24 August, and these commercial concerns were asked to consider an incentive of paying a partial salary to those of their employees who might be persuaded to join.[22] On Friday 28 August a body of employers gathered together in the town hall to see if they might be able to sponsor recruitment and make their scheme a reality. The influential newspaper the *Manchester Evening News* carried a long piece on its front page the next day, announcing the success of the initiative under the headline: 'The New Battalion. Welcomed by Lord Kitchener. An Auspicious Start.'[23]

Lord Kitchener had given his sanction to the raising of a Manchester battalion of middle-class merchants:

> Your telegram just received. Hope you will be able to raise a battalion in Manchester and thus give your signal help to the armed forces of the Crown. Any men joining the battalion will be doing a patriotic deed, and I shall hope to welcome them in the army where their comrades await them. KITCHENER.[24]

Just as had happened elsewhere, a recruiting committee was set up to guarantee that the battalion would indeed be filled to the brim. It was also to be

'Is your home here? Defend it!' A PRC recruiting poster that depicts the recruiting depots of local regiments. Pals battalions would eventually spread across Britain.

supported by a gift of £15,000 from the members present, and this was to ensure that – in clothing and equipment at least – the men of the 'Battalion of Clerks & Warehousemen' would not be wanting.

This aspect made the locally raised Pals units somewhat different from the other Service battalions of K1–K3. With the First Hundred Thousand, the recruits were passed through the ordinary recruiting process which, though creaking and groaning, had just about been able to supply its soldiers with uniforms of sorts – even if it was the detested and shapeless Kitchener blue, or even the hotchpotch of red full dress tunics, civilian caps and khaki puttees.

In Manchester, a city built on its textile trade, there would be no such poverty of military bearing. The Manchester Testing House ensured that 'every article of clothing and equipment was checked by them and passed as correct before distribution to the men'.[25] As described in *The Manchester City Battalions Book of Honour*, the resulting uniform was based on the standard service dress – though with simplifications:

> The original uniform was blue with the well-known dark grey overcoat, and very serviceable it looked; but still there was a feeling that these battalions would never consider themselves real soldiers until they donned the universal khaki. Needless to say they would have been promptly put into khaki had it not been forbidden by the War Office, who required at that time every yard they could obtain.[26]

Khaki was eventually sourced – and a 'second suit' made.

'The City expects and the City knows that every man will do his duty.' Postcard depicting Manchester's Own. Eight Pals battalions would hail from the city. Similar postcards were produced for other cities.

The Manchester City battalions wore the second type of Kitchener blue based on a simplified version of the standard service dress, with a leather-peaked cap. Equipped with shoulder straps, each one bore a special title numbered to the battalion. The soldiers wore all-brass or bronzed versions of the more usual bi-metal Manchester cap badge, depicting the arms of the city.

Not only did the Mancunians require uniforms and equipment, they would need feeding and housing. Kitchener and the War Office were fortunate that there were so many public-spirited people who were willing to devote time, effort and money to aiding recruitment. The costs of maintaining the Pals before the War Office officially adopted them would have to be met by the local citizenry. Some 165 donors – from individual citizens to textile and financial firms – would guarantee £26,701 9s 6d by 1916. Others would make donations, including 4,000 pairs of puttees from Chorlton Bros Ltd; 4,000 'holdalls for soldiers' necessaries' from Kay & Lee Ltd and a 'tug of war rope' from Henry Cardwell & Co.[27]

There would be a delay, though, with so many men coming forward. Local newspapers carried the story so that prospective recruits would not be too disappointed:

At the recruiting headquarters the fourth city battalion was yesterday rapidly completing. It is realised that it will take some considerable time to clothe all the men, and with a view to getting the battalions working the following order was issued yesterday: 'Pending issue of uniforms, recruits are invited where possible to obtain from their homes good boots, suit, and a greatcoat … Seven shillings and sixpence will be given to each man who produces [them] in good condition ...'[28]

In all, Manchester would supply eight city battalions – eight battalions of Pals forming two brigades, the 90th and 91st. Together with the 89th Brigade, formed of the Liverpool Pals, they made up the three component parts of the 30th Division – a division consisting of Lord Derby's men, who would adopt the Stanley crest as their sign later in the war.[29]

Nearby Salford, so often in the shadow of its larger cousin, was not to be outdone, however. With long-standing links to the Lancashire Fusiliers, the local MP, Montague Barlow, 'in response to many requests',[30] started recruiting for a Salford Battalion for the regiment on 3 September 1914. Salford would actually furnish the best part of a brigade, the 96th, a component of the 32nd Division.[31]

With Lancashire leading the way, it was not surprising that some of the smaller mill towns would want to join the throng. In Accrington, a town of 45,000 people nestling amongst a string of similar Lancashire mill towns, there were hopes that Lord Kitchener would accept half a battalion – it was perhaps just too much to hope that such a small town would be capable of forming its own dedicated battalion of at least 1,000 men.

The Manchester City Battalion, mostly wearing standard service dress, and illustrating the diversity of cap badge finishes – some brass, some bronzed. One man in the second row from the front, fourth from the left, still wears Kitchener blue.

There were competing pressures, too. Manchester was only 20 miles away and there were the Territorial battalions of the local East Lancashire Regiment to be filled. But then, there was a recession in the cotton textile trades that the mill towns depended upon and so there were many unemployed. Kitchener's reply to a telegram offering the half-battalion sent by the mayor, Captain John Harwood, on 31 August was disheartening – only a full battalion would do.[32]

Enlisting the help of other citizens, including the Legion of Frontiersmen, a somewhat ambiguous paramilitary organisation of Imperial daredevils, Harwood expanded his offer to an Accrington & District Battalion, opening it up to other Lancashire towns. It was the offer of 250 men from nearby Chorley – a company of Chorley Pals within the larger body – that led to the formation that became known as the Accrington Pals.[33] The raising of the Accrington Pals struck a decidedly different tone to that of most other Pals battalions, however, because in this depressed mill town, the men who joined were not drawn exclusively from 'men of the commercial classes'.

As Peter Simkins has pointed out, the root of the Pals phenomenon is the development of intense civic pride in the major cities of Britain – cities that considered themselves, like Glasgow, to be world cities, cities of Empire.[34] While London could claim a population of over 7 million people, the southern Lancashire cities of Manchester and Liverpool, and the towns that surrounded them, added a further 3.5 million. Across the Pennines in West Yorkshire and farther south, in and around the 'workshop of Empire', Birmingham, each added over 1.5 million people.[35] The major conurbations of Britain had grown from the

A studio shot of two Manchester City Battalion soldiers, c. 1916. Such images were distributed amongst family members.

country's industrial clout, most of them clustered in northern England.

Nevertheless, it was Birmingham, at England's industrial heart, which made one of the most important contributions in the drive for more men. The Royal Warwickshire Regiment, with its long history of association with the city, had already expanded with the addition of three Service battalions, one in each of Kitchener's New Armies, K1–K3, assigned to the 13th (Western), 19th (Western) and 24th (later tortuously finding its way into the 37th) divisions.[36]

On 28 August 1914, the *Birmingham Daily Post* led with an editorial that was designed to 'flush out' those men who had been reluctant to 'join the Colours' – once again, men from the commercial classes who were holding back from joining alongside manual workers. With a sizeable city, it reasoned, there would be a sizeable number of potential recruits available:

Roughly, then, it may be fair to estimate that Birmingham has contributed some 25,000 men to the defence of the national honour. Even if it be assumed, which it cannot, that all these are under 30 there would still remain 115,000 men eligible by age to join the colours. Of these probably less than half – at least 50,000 – are unmarried. What are these 50,000 men, nearly all without dependants, doing that they have not presented themselves for the service of their country?[37]

Opposite: Sewing the 30th Division formation sign – based on the Stanley crest – on to the uniform of a soldier from the 1st Liverpool Pals.

The shoulder title on Kitchener blue, of a pattern worn by most Salford Pals. The 20th Lancashire Fusiliers, a Bantam battalion from Salford, had its own title (see p.141)

No. 5 Platoon, 15th (Service) Battalion, Lancashire Fusiliers, the Salford Pals. They wear the second pattern Kitchener blue uniform, based on standard service dress; most Pals battalions wore this at first.

The Accrington Pals wore the standard East Lancashire Regiment insignia once they were in khaki.

Seizing upon the initiative already put in place in Liverpool by Lord Derby, the *Daily Post* continued to make the inevitable conclusion. Apart from holding open positions for returning soldiers, there was also the opportunity to enable men to serve with those of their own class: 'Something might also be done if the authorities would facilitate the raising of a battalion of non-manual workers. Splendid material is available, and we do not doubt that such a battalion, if associated with the name of the city, would fill rapidly.'

The response was almost immediate. After throwing down this gauntlet, the offices of the *Birmingham Daily Post* were inundated with prospective recruits answering the challenge.[38] By Monday 1 September the newspaper had taken the names of 1,200 men who were willing to serve, and by the end of the week there were 4,500 names of young men who worked in the white-collar professions. Every man who applied to join was issued with a card that instructed the applicants to attend the recruiting office to attest if they wanted to become official members of one of the three Birmingham city battalions.

In lieu of uniforms, and intended to avoid the attentions of the female white feather vigilantes, the Birmingham Battalion Equipment Fund Committee sanctioned the wearing of a specially made and enamelled buttonhole badge. These were distributed by Deputy Lord Mayor William Bowater and his wife to all original members at Thorp Hall in September 1914. There were even badges that recorded the fact that a man had volunteered and been rejected – as the need to be recognised as someone who had volunteered was an important one. This general theme was taken up in a letter to the *Yorkshire Evening Post* on 8 September:

> I notice that in Leeds those young men who have presented themselves to the recruiting officer, and, for some reason or other, have not been accepted, are given a certificate, thanking them for their patriotic offer ... Could the authorities not go a step further and present a button to each young man so disappointed? This would be ocular evidence that he has done his duty. It seems too bad that one so situated could possibly be classified as a coward or a waster.[39]

The same tack was taken up in a letter to the *Western Daily Press* from a Bristol citizen. There was clearly a growing need for such marks:

> Sir. The suggestion is being circulated that a white feather should be sent to those who are presumably unwilling to serve their country in its great need. I venture to think that a more salutary plan would be to provide those who have offered their services, and have been accepted, but are not yet in uniform, with a button with the inscription, such as 'To Serve'.

Lord Kitchener's Army.

SPECIAL RECRUITING OFFICE, No. 11,
COUNCIL HOUSE, BIRMINGHAM

CITY OF BIRMINGHAM BATTALION.

It is notified for your information that you are a member of *C* Company, No. *1* Battalion of the above unit. If you wish to draw pay on account of the 3/- per day due, you should attend at the COUNCIL HOUSE (Margaret Street entrance), on **26 Sept.** 1914 between the hours of 10.30 a.m. and 12.30 p.m. You are to bring this card with you.

JOHN BARNSLEY, Lt.-Col.,
O.C. Recruiting Station.

Recruits to the Birmingham City battalions joining at the council house were sent a card like this one, indicating their company and battalion, and instructing them when to attend to draw pay.

Recruits to the Birmingham City battalion were issued with this enamel badge in 1914 – a protection from the attentions of white feather vigilantes.

A different sort of button might also be handed to those who, though willing to serve, have, through no fault of their own, been rejected. I venture to think that every woman would look with pride and satisfaction on the wearer of either button.[40]

Packing for Kitchener's Army.

By the end of the year, all Birmingham Battalion men were clothed in Kitchener blue. But that's where the similarities with other battalions ended – blue it might be, but poorly fitting it was not. As with Manchester, the direct sourcing of khaki cloth using any extra influence that the city could bring to bear was forbidden. Nevertheless, the city's Equipment Fund Committee was well provided for, with £17,000 to be spent on the production of uniforms. Each one was cut to fit the soldier. The cloth was of the best quality and, in this city famed for its badge and button making, tunic buttons were specially made, bearing the battalion titles. And there were special cap badges and shoulder titles to reflect the individuality of the units.[41] There were never other Kitchener's Army men who could match them. Accordingly, each man was expected – and instructed – to maintain a smart turnout.

> Always appear smart and well turned out and pay attention to order of dress. Uniform should be clean and trousers well pressed, not turned up – walking out boots well blacked – hair cut close, particularly at the back of head–face well shaved except upper lip.[42]

Glasgow, another of Britain's 'cities of Empire', would equally not be outdone. The *Daily Record*, an illustrated newspaper, carried a full-page spread in early September which addressed the response of the city to Kitchener's call, and Lord Derby's initiative. Under the headline 'Glasgow has raised her first Battalion for Earl Kitchener's New Army' are depicted men in the uniform of the Glasgow Tramways, 'Nearly a thousand Glasgow tramway-men have volunteered for active service', reads the caption.[43] Quite what the men who had already volunteered for service in the 10th, 11th and 12th (Service) battalions (K1 and K2) of Glasgow's own regiment, the Highland Light Infantry, thought of this was not recorded.

Nevertheless, this was the first of four Glasgow battalions raised by the Lord Provost, the city and the Chamber of Commerce for the Highland Light Infantry in September 1914. Glasgow was proud, however, that *its* Pals would be drawn from a wider demographic:

Kitchener's man – a soldier from one of the Birmingham City battalions, dressed in Kitchener blue. The uniform worn by the Birmingham Pals was modelled directly upon the standard service dress and was of the highest quality, with special buttons, badges and other insignia.

Right: Service dress buttons specially manufactured for the Birmingham battalions, with the number of each battalion and the year 1914.

Far right: Birmingham Battalion insignia, showing the special double-scrolled cap badge and the shoulder title. The city of Birmingham was justifiably famous for its badge manufacturing.

Young men of a Birmingham battalion pose for the camera in newly issued khaki (here the simplified service dress of 1914); not all wear the special cap badge.

GLASGOW'S OWN
ALL CLASSES FLOCK TO THE COLOURS
1000 TRAMWAYMEN TO JOIN

The special battalions which Glasgow has decided to raise and equip may be said, in a sense, to be already in being. At least a couple of thousand men have either registered their names or have expressed their willingness to enlist. Many offers of service and enquiries from young men in all branches of city life have been made, and it may safely be predicted that it only requires that recruiting offices be opened to have two or three battalions enrolled straight away.[44]

The first three battalions raised by the city would be brigaded with that of Lord Lonsdale in the 97th Brigade, part of the 32nd Division and there would be a fourth, Bantam, battalion of shorter men raised in February 1915.

The cities of Leeds and Bradford together eventually contributed four battalions that would serve with distinction in the West Yorkshire Regiment. If civic pride was the main driver for the development of the Pals concept, then this can be fairly identified in the fierce pride, and once again rivalry, of these two industrial cities. The city of Leeds had been active in seeking recruits for its local regiment, particularly in the wake of Kitchener's first Call to Arms, published on 8 August 1914.[45] Prominent citizens and clergymen made impassioned speeches in public meetings, at the pulpit and even at the football grounds in an attempt to get young men to take up Kitchener's challenge. If that wasn't enough, the city corporation also resorted to the use of an 'illuminated tramcar', the whereabouts of which were noted in the local evening press:

Tonight an illuminated tramcar will pass through the streets of Leeds. This will mark the latest effort of the Lord Mayor and Corporation to stimulate recruiting among the ranks of the able-bodied citizens. The car will be brilliantly lighted, and is to be garnished with legends which will make a terse and pointed appeal to loyalty and patriotism.[46]

'Terse and pointed ...' – the mayor was vigorous in his pursuit of fresh recruits. Lord Derby's efforts in Liverpool to try to raise a 'Battalion of Pals' had not gone unnoticed in West Yorkshire, however. The *Yorkshire Evening Post* was quick to pick up on it, just four days later:

The Highland Light Infantry cap badge worn by the Service battalions of the city of Glasgow.

A card issued in 1914 directing young men to the recruiting office in Leeds.

THE RECRUITING OFFICE FOR LEEDS IS CITY SQUARE

ENLIST THERE FOR ALL BRANCHES OF THE REGULAR ARMY & TERRITORIAL FORCE

SOMETHING THAT LEEDS MAY DO WHY NOT A 'FRIENDS BATTALION?' A LEAD WANTED FOR THE MIDDLE CLASSES In one hour to-day a full battalion of commercial men was enrolled at Liverpool. Another battalion is to be enrolled forthwith. Birmingham is following Liverpool's example. Cannot Leeds do what Liverpool has done and Birmingham is preparing to do?

There is a vast recruiting ground in Leeds at present untapped. It consists of the middle class population engaged in commercial pursuits, young men from the factories, the warehouses, and the offices of the city, who desire to go to the front, but hesitate about enlisting lest they should be sent to join a regiment in which they do not have kindred spirits.[47]

'Wanted at once 5000 recruits from Leeds'. Illuminated recruiting cars were popular means of recruiting young men in many cities. Leeds' example is justifiably famous.

Once again, the appeal was made in order to provide a means of men to serve with 'their own kind'. The coming of the Leeds Battalion was announced the next day in the same paper, under the headline 'Leeds rising to the occasion':

PALS' BATTALION ON THE WAY
AN OPENING FOR THE CITY'S YOUNG MEN.
The proposal, as outlined in the *Yorkshire Evening Post* yesterday, for a Pals' battalion for Lord Kitchener's Army, to be recruited from the middle-class men who are engaged in the offices and warehouses of Leeds, is regarded on all hands as an excellent one, and if a strong committee is formed the scheme can be carried through successfully.[48]

The committee was indeed strong, headed by Lieutenant Colonel Walter Stead, a Leeds solicitor and former commanding officer of a Leeds Territorial battalion, and Lord Mayor Edward Brotherton.

Brotherton's commitment to recruitment was seemingly boundless. He made a personal pledge that the cost of raising the Leeds Pals, their uniforms and equipment, would be paid for out of his own pocket – a significant commitment.[49] The Pals would wear the city's coat of arms as their badge.

Even though the Pals were supported through the generosity of the lord mayor, there were still those wont to complain. In a letter to the *Yorkshire Evening Post*, the correspondent bemoaned the 'feather bed treatment' the Pals were receiving:

When our lads enlist on their own without fuss or bribery, they have to go where and with whom they are sent. May I suggest that

when the Lord Mayor equips his Feather Bed Battalion that he be sure and not forget dressing gowns, slippers, eider downs, whiskies and sodas, and, if he can manage it, to throw in a few billiard tables. I have no doubt the Battalion will greatly distinguish itself.[50]

Perhaps the correspondent was already a soldier – or perhaps he resented the overt reaching out to the middle classes. Either way, on the day his letter was published (8 September 1914) the battalion was declared full.

Despite claims to the contrary, there was evidence that finding appropriate uniforms was a challenge, even for a city like Leeds. Leaving for their camp at Colsterdale, the local press noted that the men were in the position of having to fend for themselves:

Lieutenant T.A.R. Willey's framed insignia, including his silver and bronzed cap badges bearing the arms of Leeds, buttons and the puggaree flash worn on his Wolseley pattern sun helmet when in Egypt.

Although the Lord Mayor will equip the battalion with khaki uniforms, boots, great-coats, blankets, etc., those materials have for the present been found to be unprocurable. Members of the battalion are therefore asked to provide their own clothes.[51]

Nearby Bradford was a city of 300,000 that had built its industrial reputation on the production of worsted woollen products. Like its neighbours, the city had aspirations to raise its own Pals and had gone so far as to form a Bradford Citizens Army League on 3 September, in order to set plans in motion. Like all the other Pals committees, it was supported by the great and the good of civic life – local politicians and businessmen (though not by the pacifist Labour MP for Bradford West, Fred Jowitt). The committee would oversee recruitment and ensure that, in this city of wool, its men were suitably clothed.[52]

The *Evening Post* recorded that the first recruits were forthcoming on 8 September, the day that the Leeds Pals had declared themselves closed for further men:

BRADFORD 'PALS' BATTALION

Recruiting began at Bradford to-day at the Mechanics Institute for the Bradford Service Battalion, West Yorkshire Regiment. From nine o'clock this morning there was a steady stream of young businessmen, and it is expected that the 1,200 men will be forthcoming at an early date. The equipment of the battalion, to cost about £7,000, will be paid for by the citizens of Bradford.[53]

By the end of the week, the diverse commercial concerns of the city had relinquished some 400 of

their workers – men who, it was hoped, might serve together, and separately, in the eight companies, one for each trade or profession. Once again, segregation into commercial classes was proposed, down to the very fibres of the battalion. It was never enacted. The battalion register was completed on 19 September.[54]

Training commenced when the battalion was moved to a former roller skating rink near the city's Belle Vue barracks. Like the Birmingham Battalion before them, there was a need while the recruits were still clad in civilian clothes for some means of distinguishing them from 'the shirkers'. It was hoped that such a mark might promote envy and therefore stimulate recruitment. As such, Sir William Priestly MP, the Liberal MP for Bradford East and chairman of the Bradford Citizen's Army League Finance Committee, commissioned enamel badges bearing the coat of arms of the city to be worn in the buttonhole in order to deter negative comment.

The Pals became almost like local celebrities. They were granted gifts from the owner of the Alhambra Theatre of brass boxes filled with comforts and bearing the badge of the West Yorkshire Regiment, and no doubt received similar criticisms to Leeds' 'Feather bed soldiers' on the way. And like their compatriots in Birmingham, when their Kitchener blue service dress uniforms arrived in November, they were of the finest quality.[55]

Bradford would go on to raise another Pals battalion in January 1915. Ultimately, both (16th and 18th West Yorkshire Regiment) were brigaded in 93rd Brigade, 31st Division together with the 1st Leeds Pals (17th West Yorkshires), and a battalion of the Durham Light Infantry. The 'Durham Pals' (1st County) had been raised in October 1914 by Colonel R. Burdon – as usual to 'give an opening

Left: A young man in the Leeds Pals proudly wearing his khaki service dress. Private 15/1545 Tom Scawbord was killed on the first day of the Somme on 1 July 1916. He is remembered on the Thiepval Memorial to the Missing.

Below left: Like many cities, Bradford was proud of its Pals battalions. The mayor paid for an enamelled badge, manufactured by the local badge-makers Fattorini & Sons, to protect recruits from negative comment while still in civilian clothes.

Opposite page
Top: Leeds Pals – a uniform from 1916. The arms of Leeds are prominently displayed as an example of civic pride.

Bottom: The Leeds Pals wore distinctive shoulder titles.

The proprietor of the Alhambra Theatre commissioned a special brass box for the Bradford Pals as a token of appreciation. It is suggested that this contained tobacco and/or chocolate. (A similar box was given to the city's Territorial battalion.)

to clerks, draughtsmen, elementary schoolmasters, and others of kindred occupations'

The senior brigade in this division, the 92nd, consisted entirely of Pals battalions from Hull, a city of similar size to Bradford. The four battalions were once again segregated according to trade, profession or calling. Biographer of the 1st Hull Pals, David Bilton, has identified the snobbery that existed between them:

The four main active service battalions came from different strata of society ... This was reflected in the social composition of the 'Hull Pals', with the Commercials being composed of men from middle-class occupations, especially from the commercials, who, the other battalions felt, thought they were better than the others.[57]

The Accrington Pals and the single Pals battalion raised by Sheffield – the Sheffield City Battalion, otherwise the 12th (Service) Battalion, York & Lancaster Regiment – served together with the two Barnsley Pals battalions in the 94th Brigade. It is no surprise that the divisional sign contained the red and white roses of Lancashire and Yorkshire.[58]

The Pals concept was inspired. Most of the Pals battalions were born at the same time that Kitchener made his appeal for his Second Army. By the time he had appealed for the Third Army, the supply and training of the Pals battalions was well underway, local authorities taking on the mantle to recruit, clothe and train Kitchener's men before they were passed over to the War Office.

The rivalry between cities was as much a part of the Pals story as the desire of the men themselves to serve with those they felt most comfortable

with. Most significantly for the Secretary of State for War, Lord Kitchener, it provided a valuable means of filling his next tranche of 100,000 men, a whole six divisions, the Pals divisions, 30th–35th, without the need for a wider call for arms.[59]

If the Pals battalion concept hinged around the recruitment of 'men of a better class', then this undoubtedly included those who had been educated in the public schools and universities of Britain. The officer corps were predominantly derived from these men, many of whom had been at least partially trained in the Officer Training Corps, a function of Haldane's reforms. It might have been expected, therefore, that most would have applied for commissions. In fact, Kitchener's appeal for officers on 10 August had been directed

In uniform, the Bradford Pals (16th and 18th West Yorkshire Regiment) were distinguished by their shoulder titles, which had the numeral '16' or '18' in addition to the standard name 'W. York'.

Sheffield – a city so involved in steelmaking and industry – was essential to the war effort in so many ways. Nevertheless, the city raised its own Sheffield City Battalion for the local York & Lancaster Regiment.

at men 'educated to a good standard', and under the age of 30, to apply for 2,000 'Commissions in His Majesty's Army'. This offer was quickly filled, but in 1914 there were men who felt the opportunity to serve had passed them by. With no possibility of a commission, there were those who felt that there was little hope they would serve their country by leading men into battle.

On 26 August, after their attendance at a meeting to help form training centres for home defence, 'eight unattached' ex-public schoolmen – men with experience on the shooting range and in marksmanship – wrote to *The Times*:

Sir, We attended the recent meeting ... to consider the formation of a corps of past

public schools men, and found that the organisers only required grey-haired, spare-time veterans. We are between thirty and thirty-five, absolutely fit and game for active service ... We have applied for commissions in the new Regulars, but find we are too old ... After endless inquiries there seems to be only one way in which our services are acceptable, and that is by joining the ranks.[60]

Once again there was a desire that men 'of their own type' would serve together. This was defended in the *Spectator* magazine: 'There is no suggestion that public school men are better than others, but it is natural to wish to spend possibly many weary months or years with people of one's own "upbringing".[61]

Though the original 'eight unattached' actually joined a Territorial battalion, their idea had planted a seed and, at a meeting at the ritzy Claridge's Hotel in Mayfair the day after *The Times* letter was published, it was decided that there would be a recruitment drive to fill a brigade, some 5,000 strong, of university and public school men.[62] A poster was issued, 'The Old Public School and University Men's Committee makes an urgent appeal to their fellow Public School and University Men', and recruiting was taken across the country. Yet the committee had acted out of turn; no official sanction had been given by Kitchener to the raising of the brigade. The committee had to approach the great man himself on 8 September, and permission to proceed was granted the next day.

The UPS, as it became known, was a familiar sight in Hyde Park in September and October 1914. Drilling in civilian clothes, the first parade made quite an impression, as described in the brigade history:

Over 2,000 mustered at this first parade. They comprised, generally speaking, the London Contingent ... And an astonishingly fine, well-set-up force they are too ... Mostly above average height, and all supple, athletic fellows of manifest strong lung capacity, they made a capital impression.[63]

To distinguish these men from the throng of civilian onlookers, 'the Committee adopted a design in the form of a cardboard disc printed with the letters "U.P.S." in the form of a monogram, attached by a red cord'.[64] It was typical of the extemporised insignia of the early Pals.

The UPS men would eventually go on to form four Service battalions of the Royal Fusiliers, the 18th–21st (Service) Battalions (1st–4th Public Schools). All four battalions would serve together in a single brigade, the 98th, the senior of the three forming the 33rd Division, made predominantly of Londoners. Yet the influence of the UPS was felt far beyond the confines of the capital. The

Lord Kitchener inspects the sturdy ranks of the University & Public Schools (UPS) Brigade.

An original UPS card badge (front and back), each numbered for the man it was issued to.

The UPS men were distinguished by a simple card badge with the UPS monogram, suspended from a cord.

Dapper recruits of the UPS wear their badges in 1914.

20th (Service) Battalion, Royal Fusiliers (3rd Public Schools) had recruited mainly from Manchester.

The UPS would not be the only route for public school men serving together, there was also the 16th (Service) Battalion, Middlesex Regiment (Public Schools), raised on 1 September 1914 in London. It was the constant fear of the UPS that it would be a target for the army in supplying men suitable for commissions – which was the intention of the original 'eight unattached'. As it turned out, that fear was justified. In February 1916, three of the UPS battalions – 18th, 19th and 21st – would be transferred from the 98th Brigade to the status of

headquarters troops, before being disbanded in April to supply much needed 'officer material' for the New Army.

If the public schools and universities felt that they stood apart as 'men of a different calibre', with Britain 'a nation of sportsmen' there was also an opportunity for just this type of man to take his position alongside the others 'of the commercial classes' who were then flocking to the Colours. The Sportsmen's Battalion was raised in September 1914 by Mrs Emma Cunliffe-Owen, a society lady and noted sportswoman who was sufficiently well connected to be able to telegraph Lord Kitchener with

the question, 'Will you accept complete battalion of upper and middle class men, physically fit, able to shoot and ride, up to the age of 45?' She was to receive the answer, 'Lord Kitchener gratefully accepts complete battalion'.[65]

It was reported in the press in mid September with, in keeping with the status of the battalion, its recruiting office set up for a month in the 'India Room' of the Hotel Cecil on London's Strand.[66] Mrs Cunliffe-Owen ran a tight ship there, overseeing all aspects of the enrolment of suitable men and assessing whether applicants could 'shoot, ride and walk well'.[67] The battalion history claimed that this set the Sportsmen's Battalion apart from others as it was open to anyone with a sporting background:

With the formation of the Sportsman's Battalion it will be admitted quite a new type of man was brought into the British Army. To begin with, it

was cosmopolitan. Practically every grade of life was represented, from the peer to the peasant; class distinctions were swept away, every man turned to and pulled his bit.[68]

Across the country, newspapers and posters encouraged such men to join its ranks:

THE SPORTSMEN'S BATTALION
FOR ACTIVE SERVICE
Enrolment is now proceeding at the HOTEL CECIL, and now is the opportunity for Sportsmen and others to enlist in this exceptionally fine Battalion. No financial obligations.[69]

Few of the many articles on the raising of this battalion mentioned Mrs Emma Cunliffe-Owen, however. Most attributed her efforts to her husband, Mr Edward Cunliffe-Owen (whether

Above left: UPS paraphernalia: a swagger stick incorporating the monogram, and a silver badge incorporating the regimental badge of the Royal Fusiliers.

Above right: *The Pow-Wow* was the brigade journal. The record of the UPS was written up as early as 1917 and published by *The Times* newspaper.

Our Country's Urgent Need.

EVERY PHYSICALLY FIT AND HARDY MAN REQUIRED AT ONCE.

JOIN THE SPORTSMAN'S BATTALIONS.

DO IT NOW

AGE 19–45.

Minimum Height **5**ft. **5**ins.
Minimum Chest - **35**ins.

Separation Allowance & Pay at Army Rate.

Apply E. CUNLIFFE-OWEN, Hotel Cecil, Strand, London, or Management.

W. STRAKER, Ltd., Printers, 13, Coventry Street, Piccadilly, W.

by accident or design is a moot point). Two Sportsmen's battalions would be raised, the 23rd and 24th (Service) Battalions, Royal Fusiliers (1st and 2nd Sportsmen's), both serving in the 99th Brigade, 33rd Division.

But there were other sportsmen in Britain. A letter to the *Edinburgh Evening News* for 2 September 1914 captured the mood of the day:

'PALS' BATTALIONS

'Old Un' writes: I venture to suggest that Edinburgh footballers follow Liverpool's example, and form battalions of 'Pals'. A Hearts and Hibs Brigade would make things hum for the Germans.[70]

It would take time for this to come to fruition. Football, the professional game, was under immense pressure. For while the men were earning money on the pitch, it was reasoned that there were other men fighting for their liberty to do so. In England and Wales, the Football Association was in a difficult position. There was a growing atmosphere of approbation for the professional game – led in part by the somewhat joyless campaigner against music halls, drink and now football, F.N. Charrington, ironically an heir to Charrington Brewery.[71] With the association proposing that the 1914–15 league season continue, an infamous cartoon appeared in the magazine *Punch*, depicting Mr Punch addressing an association footballer: 'No doubt that you can make money in this field, my friend, but there's only one field to-day where you can get honour.'[72]

Though still immensely popular, the image of professional football, north and south of the Scottish border, was being tarnished. The debate reached the House of Commons on 26 November 1914:

Far left: Shoulder strap insignia of the 23rd (Service) Battalion Royal Fusiliers (1st Sportsmen's).

Left: Alternative badge of the 1st Sportsmen's Battalion, Royal Fusiliers. A second Sportsmen's Battalion would be raised.

Sir JOHN LONSDALE asked the Prime Minister if he is aware that recruiting meetings held in connection with assemblies of men to watch football matches have produced disappointing results: and whether, in view of the gravity of the crisis and the need for recruits, he will introduce legislation taking powers to suppress all professional football matches during the continuance of the War?[73]

Lonsdale continued, was the prime minister aware that the previous Saturday, 'notwithstanding the most strenuous efforts at a number of football grounds attended by many thousands of people, only one recruit to the Colours was obtained?'

Asquith was able to reply, 'I am glad to say that in Scotland there was a very different response.'[74] He was referring to the fact that 'Old Un's' suggestion had come to fruition. The day before, on 25 November, Sir George McCrae had raised a battalion of the Royal Scots, the 16th (Service) Battalion (2nd Edinburgh), in which eleven (rising to thirteen) players of the Heart of Midlothian

football club had enlisted. They were to be joined by other professionals from across Scotland in McCrae's Battalion.[75] The prime minister was off the hook.

Hearts' lead would be followed in December, when the English Football Association relented. Early in the month, the press carried reports of a new Footballers' Battalion:

> After a prolonged discussion at the conference of London professional football clubs it was resolved that the meeting heartily favours the project of the formation of a football battalion and Mr Joynson-Hicks was instructed to see the War Office on certain points. It was also decided that all London professionals be invited to attend a conference to be held at Fulham Town Hall on Tuesday next.[76]

Every professional club in London sent delegates to the meeting, and a resolution was passed that a Footballers' Battalion be formed.[77] And ten days later, the press carried the news that 'The

Opposite: Privately produced recruiting poster for the Sportsmen's Battalion. 'Apply E. Cunliffe-Owen', referred to Emma Cunliffe-Owen, rather than her husband.

McCrae's battalion was the 16th (Service) Battalion, Royal Scots.

War Office has given authority for the formation of a Battalion of footballers, to be called the 17th (Football) Battalion of the Middlesex Regiment.[78] Initial recruits were from eleven clubs, with Clapton Orient supplying ten players. Some fifty clubs were involved before recruiting was finished, and a further battalion, the 23rd (2nd Football) would be raised the following year. Professional football matches were suspended for the war in 1915.

The 17th (1st Football) Battalion would be placed with the 16th (Public Schools) Battalion in the 100th Brigade, 33rd Division, alongside the 13th (Service) Battalion, Essex Regiment. Raised in December 1914 by the Mayor of West Ham, this battalion included many West Ham supporters, with traditional claret and blue recruiting posters declaring 'Join the "Hammers" and Hammer the Huns'.[79] Football had found its way.

The industrial cities of northern England held no monopoly on the raising of local battalions for Kitchener's New Army. The city of Bristol, with a population of around 400,000, had taken a direct interest in garnering troops for the nation from relatively early on. Four days after the Secretary of State's Call to Arms, a meeting chaired by the Lord Mayor of Bristol had led to the creation of the Bristol Citizen's Recruiting Committee, chaired by Sir Herbert Ashman – a prominent Bristolian who had been the city's first lord mayor in 1899.

The committee set to work raising volunteers for the Service battalions of the Gloucestershire Regiment, using the prominently placed Colston Hall as the recruiting centre.[80] With recruitment steady and sound, the chairman approached Kitchener on the day that Lord Derby was announcing his Pals concept in the Liverpool press (27 August 1914). Recruitment for the new Bristol battalion was to tread the same path as most other Pals. It was to be solely for the use of men of the 'professional and mercantile classes', and the committee acted as scrutineer to ensure that this was actually the case. Articles in the Bristol press were clear on the matter. The *Western Daily Press* for 5 September 1914 carried a front-page advertisement for the 'New Bristol Battalion, Gloucestershire Regiment' (which would be repeated on successive daily editions) and an editorial advising prospective recruits of the conditions of application:

Those who are eligible for the new Bristol Battalion should obtain one of the forms that are to be had at Colston Hall; at banks and insurance offices; at the Commercial Rooms, and the Liberal, Constitutional and Clifton clubs, Stock Exchange, etc ... They will then be gone through and notifications sent in due course to each approved candidate. It is scarcely necessary to emphasise the fact that the scheme has in view the enlisting of young fellows connected with the business life of the city.[81]

Applications were strictly vetted: 'It cannot be too strongly emphasised that the battalion is for mercantile and professional men only, and it will save the committee a lot if those not qualified will refrain from filling up the forms.'[82]

The fact that, in some circles, the new unit was being referred to as 'the businessmen's battalion' – and therefore relatively well-heeled – was causing some confusion. A few days after the announcement, the Bristol press had to clarify for prospective recruits that rather than having to supply their own kit it would be provided free of charge 'with everything on the same footing as the Army Regular'.[83]

The new battalion was still below strength by the time of its parade on 21 September 1914,[84] but nevertheless made an impression on the local citizens. 'This was the first opportunity Bristol has had of witnessing actually the progress made in the recruiting of the new Battalion, and it is safe to say that thousands of citizens were agreeably surprised at the smartness and military aspect of the recruits.'[85]

Yet, unusually, none of the recruits were in uniform. The Bristol Citizens Recruiting Committee had spurned the opportunity of wearing Kitchener blue. Instead, the battalion would wait until khaki service dress was available – not until December.

The Bristol Citizens' Recruiting Committee sought recruits for a new battalion of the Gloucestershire Regiment. The recruiting office was in the central Colston Hall, Bristol. Recruits were issued with card badges on enlistment to protect them.

In the meantime, they too would escape the white feather by the issue and wearing of buttons on the lapel – in cardboard at first, and then celluloid, bearing the arms of Bristol superimposed on the Union flag.

Arguably the greatest commitment to recruitment came from Tyneside. In addition to the seven battalions (and one Reserve battalion) that were added to the roster of the Northumberland Fusiliers as part of the first three of Kitchener's armies, K1–K3, the Tynesiders added a further twelve Pals battalions and a further seven Reserves – a truly prodigious achievement.[86] The first inkling that Lord Derby's Liverpool Pals had made an impact this far north came when a new 'commercial' battalion was mooted in the *Newcastle Journal*,

Recruits to the new Bristol Battalion were not issued with Kitchener blue; instead they wore button badges like this one, before becoming the 12th (Service) Battalion, Gloucestershire Regiment (Bristol).

Men of the Gloucestershire Regiment at camp – Bristol's Own wore no specific identifying insignia.

to be formed along the exact lines that had first been developed amongst the commercial houses of Liverpool and Manchester:

COMMERCIAL BATTALION
NEW UNIT TO BE FORMED IN NEWCASTLE
Permission has been obtained for the formation of a commercial battalion in Newcastle for Lord Kitchener's Army. The announcement was made amid much enthusiasm ... by Mr C.W.C. Henderson, who explained that young business men, clerks, and shop assistants would be eligible for the new unit. Already 300 men were waiting to form a nucleus. The War Office had told them that they must not only raise this battalion themselves, but equip it, and it fell to the lot of the committee of the Chamber of Commerce to get the unit ready and take it over.[87]

This mirrored most of the other local battalions, and recruitment to it was complete by 16 September. But a real departure was the idea that there would be mileage in the raising of a battalion of ex-patriot Scots or at least, those Tynesiders with a penchant for all things Scottish.

The idea was an old one. During the Boer War there had already been a suggestion on the table that men of Scottish descent might be willing to join the army as volunteers, so long as they could serve together as a recognisably Scottish unit. At that stage in the South African war the need was greatest for mounted infantry – the Imperial Yeomanry – and as such the offer was not taken up by the War Office. But with the development of Kitchener's Army in this new war, it seemed that this might be an excellent way of adding at least a

battalion to the roster of locally raised units from Tyneside. The idea was raised in the local press on 8 September 1914:

SCOTS ON TYNESIDE
PROPOSED FORMATION OF LOCAL
BATTALION
It will be remembered that at the time of the Boer war in 1901, a few Scotsmen living in Newcastle, including Mr Farquhar Laing and Sir Thomas Oliver ... made an appeal for the formation of a Tyneside Scottish Battalion. Nearly one thousand names were enrolled within a week ... The movement fell through because mounted infantry were then particularly needed. Since the present war began, Sir Thomas Oliver ... with a view to ascertaining if the present time is opportune for reviving the Tyneside Scottish has received from the War Office a letter stating that Lord Kitchener would be willing to accept a battalion of Scotsmen from Newcastle if a thousand men can be got. They could be taken up to 45 years of age.[88]

In fact, as discussed by recent historians of the Tyneside Scottish, it was as much of a struggle to get the 1914 version on the books as it had been in 1900.[89] The intention was that the Tyneside Scots would be kilted, with Sir Thomas Oliver fighting the corner for the distinctive dress with the War Office: 'It was strongly expressed that the regiment proposed to be raised should be a kilted one, the original idea being on the basis, so far as dress was concerned, of the London Scottish.'[90]

The financial burden of raising a local battalion, especially a kilted one, was a challenge and the

persuaded Kitchener to accept the battalion and to think ambitiously, combining it with a proposed Tyneside Irish Battalion and the already formed Newcastle Commercials to create a brigade. The *Newcastle Journal* reported the news:

WAR OFFICE SANCTION

The Lord Mayor of Newcastle received a telegram last night from the War Office, authorising the formation of three local battalions, to be known as the Tyneside Scottish, The Tyneside Irish and the Tyneside Commercial Battalions.[93]

The battalion would not be kilted:

There had been some talk to the effect that men would not join unless they could wear the kilt. He hoped that no one would be exacting in a manner of that kind. The intention was to go on with the Tyneside Scottish Battalion, and to serve in the ordinary uniform (trousers); and probably they might be able to get some distinctive badge for the cap, which would show the men belonged to a Scottish Battalion.[94]

Recruiting was now so strong that it was difficult to keep up with it. Battalion followed battalion. Each time the committee making an application to the War Office for official sanction and each time receiving it. By 16 November 1914, four battalions had been raised.

None of these men would have to suffer the indignity of wearing Kitchener blue. Instead, like Bristol's Own, the organising committee decided to hold out for khaki, all the while wearing civilian

raising committee hesitated, expressing the view to the War Office that the battalion would have to be kept on hold. In any case, Kitchener seemed reluctant to sanction formations that could be said to be 'semi-nationalist' and the raising of an overtly Scottish battalion certainly fell into this bracket.[91] The War Office wrote to Sir Thomas to decline the offer of the battalion on 18 September.

Despite this blow, the committee continued its work. With an obvious decline in recruiting in the latter part of September, but the donation of a sum of £10,000 to the committee by Colonel Joseph Cowen, some of the obstacles were starting to be removed.[92] A visit of the Lord Chancellor Lord Haldane to the city on 10 October provided the opportunity for work to progress. Haldane had

The Tyneside Scottish Brigade recruited from Scots living in Newcastle and the surroundings – or those men who admired the traditional Scottish dress. The Tyneside Scots were denied the kilt, although this brooch, bought in Alnwick while the Tynesiders were training there, clearly shows that the men still hankered after it.

clothes. With no protective button badge, these men wore simple Royal Stewart tartan armbands with the letters 'TS', in order to distinguish them from those who had not the inclination to serve.[95]

With the disappointment over the kilts, the fact that the four battalions would wear the distinctly Scottish glengarry bonnet was significant, as was the choice of a recognisably Scottish cap badge, to be designed by Major Hopkins of the Recruiting Committee. In fact, there would be four variants before the war's end.[96] And although this remained the only distinctively Scottish mark, the battalion pipers did indeed wear the kilt, which included

the startling black-and-white checked Shepherd's or Northumberland tartan for the 1st Tyneside Scots, with Campbell of Loudon or Campbell of Argyll denoting the others (2nd and 4th, and 3rd Battalions respectively).[97]

The Recruiting Committee had successfully raised a whole brigade – the 102nd – and just out of men wanting to serve with the Tyneside Scots. There was now a battalion of Irishmen to fill. An idea that Haldane himself was keen on – as noted in the local press. There seemed to be no shortage of recruits even while the other battalions were under way:

An officer's uniform of the Tyneside Scots. Denied the kilt, these men were granted the glengarry and 'distinctively Scottish' badge.

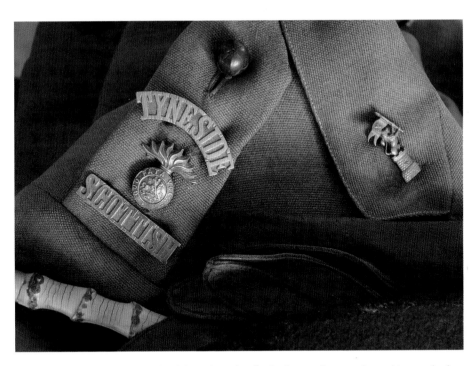

The four successive patterns (left to right, top to bottom) of the Tyneside Scottish badge, 1914–16. The first pattern (top left) was deemed to be too small.

Officers wore this distinctive shoulder title and collar badge. Rank was indicated in standard fashion on the sleeve.

Other ranks wore titles like these, although with different numerals to indicate their battalion (2–4 in brass, rather than white metal).

Pipers of the 2nd Tyneside Scottish. The first battalion wore the traditional houndstooth 'Shepherd's tartan'.

THE TYNESIDE IRISH

The number enrolled, up to yesterday for the Tyneside Irish was 2,815. The work of attestation is progressing very rapidly. Those who have already enrolled are pressing for attestation as quickly as possible, and this work is being carried out with the least degree of delay. The contracts for clothing, etc., are well in hand, and uniforms will very shortly be supplied to the men.[98]

The Tyneside Irish Brigade (the 103rd) was complete by 12 January. Their Irish roots were denoted only by the crowned harp of Erin worn on their shoulder straps.[99]

The raising of the two brigades was a spectacular achievement. The gift of £10,000 (increased to £15,000) had provided the means of getting over the initial obstacles, but this figure was much less than the actual expenditure. As noted by the first historian of the Tyneside Scottish, 'the liabilities of the trustees reached nearly £100,000 before there were any reimbursements from Government, and their total expenditure exceeded £500,000 before the Brigades were taken over by the War Office'.[100] It was a magnificent achievement. Both

A signaller with the Tyneside Irish Brigade, the men of which wore a distinctive shoulder title with the Harp of Erin and 'NF'. It was usual to have the battalion number above the harp.

ENLISTMENT IN THE REGULAR ARMY.

HEIGHT NOW REDUCED TO NORMAL STANDARD FOR INFANTRY OF THE LINE.

CONDITIONS TILL FURTHER ORDERS:

HEIGHT - 5 ft. 3 ins. and upwards.
CHEST - - 34½ ins. at least.
AGE - - - 19 to 38 years.

5th November, 1914.

W 7532—3692 50,000 11/14 H W V

brigades would serve as components of the 34th Division, while the Newcastle Commercials, designated simply as the 16th (Service) Battalion Northumberland Fusiliers (Newcastle), would serve in the 96th Brigade, 32nd Division.

A significant issue for recruitment to Kitchener's Army was the question of the minimum standards of height and chest expansion that had been set in the original Call to Arms, published in early August. Soldiers had to be a minimum of 5ft 3in tall, with a chest expansion of 34in. In fact, as a brake to recruiting on 11 September, the War Office had actually upped the restriction to 5ft 6in – pretty much the upper estimate of the average height of British men in 1914.[101] With resources stretched, this approach was intended to give respite to those who had to train, house and equip the battalions of Kitchener's Army that had been flooding through the doors of the recruiting offices in late August. This had an immediate effect on restricting recruitment, and the figures fell. By 5 November 1914, however, the original height of 5ft 3in was restored as the minimum.

In early October the MP for Birkenhead, 6ft tall Alfred Bigland, spotted an opportunity to open up an untapped avenue for recruitment. According to the regimental history, the Bantams were born when four under-height Durham miners – men who had been unable to join other northern battalions – marched into the town's recruiting office.[102] Reputedly offering to fight any man to prove their worth, the plight of such men lodged in the mind of the MP, who saw the opportunity that presented itself – to take small but otherwise fit men and turn them into a likely source for recruits.

Although the actual veracity of this story has been disputed, the idea was soon embraced by both the press and popular opinion, fitting the idea of the truculent bantam cock.[103] An apt poem appeared in the Cheshire Observer:

Increasing the minimum height was used as a brake on recruiting. By November the fall-off in numbers meant that it had to be reset at the original levels.

Birkenhead Town Hall – 6ft MP Arthur Bigland oversees recruitment to his Bantam battalion of under-height men.

BIGLAND'S BANTAMS

Where are you going to, my little man?
I'm going to France to fight, if I can!
But you are too small to fight Germans, I said.
Just take off your coat and I'll fight you
    instead.

But what is your Regiment, if I may enquire?
The 1st Bigland's Bantams – a name to inspire
Those men who are longing to prove to the foe
That their spirits are right, if their stature is
    low.[104]

Bigland approached the War Office for 'special dispensation', and received it. Within three days of receiving permission to recruit under-height men – though still over 5ft, and with the same rate of chest expansion – Bigland was mobbed by smaller men who were seeking a chance to join Kitchener's Army:[105] 'Men have arrived from various parts of the north of England to join the Bantams Battalion at Birkenhead, which is now complete.'[106]

Eventually some 3,000 men had enrolled at Birkenhead, and two battalions of the Cheshire Regiment, the 15th and 16th, were raised. 'Bigland's

Men' were somewhat different from the average men of the Pals battalions. They were united by two things: a desire to serve, and a stature that put them below the minimum then operating – it had nothing to do with class or status, as so many of the others did.

The *Daily Sketch* for 1 December 1914 devoted its front page to the phenomenon, under the headline, 'Brisk Recruiting for Birkenhead Bantams – "Quality, not size, wanted"'.[107] Each man received a specially commissioned celluloid badge bearing a pugnacious bantam cock, and the monogram BBB – 'Bigland's Birkenhead Bantams'.[108] The concept spread like wildfire and ultimately twenty-four Bantam battalions were raised across the country, forming the 35th (Bantam) Division.

The Cheshire Regiment was also the home to other Service units, including the 13th (Service) Battalion, a Pals battalion in all but name. It had been raised on 1 September 1914 as the 'Wirral Battalion' at Port Sunlight, mostly from the workers of Lord Leverhulme's famous soap factory, by local MP Gershom Stewart.[109] It would be the only Pals battalion without a special title. There was also the unusual 1st Manx Service Company, an 'active service' company of volunteers from the Isle of Man who volunteered to serve overseas in March 1915. The governor of the Isle of Man, Lord Raglan, was instrumental in getting War Office sanction for the men to stay together as a special 'service company', and they were distinguished from other soldiers of the 2nd Cheshire Regiment, their eventual home, by a special 'Legs of Man' badge on their shoulder straps.[110]

Lord Rosebery, the former Liberal prime minister, followed Bigland's lead in identifying the opportunities for recruiting fit but under-height

Bantam recruiting tramcar with distinctive bantam cock insignia at Woodside, the ferry terminal for the Mersey crossing.

'Bigland's Birkenhead Bantams' – the distinctive button badge manufactured for the first of the Bantam soldiers.

men. He was instrumental in raising a Scots Bantam battalion, the 17th (Service) Battalion, Royal Scots (Lothian Regiment) (Rosebery), a unit distinguished by a yellow-enamelled silver badge worn on the collar, a gift from Lord Rosebery himself.[111] This dainty badge, a primrose, alluded to his family

In action, the Cheshire Bantams wore the standard service dress with no special distinctions.

Below left: The 1st Manx Service Company was raised from Isle of Man volunteers who wished to serve overseas. They were initially posted to the 16th (Service) Battalion, King's Liverpool Regiment, before being transferred to the 3rd Cheshires, a Regular battalion. They wore this distinctive 'Legs of Man' insignia.

Far right: Lord Rosebery was instrumental in raising a Bantam battalion, the 17th (Service) Battalion, Royal Scots (Rosebery). Each one of the original members was issued with a delicate primrose badge, a reference to his family name.

name. Rosebery made a rousing address in favour of the under-height soldiers in February 1915, reported in the *Daily Record*:

> Is not courage the principal qualification in the soldier? And we desire to know where is the analogy between courage and the six foot rule (Laughter). Is courage to be measured by the yard? (Laughter). Or are men, like barrels, to be gauged in order to find out their contents? (Laughter).[112]

A letter to the editor of the *Falkirk Herald* in regard to Rosebery's battalion actually claimed that the advantage lay with 'the smaller man':

> In modern warfare the advantage, if anywhere, is with the smaller men; and with examples before us of such armies as the Japs and the Gurkhas, and of such a soldier as Lord Roberts ... there is no more to be said for a 5ft or a 5ft 6in limit. The one thing is that the men be physically strong and fit.[113]

The Rosebery Battalion (106th Brigade) took its place alongside the lads from Birkenhead (105th Brigade) and others from Lancashire and Salford, including the 20th (Service) Battalion Lancashire Fusiliers (4th Salford) raised by the redoubtable Salford MP Montague Barlow, in the 104th Brigade. The Bantam experiment would continue, with at least part of the 40th Division being formed of under-height men – although eventually it was to suffer as unfit men, in the language of the day, were 'weeded' or 'combed' out.[114]

The final tranche of Kitchener's 500,000 men were formed by other, slightly more unusual,

locally raised units – from Northern Ireland or Wales – together with reserve Kitchener battalions, making up the remainder of what would have been K5, the final 100,000, and the 36th–41st Divisions.

These later battalions had a different flavour to them, though. Kitchener was now in the business of inviting prominent citizens to take on the mantle of recruiting. This was particularly the case in London. With the capital being an agglomeration of over 6 million people, individual boroughs were in a position to raise their very own battalions to rival those of other towns and cities. As Peter Simkins has pointed out, the London boroughs of 'Battersea, Bermondsey, Islington, Lambeth, Lewisham, Shoreditch, St Pancras, Wandsworth and West Ham' all produced infantry battalions in the period from November 1914 to July 1915.[115]

The distinctive shoulder title of the 20th Lancashire Fusiliers, a Salford Bantam battalion.

Bermondsey is an inner city borough of London, situated south of the River Thames. In 1914 it had a total population of around 124,000 people, and had a mortality rate that was much higher than the average outer London borough (and the nearby borough of Wandsworth).[116] It was relatively poor compared to some. With recruiting on the slide, 'Lord Kitchener issued an appeal to the mayors of boroughs', and Bermondsey would be one of them: 'Mr John Hart, Mayor of Bermondsey, received a request from the Secretary of State for War to raise a battalion of infantry, and this letter was discussed at a meeting of the borough council on May 4th 1915.'[117]

The council was asked to consider their responsibilities. They would not only have to recruit the necessary men, but in accordance with the precedent set since Lord Derby's Pals appeared on the recruiting scene in August 1914, they would have to be trained, fed and paid by the borough until taken over by the War Office. When this was taken to the council members, there were objections, particularly because a London Territorial Battalion raised from the borough was already in existence. Nevertheless, the motion was passed, and recruiting started on 24 May 1915. The battalion history noted that this was a tough call indeed at this stage in the war:

> The task of recruiting was not a light one. All sorts of schemes were adopted to try to get the men to enlist ... recruiting meetings were held throughout the district. Special appeals were made at the Globe Picture Palace ... where a patriotic picture was being exhibited, and at the South London Palace Music Hall ... where a war play depicting the agony of Belgium was being performed.[118]

There were lectures – one from a Victoria Cross winner, Lance Corporal E. Dwyer – as well as Harry Lauder's pipe bands, mass marches, parades and even knocking door-to-door, enquiring whether there were men of military age there. (Men so doing were subjected to some scrutiny, with the rebuff, 'My boy is already over there; when are you going?', or worse, if their son had been killed.)[119]

Eventually, a battalion was recruited, with a somewhat different make-up to those Pals units raised in the first flush of enthusiasm, when 'no undesirables' were required, and where 'scrutiny' ensured that only men of the 'commercial classes' were permitted to join. The battalion history continued:

> Over 1,000 men joined, the bulk of the local recruits being dock and riverside workers with a good sprinkling from the tanneries. A great many 'black-coated' workers living or working locally also helped to swell the ranks. There was a fairly big proportion of youths under and men over military age, and some not properly fit physically for the rigours of active service.[120]

It was not quite what Lord Derby had originally had in mind. Particularly as, in some cases, recruits would join, take their first day's pay and clothing – and abscond.[121] Perhaps not surprising, though, in an inner city borough.

Nevertheless, the mayor and his council were justifiably proud of their achievement in raising the battalion, which became the 12th (Service) Battalion, East Surrey Regiment (Bermondsey). Colonel Beaton, commanding the battalion, recalled that 'the Mayor wished us to identify ourselves with the Borough, and suggested we

The Bermondsey Battalion of the East Surrey Regiment wore the arms of the borough on uniform collars.

should change our cap badge for one incorporating the Arms of Bermondsey'. On this matter, the colonel would not budge – as a battalion of a famous regiment it would be an insult to wear another badge. Despite his objections, he relented somewhat. If the mayor could get permission 'for the men to wear the Borough arms on their collars, we should be pleased to let them do so'.[122]

Permission was indeed given, but such things were seemingly less important to the somewhat more wealthy and nearby borough of Wandsworth. On raising their battalion a month later the arms of Guildford, so prominently displayed on the East Surrey's cap badge, were replaced with the arms of the borough. Such was the nature of local pride.

While the colonel of the Bermondsey Battalion refused to spurn the standard East Surrey Regiment cap badge due to its distinguished history, nearby Wandsworth had no such qualms. It replaced the arms of Guildford with the arms of the borough.

THE IRISH DIVISIONS

Irish recruits filled three volunteer divisions, the 10th (Irish) – southern but not exclusively nationalist, the 16th (Irish) – southern and almost exclusively nationalist, and the 36th (Ulster) – northern and overwhelmingly unionist.[123]

Irish battalions had already been added to the roster of Kitchener's First and Second Armies. The 10th (Irish) Division was an integral part of the First Hundred Thousand and was actually composed of battalions from across Ireland, with many men who had been old soldiers who had rejoined. But there were others too. Bryan Cooper, the divisional historian, described its demographic:

Of the Irish recruits, but little need be said. Mostly drawn from the class of labourers, they took their tone from the old soldiers. [However], recruiting in Ireland in August, 1914, was not as satisfactory as it was in England, and in consequence, Lord Kitchener decided early in September to transfer a number of recruits for whom no room could be found in English regiments to fill up the ranks.[124]

This gave rise to the suggestion that the 10th Division was 'Irish only in name', which was certainly an exaggeration.[125] However, it was the case that recruiting had been a significant cause for concern.[126] The 10th was one of the first New Army divisions to see action, and yet has been overshadowed somewhat by debate surrounding the recruitment of two other Irish divisions, the 16th (Irish) and the 36th (Ulster).

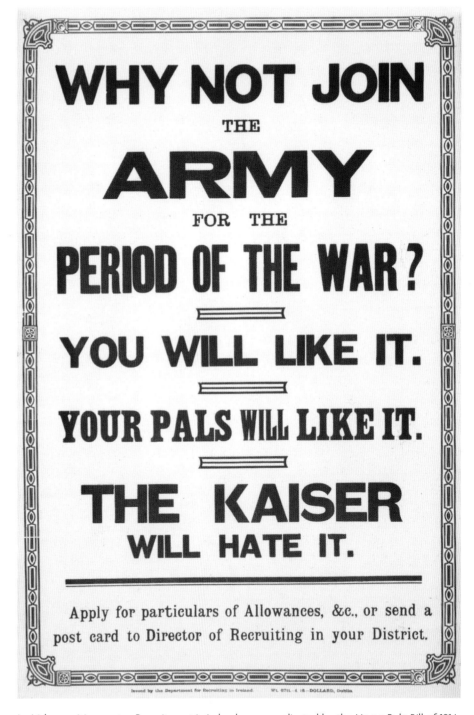

An Irish recruiting poster. Recruitment in Ireland was complicated by the Home Rule Bill of 1914.

In truth, the question of the supply of recruits in Ireland was a controversial one, with Asquith's Home Rule Bill creating a rift in the country that was only put in abeyance by the war emergency. Paramilitary Unionist and Nationalist militia forces had been raised and were on the brink of civil war. The first of these was the Ulster Volunteer Force (UVF), a 'private army' of 100,000 men raised in January 1913 by the Ulster Unionists, a party with the direct support and sympathy of the British Conservatives.[127] The UVF was open to any man who had actively signed the 'Ulster Covenant', a document that pledged opposition to the enforcement of Irish Home Rule, with an Irish government administered from Dublin. Anathema to the Ulstermen, signing the covenant and joining the UVF created the direct threat of armed struggle in Ireland through the pledge, 'In the event of such a Parliament being forced upon us we further solemnly and mutually pledge ourselves to refuse to recognise its authority'.[128]

Sir Edward Carson was first to sign, a prominent Unionist who campaigned against Home Rule. Carson would be a significant figure in the recruitment of the UVF, and later, of men to join Kitchener's New Army. The UVF was organised on military lines in political divisions: its regiments and recruiting areas matched and reflected parliamentary constituencies.[129] The existence of the UVF was to have a far-reaching effect on British politics, leading to the near mutiny of British Army officers at Curragh in March 1914.

If the UVF were prepared to stand and fight for their rights to refuse Home Rule, then it was inevitable there would be men of equal conviction who would fight to see Home Rule become reality. The raising of the UVF in 1912 was followed by the creation of the Irish Volunteers in 1913, born of the Irish Republican Brotherhood (IRB), a long-standing political organisation committed to the establishment of an Irish Republic. Though not being seen publically to raise the Volunteers, the IRB's influence ensured that it came about. On their formation on 25 November 1913, the Volunteers pledged to uphold the rights of all Irishmen in gaining Home Rule.

The raising of such diametrically opposed bodies of men inevitably led to uniforms, drill and posturing. The two private armies drilled every week, in neighbouring parts of the city of Belfast and that inevitably led to tensions.[130] It led also to gun-running, with first the Unionists and then the Nationalists looking beyond the territorial boundaries of the United Kingdom to satisfy their aims of creating bodies of men both willing and capable of fighting for their rights over Home Rule. Ireland was on the verge of a civil war, and with Carson sponsoring the rights of the Unionists, John Redmond MP, leader of the Irish Parliamentary Party, became a prominent voice in support of the National Volunteers.

But by 1914, the machinations of domestic politics were set to take a back seat. With the deteriorating international situation, both bodies, Nationalist and Unionist, were in the sights of the British Government. The UVF in particular was identified as a valuable manpower resource. Kitchener didn't waste any time in sounding out the possibilities. According to the historian of the 36th (Ulster) Division, two days after his appointment the new Secretary of State summoned Colonel T.E. Hickman, the Wolverhampton MP and president of the British League for the Defence of Ulster, to attend the War Office. Hickman was

Opposite: Cap badges of Irish regiments. *From left to right, top*: Royal Irish Fusiliers, Royal Munster Fusiliers, Connaught Rangers; *bottom*: Royal Dublin Fusiliers, Leinster Regiment.

Recruiting tram for Kitchener's Army in Ulster – Kitchener's recruiting poster is prominent (centre).

The Ulster Volunteers in 1912; they would be uniformed later.

nothing would happen while the war was being fought and, after it had ended, Ulster would have some form of recognition.

The UVF was duly taken on board to form a whole division – the 36th – with a concession that it would be allowed to retain the subsidiary title 'Ulster'. Its brigades were formed of new Service battalions of the Royal Irish Rifles and the Inniskilling Fusiliers, while the choice of battalion was in part a function of the old UVF recruiting boundaries.[132]

The brigades reflected this. For example, the 107th was formed of the 8th, 9th, 10th and 15th Battalions of the Royal Irish Rifles, and in turn, the East Belfast, West Belfast, South Belfast and North Belfast Volunteers.[133]

Sir Edward Carson, the Unionist MP who was such a towering figure in the development of the Ulster Volunteers.

36th Ulster Division cap badge produced by Belfast jeweller Sharman D. Neill and issued in 1915. It would soon be replaced by the regimental badge, though a cloth rendering of the traditional Red Hand of Ulster would later be worn on the sleeve.

a prominent member of the UVF, and Kitchener made the bold statement, 'I want the UVF.'[131]

Hickman was clear – the man to see was Carson. In actuality, many of the UVF men had already joined the British Army, but the fact that there was a tantalising quasi-military unit under the influence of Carson meant that obtaining his blessing was significant. And to obtain this meant some form of guarantee that Home Rule would not be forthcoming during the period the UVF men were away. This was not a guarantee that could be given, and Home Rule became law on 18 September 1914. Nevertheless, some concessions were made:

It had been intended that all men of the division would wear the Red Hand of Ulster on their caps.

The badges arrived, were issued, and of course worn, since an order is an order, but regimental tradition prevailed ... Protests reached Divisional Headquarters, in such large numbers ... that within a week the Royal Irish Rifles badge was in every cap.[134]

One battalion, the 14th Royal Irish Rifles, was formed from the Young Citizen Volunteers (YCV) of Belfast, a Volunteer corps intended to tap into the post-adolescent youth of Belfast. It was the brainchild of Fred T. Geddes, a prominent member of the Belfast Citizens Association.[135] As reported in the *Dundee Courier*, the Volunteers were first raised on 10 September 1912 at City Hall, Belfast:

The Lord Mayor, who is president of the organisation, explained that the objects of the Corps were to develop a spirit of responsible citizenship and municipal patriotism, to cultivate by means of military and police drill a manly physique, and to assist as an organisation when called upon in the maintenance of peace.[136]

ULSTER VOLUNTEERS, BELFAST   3828-6

The Ulster Volunteers march through Belfast in 1916.

The YCV would take their place in the 36th Division, within the 109th Brigade, and would be the only battalion to maintain its original badges and titles while in khaki.[137]

Both Carson and Redmond envisaged that their armies could be used to defend Ireland as a kind of home defence corps. Both made it plain that their responsibilities lay with the Allies in defeating German militarism, and that the government could rest easy that the security of Ireland was safe in the hands of the paramilitaries. Nationalist MP John Redmond went further. He asked the government to recognise the importance of gathering Irishmen together in order to combat the common foe. In September, *The Times* reported on Redmond's response:

> Mr. John Redmond has issued a manifesto calling upon the Irish people to keep faith with the democracy of Great Britain, who have kept faith with them and given back to Ireland her national liberties. He calls upon her people to take their part and share in the burdens and sacrifices imposed by this war — a war for high ideals of human government and international relations. Mr. Redmond appeals for an 'Irish Brigade,' for the Expeditionary Force — that Irish recruits should be kept together as a unit, officered by Irishmen, and made up into county battalions. Simultaneously, he adds, the Irish Volunteers must be made efficient for the defence of the country at home.[138]

The account noted that Redmond asked that 'Irish recruits for the New Army should be kept as much together as possible and should be officered

The Young Citizen Volunteers of Belfast became the 14th (Service) Battalion, Royal Irish Rifles (Young Citizen Volunteers). They wore distinctive shoulder titles and a cap badge with the Red Hand of Ulster.

by Irishmen'.[139] Redmond's appeal started to gain traction. In throwing his lot in with the British and identifying Germany as the common enemy, recruiting in Ireland took a step forward and the 16th (Irish) Division, a component of the Second Kitchener's Army (K2), was the result.

Nevertheless, recruiting for the division was still a struggle, even with Redmond's support, who viewed the 16th as a Nationalist contribution to the war effort, to balance that of the Unionist efforts, and ultimately to be the basis of the 36th Division.[140] *The Times* continued to have an active interest in Redmond's activity:

> Mr. Redmond reviewed a body of Volunteers nearly 5,000 strong at Waterford. [A] lie which he wanted to deal with was that which had

been put forward by another class of his enemies – that the Irish Nationalists were funking this war, and that the appropriate emblem for Ireland would be the white feather. That was an infamous misrepresentation. At this moment in the firing line Ireland had a larger proportion of her sons than either England, Scotland, or Wales. In addition to that it should not be forgotten that from the ranks of the volunteers thousands of Reservists had been called to the Colours, and had gone willingly.[141]

Famously, both divisions would serve together, side by side, during the Battle of Messines, on 7 June 1917.

Irish Nationalist MP John Redmond, who was instrumental in raising the Irish National Volunteers. His brother, Major William Redmond, was killed in action serving with the 6th (Service) Battalion, Royal Irish Regiment, a K2 battalion that formed part of the 16th (Irish) Division.

THE WELSH ARMY CORPS

I should like to see a Welsh Army in the Field. I should like to see the race that faced the Norman for hundreds of years in a struggle for freedom, the race that helped to win Crecy, the race that fought for a generation under Glyndwr against the greatest Captain in Europe – I should like to see that race give a good taste of their quality in this struggle in Europe.[142]

The raising of a whole army corps – two divisions – of Welshmen was born out of the inspiring oratory of Chancellor of the Exchequer David Lloyd George.[143] Speaking in London on 21 September 1914, he addressed an audience of 'London Welshmen', people in a position to influence recruiting. The meeting was reported widely in the press:

INSPIRING ADDRESS TO LONDON WELSHMEN

Mr Lloyd George addressing a great meeting of London Welshmen for the promotion of recruiting, met with an enthusiastic reception. He was accompanied on the platform by politicians of all parties. The floor of the hall was set apart mainly for probable recruits, and patriotic airs were sung with great heartiness in both English and Welsh. The Chancellor of the Exchequer said he had come to talk to his fellow countrymen about the Great War and the part they should take in it.[144]

For Lloyd George, that part was a direct engagement of Welshmen fighting together in a peculiarly Welsh corps. His eloquence was widely praised in the press:

The Lloyd George meeting here was an immense success, as every recruiting meeting is, and the great little man was never in finer oratorical form. He spoke with a vigour and elocutionary force which alternatively held his audience spellbound and lifted them to the heights of demonstrative enthusiasm ... Oratory such as this should make him the best recruiting officer in the Kingdom.[145]

With such praise for his actions and ideas, the Chancellor called another meeting of prominent Welshmen at 11 Downing Street two days later. 'From that moment, there was no looking back.'[146] The Cardiff-based *Western Mail* reported its outcome:

An all-important development which was made to-day in regard to the proposal, which Mr Lloyd George referred to in the course of his great speech on Saturday, to bring into being an army corps for Wales.

Obviously, before any steps could be taken in the direction he indicated, the first and indispensable move would be to secure the sanction of the War Office to what he has proposed. Mr Lloyd George, however, took an early opportunity to-day of laying before Lord Kitchener the outline of the scheme. There is the highest authority for stating that the Secretary of State for War was not only favourably impressed by the project, but has actually sanctioned it.[147]

In fact, there was evidence that Kitchener was reluctant, not generally in favour of the development of national formations, and that Lloyd

David Lloyd George, Liberal MP and instigator of the call for the Welsh Army Corps.

George was aware of this.[148]

There were already pre-existing Welsh regiments – the Welsh Regiment, the Royal Welsh Fusiliers and the South Wales Borderers – with their complement of Regular, Special Reserve and Territorial battalions to fill (with the Welsh Guards to join them in February 1915). But the chancellor was convinced that 'the possibilities of recruiting in the principality on a National basis, had not, perhaps, been appreciated to its full value'.[149]

In any case, sanction was given, and a circular letter was drawn up on 24 September that announced the birth of the new corps, and the creation of a committee to maintain and develop it chaired by Lord Plymouth.[150] Five days later, as recorded in the documents of the executive committee, the corps was discussed at a conference in Cardiff:

Realising the righteousness of the cause for which the British Empire was fighting, the delegates at the Conference expressed their readiness to work whole-heartedly in raising this great Cymric Army to supplement the large contribution which Wales had already made to the British Forces since mobilisation had begun.[151]

The newly constituted Welsh Army Corps National Executive Committee (WNEC) met on 2 October. The task ahead was huge – the corps would have to compete with the Regulars and Territorials for men out of an available population that amounted to just 404,726 (within the age range of 20–40).[152] There would have to be recruitment of Welshmen from within the principality, and those of the wider diaspora across Britain, particularly in London, the borders and northern England, thereby competing with other locally raised Kitchener battalions.

At the heart of their planning was reliance on 'county patriotism', with 'County Committees' being created, headed, it was hoped, by the relevant Lord Lieutenants, which would act to persuade men to join comrades from their home county.[153] As Robin Barlow has pointed out, this expectation was perhaps overplayed, with little evidence to suggest that men were motivated to join for this reason.[154]

The WNEC proposed that Kitchener battalions that had come through the usual route (those which had not been 'locally raised') could form the basis for the corps, and that they would be combined with the new Pals battalions that were in the process of being formed across Wales. And with the War Office having increased its minimum height to 5ft 6in, it was hoped that in the case of

the hardy men of Wales this could be reverted to the original stature of 5ft 3in.

It was a lot to ask. To raise a whole army corps required some 40,000 men. There would have to be infantry units, engineers and artillerymen. There would have to be at least twenty-four battalions, all of them newly raised, none of them transferred over from Regulars or Territorials. The task was an enormous one. Too great, in fact, as it would turn out.

In October, the first four battalions were being raised. The 13th (Service) Battalion Royal Welsh Fusiliers (1st North Welsh) was formed at Rhyl in early September, reputedly as a University & Public Schools battalion, but transferred to the WNEC on 10 October. The recruitment of the 10th and 13th (Service) Battalions of the Welsh Regiment (1st and 2nd Rhondda) was supported through the vigorous efforts of the local Rhondda MP, David Watts Morgan, who himself initially enlisted in the 10th Battalion, and Colonel A. Person RE. Finally, the 14th (Service) Battalion Welsh Regiment was raised through the efforts of the mayor and corporation of Swansea.[155]

However, by the close of the month these four units could only number 3,000 men. Recruitment was in decline and by the end of February 1915 the strength of the corps stood at 20,000. It had taken five months to raise half the corps, the infantry and all that went with it. Although over 40,000 men had been recruited by October 1915, the WNEC knew that supplying the whole corps and its reserves was an impossible task.[156]

These men would become the only division, the 38th (Welsh), though originally numbered the 43rd. Together with the 36th (Ulster), these two were the only ones of the Pals divisions to use specific

The 38th (Welsh) Division wore the red dragon, the national symbol of Wales.

local titles — titles that differed from the original regional format used when drawing up the K1 and K2 divisions.

The diversity of units and locations was well expressed in a poem by 'Tok-Emma', published in 1918:

THE WELSH

Borderers, Welsh and Fusiliers,
Guns and Mortars and Engineers,
Machine-gun wallahs and Pioneers,
We're the Welsh, the 38th.

Swansea and Cardiff and Pwllheli,
Rhondda and Merthyr and Cydweli,
Aberteifi and Abergele,
Sent the Welsh, the 38th.[157]

The formation of Welsh units from outside of Wales had been an ambition first expressed by Lloyd George in his initial meetings in London. Although it had proven too difficult a task to raise battalions in nearby Liverpool and Manchester, competing with the 'great push' on Pals battalions there, more success was achieved in London. The 'London correspondent' of the *Western Mail* reported the possibility of a London Welsh battalion in early September:

Mr Tim Evans, the treasurer of the London Welsh Rugby Football Club, has had a further interview today with highly placed officials on the subject of the formation of the London Welsh Regiment [*sic*] – the movement he initiated early last week in conjunction with Mr A.E. Jones, treasurer of the London Welsh Male Voice Society. [They] have now decided to issue an appeal to London Welshmen between the ages of nineteen and thirty-five who wish to serve in the defence of their country ...[158]

Official War Office sanction was received for the raising of a London Welsh Battalion a month later, at a meeting of the executive committee:

The 15th (Service) Battalion, Royal Welsh Fusiliers (1st London Welsh) wore this distinctive shoulder title. Simple embroidered arcs were also worn.

A soldier of the London Welsh with his sister in Llandudno. He wears the second pattern of Kitchener blue.

This meeting was called by the Assistant secretary on receipt of the following telegram: 'War Office Approval received. You may proceed with arrangement for London Welsh Battalion. Signed Ivor Herbert.' The Secretary read the above and also the letter received from Gen. Sir Ivor Herbert confirming same in which he stated that the London Welsh Battalion would form part of the Welsh Army Corps.[159]

The London Welsh joined the 38th Division in April 1915 as the 15th (Service Battalion) Royal Welsh Fusiliers (1st London Welsh).[160] They were so distinguished on their shoulders, first with brass, then in simple embroidered titles.[161]

In keeping with its position as the capital of Wales, Cardiff raised two battalions of the Welsh Regiment that were specifically linked with the city, though only one of them would serve with the 38th Division. The 11th (Service) Battalion was raised as a Pals battalion by the Cardiff Chamber of commerce in September 1914. It would certainly start its journey along lines similar to those of all other Pals battalions in northern England. The *Western Mail* reported on progress:

THE 'PALS' BATTALION
ONE THOUSAND CARDIFF MEN WANTED
AT ONCE
Captain Percival Hope attended a meeting
of the Cardiff Chamber of Trade on Monday

A fresh-faced soldier of the 11th (Service) Battalion, Welsh Regiment – the Cardiff Commercials. He wears his khaki service dress cap with the card badge that was first worn by this battalion. Prior to the twentieth century, Welsh regiments had used the archaic spelling 'Welch'. Though the metal cap badges used 'Welsh', the newly formed Cardiff Commercials insisted on the older spelling on these card badges.

These badges had much in common with those manufactured to be given as entry tokens to horse races (and similar to the 'Kitchener's Army' badge illustrated on p.56).

evening, and asked for the assistance of members in obtaining commercial men as recruits for the 'Pals Battalion'. He had already succeeded in getting half the requisite number.[162]

In common with all other Pals battalions, the aspiration was for men of the commercial classes, although, according to one recent account the unit was more heterogeneous than this, consisting of 'shopworkers and solicitors, schoolteachers, coal miners and dockers'.[163] Certainly the commercial heart of Cardiff got behind the 'Cardiff Commercial Battalion', as it was depicted on the cardboard badges issued in its early stages, or the 'Cardiff Pals' as it was styled for public consumption. There was a special Pals magazine for the Cardiff

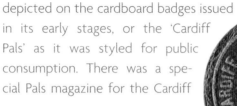

Commercials Gift Scheme, sold for 2*d* and intended as a fundraiser for the men themselves. It bore as a motto the background to these locally raised units:

THE CARDIFF (PALS) COMMERCIAL
BATTALION
11TH WELSH REGIMENT
Dear Old Pals ... Jolly Old Pals
Clinging together ... In all sorts of weather
Dear Old Pals ... Jolly Old Pals
Give me the friendship ... of dear Old Pals[164]

A pin badge, designed by the editor of the *Pals* magazine and manufactured by a local jeweller, was marketed for sale at 1s each, with 'every penny of profit' going to 'the Gift Scheme for our Boys'.[165] Despite all the trappings of a full-blown Pals battalion, the Cardiff Commercials would simply end up as a K3 battalion in September 1914. It was destined to serve with the 22nd Division, and from France, would be bound for Salonika in 1918.

By way of contrast, the 16th (Service) Battalion (Cardiff City) was first raised in November 1914 as part of the drive to fulfil the needs of the Welsh Army Corps. A resolution of the City Corporation was passed on 14 December that accepted the responsibility for the battalion:

RESOLVED – That the Corporation, in pursuance of the request made to them comprised in the resolution of the Committee convened by the Lord Mayor (Alderman J.T. Richards, OBE), on 17 November, in conjunction with the Military authorities, agree to take steps to establish for Cardiff and the neighbourhood a Cardiff City Battalion.[166]

The Cardiff Commercials' *Pals* magazine, issued to raise funds for the Pals Gift Scheme.

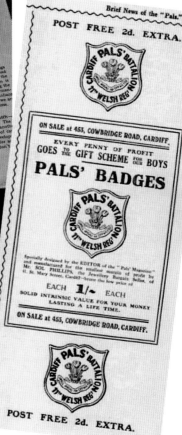

A local Cardiff jeweller, Mr Sol Phillips, created a special 'Cardiff Pals' gift badge from a design by the magazine editor, to help raise money for the gift scheme.

Recruiting was carried out at the most difficult time, but nevertheless its full complement was achieved on 11 January 1915.[167] As a distinctive mark of its status, the city's coat of arms was worn as collar badges on the standard khaki service dress, and it is reputed that this was only worn by those of the first 1,000 men to join.[168] Unusually, the 16th Battalion also adopted an all-brass (gilding metal) cap badge with the archaic spelling 'Welch', held to be more correct than the anglicised spelling 'Welsh' used by the remainder of the battalions.[169] Unlike the 11th Battalion, the 16th was brigaded with other locally raised Welsh units in the 115th Infantry Brigade, a component part of the 38th (Welsh) Division.

The 'Cardiff Pals' gift badge.

Wounded soldier of the Cardiff City Battalion wearing the distinctive collar badges.

The 16th (Service) Battalion, Welsh Regiment (Cardiff City). This battalion wore the arms of Cardiff as collar badges.

Unique amongst wartime battalions of the Welsh Regiment, the Cardiff City Battalion used an all-brass ('gilding metal') cap badge with the ancient 'Welch' spelling.

The 38th (Welsh) would serve with distinction and, like the 36th (Ulster), would receive its first true test on the Somme in 1916.

Silver sweetheart brooch given by a soldier of the Cardiff City Battalion to his loved one.

For God, For King & For Country.

Y.M.C.A.

Y. M. C. A.

WITH

FORCES ON ACTIVE SERVICE.

CARDIFF

ROAD TO THE SOMME

Who are the boys that fighting's for,
Who are the boys to win the war?
It's good old Kitchener's Army.
And every man of them's très bon,
They never lost a trench since Mons,
Because they never saw one.[1]

PUNCH, OR THE LONDON CHARIVARI.—December 30, 1914.

THE NEW ARMY TO THE FRONT.

'New Army to the Front' – a cartoon from *Punch* published at the end of 1914 expresses the challenges of the new year.

For the New Army men, training and assembly meant that they would have to wait some months before they could be committed to action. Many champed at the bit – after all, most had joined to 'go to the front' – and for most there was a delay of at least six months before they were ready to take their part in the line.

The first New Army divisions to go were the 9th (Scottish) and 14th (Light) Divisions, arriving in France and Flanders in May 1915. With four divisions committed to other theatres (Gallipoli and Egypt), the remainder would transfer to France in the latter part of 1915 and into the spring of 1916, ready for their part in the coming offensive on the Somme in July. The transfer was shrouded somewhat in secrecy, as war correspondent Philip Gibbs noted:

It was not until July of 1915 that the Commander-in-Chief announced that a part of the New Army was in France, and lifted the veil from the secret which had mystified

The departure of Kitchener's Army for France was of immense interest to the general public. This gramophone record of *c.* 1915 contained a dramatic reconstruction in words and music.

people at home whose boys had gone from them, but who could not get a word of their doings in France.[2]

As recorded in its divisional history, the 9th (Scottish) Division, first to go, received the first of many similar messages from the king:

> You are about to join your comrades at the Front in bringing to a successful end this relentless war of more than nine months duration. Your prompt patriotic answer to the nation's call to arms will never be forgotten. The keen exertions of all ranks during the period of training have brought you to a state

The divisional insignia of the 9th (Scottish) Division, the first of the Kitchener's Army men in France.

You'll see by this Card my lot I now share
With the Brave Highland Regiment
whose Badge I now wear,
And whatever, perchance, be my station,
In Camp or in Field, or when under Fire,
It will be my great aim, and my only desire,
To live up to their grand reputation,
And whether I live or my blood be spilt,
I swear I will never disgrace the Kilt.

From ·
One of the
GORDON HIGHLANDERS.

'I will never disgrace the kilt' – a postcard bought by a New Army soldier serving with the Gordon Highlanders, part of the 9th (Scottish) Division.

of efficiency not unworthy of my Regular Army. I am confident that in the field you will nobly uphold the traditions of the fine regiments whose names you bear.[3]

The New Army men of the 9th (Scottish) Division were only too aware of the burden of responsibility they held. No time was wasted in moving the men to the front line. The 9th was concentrated around St Omer, and with the other branches of the division farmed out for instruction with experienced formations, the infantry came under the wing of the Regular 6th Division in and around Armentières. Here they became acquainted with the reality of trench warfare, the domination of

125. THE EAST YORKS GOING INTO THE TRENCHES.

"Daily Mail"
Official Photograph
Crown Copyright reserved

'The East Yorks going into the trenches' – one of the *Daily Mail* 'Official War Postcards' series. This image depicts men of the 10th (Service) Battalion East Yorkshire Regiment (1st Hull) – the Hull Commercials – near Doullens on 3 July 1916.

no-man's-land, and the value of the bomb (as grenades were referred to at the time).

The divisional history continued its story: 'In spite of the immense preponderance that the enemy enjoyed in artillery, the men found in the life more of interest than of peril. Patrolling was a new form of enterprise that appealed to the bolder spirits.'[4]

The division received its acclimatisation to trench life from the end of May through to August. This would be matched by the other New Army divisions that were transferred to France and who were sent into the line to get their first experiences of being at the front. In all cases, their transport into the battle zone was a slow process, more often than not on slow-moving rail trucks that would carry them into an advanced location still behind the lines. Private Ernest Parker's journey in May 1915, with the 10th (Service Battalion) Durham Light Infantry (K1, 14th Division), was typical of so many others: 'Our cattle truck, like its neighbours, was marked plainly *Hommes 40: Chevaux 8*, but a wonderful feat of compression squeezed fifty of us into it and it was with difficulty that we converted our packs into seats.'[5]

Detrained, and eventually moving forward on foot, the New Army men would enter through communication trenches (CTs), avenues that linked the forward or fire trenches to the reserve lines and beyond to the rear areas. CTs permitted men, munitions and supplies to travel up to the line, as well as wounded soldiers to come out of it.

Unwary soldiers entering the line at this point could also suffer casualties. Private Dick Read of the 8th (Service) Battalion Leicestershire Regiment (37th Division) first went into the trenches at Wulverghem in 1915:

A communication trench. A wounded soldier struggles to cross the battlefield at Ginchy in September 1916.

Our first casualty was just as we were entering the communication trench. As we passed him we heard the wounded man gasping as stretcher-bearers tended to him. He had been hit in the stomach and subsequently we were told that a sniping rifle was laid on this point by day and fired at intervals by night.[6]

New Army men moved up to the front line from the rear areas along these crowded CTs at night. They were bustling, narrow thoroughfares 6ft deep, with barely enough room for men to pass. The relieving battalions would be guided to the front by experienced soldiers from the battalion who were about to be relieved – important, as not all trench systems followed the ideal. Irvine Clark was one of Tunstill's Men, a K3 volunteer serving with the 10th (Service) Battalion, Duke of Wellington's Regiment (23rd Division). In a letter home to his family in March 1916, he described the conditions he found when the British took over the line from the French:

> The trenches are only thirty yards apart; although I am calling them trenches they are only shell holes and ditches. There were six of us in one shell hole during the night time; we dug holes to get into in the day time and some of the chaps had to sit on a dead German all day.[7]

In many cases, particularly in the winter of 1915, conditions were dismal. Lance Corporal Norman Roberts, one of Tunstill's Men and serving in the 10th Duke of Wellington's, experienced the misery first-hand in November:

On the 3rd we left for the real thing. It was raining, the communication trench was over the knees in mud and water and it was 'some work' with a pack to get through. We manned the bags immediately and remained on duty until noon the next day. Twenty hours out of the day are devoted to some duty or other, but from 12 pm to 3.30 pm you are free to sleep – if you can get it. The dug-outs are all wet and one can hardly get inside. It is an awful time.[8]

Some shelter was provided by dugouts, which evolved from simple scrapes in the trench slopes providing little cover or security (known to the men as 'funk' or 'cubby' holes) to deeper affairs providing greater protection from the attentions of

54. "TOMMY'S" LOOK-OUT IN A CAPTURED TRENCH AT ORVILLERS.

OFFICIAL PHOTOGRAPH, CROWN COPYRIGHT RESERVED.

A classic *Daily Mail* Official War Postcard illustrating the nature of the front-line trench. This is a captured German trench that has been 'reversed', shown by the soldier asleep on the original fire step and the sentry on guard facing the Germans on a newly dug example.

Soldiers in 'funk' hole dugouts
at Guillemont on the Somme,
in September 1916.

howitzer shells and trench mortars. Dick Read of the 8th Leicesters came across one of these on his first tour of trench duty in 1915:

> The Lance-Corporal of the Middlesex machine-gun section took our corporal under his wing and a few moments later we were sharing a shelter made in a traverse about three feet six inches high, with several sleeping Middlesex men. There appeared to be a kind of front porch consisting of two pieces of galvanised sheeting laid across two sandbag walls, with a few bags laid across the top for added protection.[9]

These barely provided sufficient protection, and deep dugouts would come later in British service.

German deep dugouts were encountered in the aftermath of the battles of Loos (September 1915) and the Somme (July–November 1916). Here, New Army men came across their deep, dry shelters dug in the hard chalk. They were often equipped for a long period of occupation, as was found by Captain G.M. Brown, an officer in the 9th (Service) Battalion, Suffolk Regiment (K3, 24th Division):

> The dug-out that has been allotted to me ... is an old divisional HQ of the German Army, fitted as though it were impregnable, armchairs, bureaus, cabinets, framed pictures and electric lights, and upstairs with double and single bedrooms, more like a week-end cottage than a dug-out.[10]

A *Daily Mail* Official War Postcard illustrating a heavily revetted German trench, with its dugout entrance, at La Boisselle on the Somme.

127. A CAPTURED DUG-OUT NEAR LA BOISELLE.

"Daily Mail"
Official Photograph
Crown Copyright reserved

British trenches were laid out by the Royal Engineers, but were invariably dug by the infantry. The time for digging a man's length of fire trench – two paces, or 45 cubic feet – was estimated in 1914 to be 100 minutes under normal conditions.[11] Under *normal* conditions …

With the reality that trench warfare was demanding, some battalions of the Kitchener armies were designated as pioneers in late 1914. Men of the pioneer battalions were equipped and trained as fighting soldiers, but were skilled enough to provide essential labour building roads, digging dugouts and maintaining services. For this reason, all men designated as Pioneers bore distinctive collar badges of a crossed pick and rifle – a badge first introduced in 1915.[12] In fact, some sixty-eight infantry battalions would be transformed into pioneers from November 1914, and each division received one of these newly designated units.[13]

The pioneers were created to help relieve pressure on the engineers, supplying men with a modicum of engineering or practical skills, while still training them to take on the role of infantry. Some New Army infantry battalions forming in 1914–15 would be redesignated as pioneers. This was certainly the case for the Oldham Comrades, a Pals battalion that had been raised by the mayor of this predominantly cotton-spinning town with the assistance of an 'illuminated tramcar', like so many other boroughs at the time. Though landing in France in November 1915 as infantry, on 22 May 1916 it was redesignated as a pioneer battalion – the practical skills of its men self-evident. The unit served as divisional pioneers with the Regular 7th Division for the rest of the war.[14]

But with the concept of the pioneers came a new opportunity for raising New Army units with special skills, Pals battalions that would be linked

130. A BRITISH LABOUR BATTALION AT WORK.

"Daily Mail" Official Photograph Crown Copyright reserved

'A British Labour Battalion at Work' – a *Daily Mail* Official War Postcard. Organised labour was an important part of the modern battlefield, and many Kitchener's battalions found themselves redeployed as pioneers.

The 'Cotton Town Comrades', the 24th (Service) Battalion, Manchester Regiment (Oldham) (Pioneers). The distinctive crossed pick and rifle collar insignia was worn by all pioneer battalions.

Right: A cap worn by an officer of the 18th or 19th Middlesex Regiment. These pioneers were raised by North London MP Lieutenant Colonel John Ward as the 1st and 2nd Public Works battalions.

Far right: An other ranks cap badge of the 18th and 19th (Service) battalions of the Middlesex Regiment (1st and 2nd Public Works Pioneers).

to tramways departments, railway engineers or corporation public works. There were twelve such battalions, raised in 1914–15.[15]

Perhaps the most well-known were the three Middlesex Public Works Pioneer Battalions, serving as the 18th, 19th and 26th (Service) Battalions of the Middlesex Regiment. The battalions were raised by John Ward MP, a prominent citizen and former manual labourer or 'navvy', who had also been the founder of the Navvies, Bricklayers Labourers & General Labourers Union in 1889. These battalions served overseas in the 33rd, 41st and 62nd divisions. With Ward's connections, it is not surprising that these units became known as the Navvies' battalions, reported widely in the Empire press:

THE NAVVIES' BATTALION

Mr John Ward, the navvies' MP, is going to lead his men in war, as he has led them in peace. He has become a captain of the Navvies' Battalion, which has been formed to do trench digging at the front. Its official name is the Public Works Pioneer Battalion, 18th Middlesex, and recruits are coming in at a rate of fifty a day. The men are undergoing the usual military training, but fighting will naturally be only a secondary part of their work. In these days of trench warfare a company of navvies will be invaluable to any brigade.[16]

As described by the regimental history, the work of the pioneers was hardly glamorous, however:

They were Pioneers, and these brave fellows led an almost unselfish existence. They had no opportunities (or seldom had), such as fell to infantrymen in the front line, of engaging in exciting contests with the enemy, they could not retaliate when fired upon, though they worked almost always under shell fire ... They just kept on with their work, repairing or making fresh defences, building machine gun posts and emplacements, laying duckboards in the trenches, digging communication trenches, wiring the front of the trenches in 'No Man's Land'.[17]

No-man's-land was that strip of contested ground between the opposing trenches. Tactical possession of no-man's-land was claimed by many, and aggressive patrolling, raids and observation were common practice in British battalions. With no-man's-land observed by both sides through trench periscopes set up for the purpose, it would have been virtually suicidal to look over the parapet that protected the trench top. Lance Corporal Norman Roberts of the 10th Duke's was well aware of the situation on Guy Fawkes Night, 1915:

The Germans have our parapet well marked with guns and rifles, which were apparently set during the day. It is most dangerous to

put one's head above the top. I gave them about one hundred to two hundred rounds to commemorate the fifth.[18]

The forward trenches either side of no-man's-land were protected by belts of barbed wire, and it was to need constant attention. Wiring parties on both sides entered no-man's-land under the cover of darkness in patrols of two to three, or in larger fatigue parties – gangs of anywhere between twelve to eighty men – to repair and improve the front-line wire.

Private Robert Price, aged 42, was a Lancashire miner who joined the 1st Rhondda Battalion 10th Welsh Regiment, 38th (Welsh) Division. Service in the Ypres Salient in 1916 was wearing him down:

OFFICIAL PHOTOGRAPH SHOWING BRITISH ADVANCE IN THE WEST. TAKEN BY PERMISSION OF THE C.-IN-C. OF THE B.E.F.

Supplied by The Sport & General Press Agency, Ltd., 45, Essex Street, Strand, London.

CAPTURED GERMAN TRENCH.
Wire not destroyed.

Crown copyright reserved
F 17864

A postcard depicting the German barbed-wire defences at Loos in 1915.

A British wiring party in 1916, one of the *Daily Mail* 'Official War Postcard' series.

135 Crown Copyright reserved **A WIRING PARTY GOING TO THE TRENCHES** " Daily Mail "
Official Photograph

Well my dear I was out last night working putting barb wire down until 12 midnight, so you see I have not got much rest. We are on the go night and day out here. I wish it would soon come to an end. I hope your Jack has never to come out here, he will know it if he does, the same as we know.[19]

On average, men spent a period of four to eight days in the front line, but this depended very much on circumstance, with some battalions spending longer in hard-pressed areas. Sergeant Blencowe, of the 1st Public Schools Battalion, the 18th (Service) Battalion of the Royal Fusiliers (33rd Division), recorded a typical spell in the trenches in January 1916:

We are just out again and with any luck shall not go in again for about a month. We have done a month in and out of the trenches, this last time we were in for 9 days – 4 days in support and 5 days in the firing line. I wish I could tell you where it was but I shall only get the letter torn up by Old Man Censor! Anyway it was a very well-known place and a very hot corner and I am glad to say I got through this time without having any more casualties in the platoon.[20]

Private Humphrey Mason, of the 6th (Service) Battalion Oxfordshire and Buckinghamshire Light Infantry, also clandestinely recorded his trench duties while serving in the 20th (Light) Division at

Ypres. In 1915–16 his tours of the trenches lasted between four and eleven days in the salient, and this was typical for many. There would be random attacks, trench raids and flash bombardments to survive while he was in the Ypres Salient, as his brief diary entries so often record:

Tuesday 11 April, 1916. Went into trenches again to relieve 7th D.C.L.I. [61 Brigade, 20th (Light) Division] German attacked 2 or 3 times during the relief and before and bombarded the dumps and roads and canal very heavily.[21]

While some men were in the front fire trenches, others would occupy the support lines behind, ready to provide reinforcement when hard pressed in an attack or raid. There was to be a rhythm to trench warfare, with typically five days in the front line, five in reserve and then five at the front again and five days in reserve. Relief, when it came, saw the battalion removed from the front-line trenches and taken to the rear areas.

For both sides, there was a daily trench routine that usually commenced with 'stand to' ('stand to arms') at one hour before dawn, when all troops in the front line would stand upon the fire step armed and ready to confront an attacker – the theory being that most attacks would take place at dawn. Following 'stand to', most men were stood down with a tot of rum issued to each man, leaving sentries on duty, one per platoon, to man the fixed box periscopes. Breakfast followed, with the meal comprising rations that had been brought up at night and were meant to last a forty-eight-hour period. Tea, bacon, bread – these were the staples of trench food, but often it could be simply bully beef and biscuits.

Private Ernest Parker of the 10th Durham Light Infantry found his journey as one of a ration party moving up to the firing line in 1915 a tense experience:

All the Regular occupants seemed so desperately stealthy and noiseless. Alertness was written on every face, yet in spite of this awareness of the imminence of danger, when we visited the front line by day dixies of tea were boiling in every fire bay.[22]

During the day, most men not on 'sentry go' were detailed for fatigues (work duties) to repair

KEEPING A SHARP LOOK-OUT
Crown Copyright reserved　　140　　"Daily Mail" Official Photograph

Daily Mail Official War Postcard illustrating a sentry at a sandbagged loophole, in 1916. In reality, this would be dangerous in daylight, as such apertures would be targeted by snipers.

trenches and engage in similar activities, only broken for a rudimentary lunch – drawing upon the rations brought up to the front line – and an evening meal at around 6 p.m. No soldiers in their right minds would place themselves at risk moving around the front line in daytime; they had to be vigilant at all times. Bombardments and *Minenwerfer* mortar attacks were common, especially where there was out of the ordinary activity; one of the many challenges to the unwary in the front line.

Night routine would commence with another 'stand to' before dusk. Norman Roberts of the 10th Duke's found it challenging to describe the nature of the trenches at night in a letter home:

> It is awfully cold and dismal at nights. I would refer you to Rudyard Kipling for a description of the dawn and the close of the day, when soldiers stand to arms, to give you a truer idea of something no-one but a good poet can describe.[23]

An exhausted British soldier asleep on a fire step at Thiepval.

In Memory of
Field Marshal the Rt. Hon.
H. H. Lord Kitchener of Khartoum,
K.G., K.P., G.C.B., O.M., G.C.S.I., G.C.M.G., G.C.I.E.,
Born June 24th, 1850, Died June 5th, 1916,
Who was drowned off the Coast of Scotland, by the sinking of H.M.S. "Hampshire,"
On MONDAY, June 5th, 1916.

Now the labourer's task is o'er,	Lands the voyager at last.
Now the battle day is past ;	FATHER, in Thy gracious keeping,
Now upon the farther shore	Leave me now Thy servant sleeping.
	HYMNS A. & M.

A memorial card to Lord Kitchener, lost at sea on 5 June 1916.

Opposite: Suvla Bay, Gallipoli – where the New Army men came ashore in August 1915.

At night the trenches were a hive of activity, and sentries had to maintain a high level of alertness, even though their lack of sleep during the day would tempt them to nap – a military crime of a most serious nature. The cloying darkness magnified the noises that emanated from no-man's-land. As such, no-man's-land was regularly lit up brilliantly by Very lights, flares and star shells. With most of the activity in the front line boiling down to combating the fatigue and enduring, the men of the New Army would peer into the gloom.

With the New Army deployed in France, and about to be deployed elsewhere, Lord Kitchener was set to behold the coming of age of his grand plan. But it was not to be. Lord Kitchener was lost at sea when his ship, HMS *Hampshire*, bound for Russia on a diplomatic mission, hit a mine on 5 June 1915. And cruelly, there was a strange coincidence that 'the last of the 70 Divisions was on the way to France when their creator embarked on his fatal voyage'.[24] He would not be witness to the first day on the Somme.

GALLIPOLI AND EGYPT

We had never heard of Suvla Bay – we didn't even know what part of the Peninsula we had reached. The mystery of the adventure made it all the more exciting. It was to be 'a new landing by the Xth Division' – that was all we knew.[25]

Not all of Kitchener's men were destined to serve in the mud and trenches of the Western Front. Others would serve in Gallipoli, or in Egypt. The first landings in Gallipoli had been carried out with Regulars of the 29th Division and the untried Australian and New Zealand Army Corps (ANZAC) on 25 April 1915. The landings had been intended to remove the threat of the coastal defences and provide the opportunity for the Allied navies to pass through the Dardanelles and threaten Constantinople.

The landings had largely been checked, and the Allies, including the French, were constrained to two small sectors of the peninsula, forced to fight frontal assaults against challenging odds. By July 1915, the campaign had run aground. Lord Kitchener, originally reluctant to commit troops to the enterprise, made the decision to reinforce the beleaguered commander, General Sir Ian Hamilton.

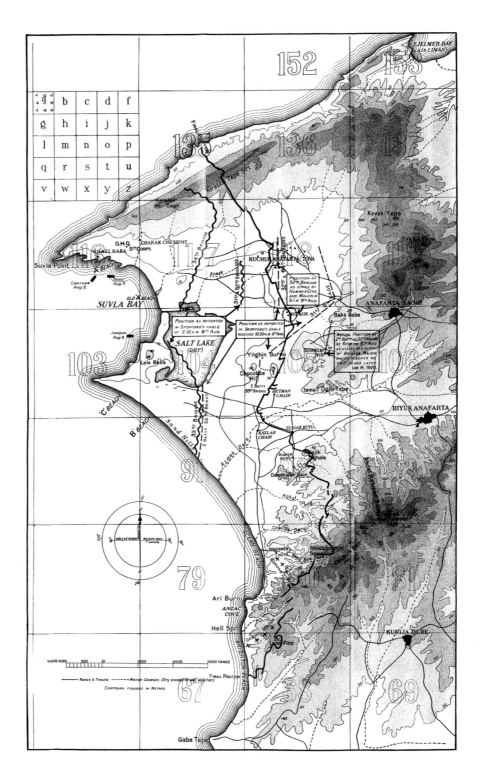

Two New Army K1 divisions, the 10th (Irish) and the 11th (Northern) of General Stopford's 9th Corps would be deployed in new landings at Suvla Bay, and a third, the 13th (Western), would be sent to relieve the 29th at Helles and support the operations elsewhere.

The landings at Suvla were made on 6 August 1915. Stopford's orders were simply to capture the bay in order to make it safe as a British base of operations. Lacking detailed orders to the contrary, and lacking initiative and drive, Stopford felt he had achieved his objectives when his troops came ashore successfully. First to land at Suvla, on the evening of 6 August, was the 11th Division. Here, the first of Kitchener's New Army to see action, the 6th (Service) Battalion, Yorkshire Regiment (32nd Brigade), were deployed against a hill known as Lala Baba, eventually carrying it at the high cost of one-third casualties. The commander-in-chief of the Mediterranean Expeditionary Force, General Sir Ian Hamilton, recorded his impressions in his official Despatches:

The units of the 10th and 11th Divisions had shown their mettle when thy leaped into the water to get more quickly to close quarters,

Lala Baba, Suvla Bay – a hill contested by men of the New Armies in August 1915.

or when they stormed Lala Baba in the darkness. They had shown their resolution later when they tackled the Chocolate Hills and drove the enemy from Hill 10 right back out of rifle range from the beaches. Then had come hesitation.[26]

Other battalions, the 9th Lancashire Fusiliers and the 11th Manchesters (34th Brigade) were ordered to capture all similar hills on the open Suvla Plain – Hill 10, and Chocolate and Green Hills – while the Manchesters found their way up onto the Kiretch Tepe Ridge along the Aegean coast. Two of the 10th (Irish) Division brigades came ashore in order to assist in these assaults – but no real effort was made to push on to the heights. Forced by Ian Hamilton, Stopford finally made the decision to try and dislodge the now growing Ottoman threat from the larger hills dominating the Suvla Plain. But it was too late; the New Army men would not leave the plain.

While the landings were taking place, a mixed force of New Zealanders and Gurkhas were attempting to break out of the Anzac perimeter and outflank the Ottoman troops holding the heights. The ground was terribly broken and confusing, but by dawn on 7 August some had reached a spur that led right up to the heights. Dug in as best they could, the New Zealanders were reinforced by two newly arrived battalions of the 13th (Western) Division, the 7th Gloucestershire, and the 8th Welsh – both K1 battalions. At 3 a.m., the peak of Chunuk Bair was taken by the New Zealanders and the Gloucesters, men who faced a determined counter-attack in the small hours. By the following evening, the New Zealanders and New Army men held on grimly, their casualties mounting.

Hill 10 Cemetery, Suvla Bay. Here lie many men of the 10th (Irish) and 11th (Northern) divisions.

The beach at Suvla Bay, with the Anzac sector visible as the high ground in the distance.

With Chunuk Bair holding, a mixed force of four battalions from the 13th (Western) Division, and two battalions from the 29th Brigade of the 10th (Irish) Division assaulted another feature known as Hill Q. They met stiff opposition. And after an overwhelming Ottoman counter-attack on 10 August, the exhausted New Zealanders had been relieved by the 6th Loyal North Lancashires, K1 men who had arrived at 10 p.m. But the force of an Ottoman attack was to prove too much for the

newly arrived British battalions, breaking them and sweeping them down the slope into the confusion of gullies below. The heights so fleetingly held by the Allies were now firmly back in Ottoman hands.

The performance of these New Army men at Gallipoli has been criticised by some, particularly by the Australian correspondent (and later official historian) Charles Bean. Writing in 1924, Bean simply considered them to be inadequate for the job; he was, in a way, attacking them instead of the inadequacies of the command:

> The men had doubtless the high qualities of their race, among them orderliness, decency and modesty; they could follow a good leader anywhere as bravely as any troops ... [but] a large proportion of the new force had come straight from the highly organised life in or around overcrowded cities, and as a result they lacked the resourcefulness required for any activity in open country. Further, though many reports had been heard concerning the excellent physique of the New Army, the standard in that respect was very uneven.[27]

Bean's view was to inform a generation of Australians; yet he perhaps took his lead from a letter sent by the Australian journalist Keith Murdoch who wrote to the British prime minister before the campaign was over. It contained equally challenging assertions about the New Army:

> The physique of those at Suvla is not to be compared with that of the Australians. Nor is their intelligence. I fear also that the British physique is very much below that of the Turks. Indeed it is obviously so. Our men have

Private Robert Wheatley of the 6th (Service) Battalion, Yorkshire Regiment, 11th (Northern) Division, who was killed at Suvla Bay. He has no known grave.

found it impossible to form a high opinion of the British K. men ... They are merely a lot of childlike youths, without strength to endure or brains to improve their conditions.[28]

It was challenging stuff, and General Sir Ian Hamilton was not willing to accept this view: 'I know that Mr Murdoch will find not one member of the Suvla Bay force who will endorse his cruel travesty of the soldiers who compose it.' He continued, directing his question to the War Office, and Kitchener himself, 'Again, I ask, is this accepted as a fair description by those who send me the troops?'[29] Certainly it would be New Army men who would face their determined enemies at Loos in September 1915, or on the Somme on 1 July 1916. Neither Murdoch nor Bean's judgement was shared widely in Britain – though it lingers today in Australia, unfair today as it was then.

The 10th, 11th and 13th Divisions were not the only New Army men to make it to the Middle East, however. There were those who faced a move to Egypt, part of a desire to maintain a substantive force to ward off the threats of the Ottoman Empire, who hoped to wrest control of the Suez Canal from the British. That the threat to the canal was a real one was identified by the fact that it had already been under attack in early 1915. It had been a failure, but this demonstration left the British nervous of further attempts to take the canal, and nuisance raids continued to test the British defences throughout 1915.

Kitchener was resolved to supporting the Egyptian commander, Lieutenant General Sir John Maxwell, and had planned to send two new army divisions – the 14th (Light) Division and the 31st Division, together with the Territorial 46th

The Leeds Pals in Egypt. Private Firth in a trench, 1915.

(North Midland) Division.[30] However, the failure of the Gallipoli Campaign meant the transfer of divisions from the peninsula, the new ones being no longer needed. Though the 31st Division made it to Egypt with its complement of Pals battalions – the Hull Pals, the Accrington Pals, the Sheffield City Battalion, both battalions of Barnsley Pals, both Bradford Pals battalions and the Leeds Pals[31] – the move of the other two divisions was cancelled. The 31st would spend just the briefest of time there, serving in the northern sector of the Suez Canal defences before being recalled to France. They landed at Marseilles in February 1916 – in time to serve on the Somme.

LOOS

Our division was all part of the new army [Kitchener's Second Army] and we took it as an honour that we should be given the most important part of the position to attack, and I think we proved that the new army is fit to rank with the best of British – and better still – Scottish, infantry.[32]

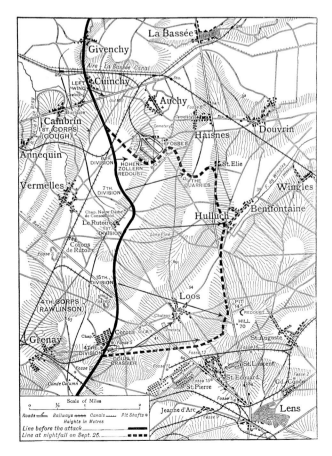

The Loos battlefield.

The Battle of Loos, fought from 25 September 1915, was the first time that the New Army had been committed to battle on the Western Front, and the first major test of the conditions that other New Army divisions would face a year later, when the Pals battalions would infamously be pressed into action on 1 July 1916.

The British commander-in-chief, Field Marshal Sir John French, was well aware that the British Expeditionary Force was not ready for an all-out British assault on the Germans. There were too few men, and even fewer munitions. If he could stand on the defensive long enough, then he would be in a position to fully deploy the trained Kitchener's Army divisions, supported by the output from newly energised and reorganised munitions factories.

But with General Joffre, commander of the armies in Northern France, pushing for British involvement to support French plans to relieve pressure on Paris through attacks in Artois and Champagne, there was little he could do. With Russia under severe pressure, Kitchener directed French to relent. The stage was set for the first major British offensive on the Western Front – and the first use of Kitchener divisions as a major part of it.

The area from the La Bassée Canal south to Lens in French Flanders was selected as the battlefield for the British in support of the French to the south, close to Vimy Ridge. General Sir Douglas Haig, commander of the British First Army, was ordered to make an assessment of the ground – he found it to be unfavourable to assault without adequate artillery preparation. With the British still suffering from the scandal of a 'shells shortage' that broke in the news in May 1915 (and which tarnished the reputations of Kitchener and the War Office, who at this point had control over production), it was unlikely

The Loos battlefield; bombardment of the Hohenzollern Redoubt in 1915.

that the assault would gain much traction. However, with the Germans using gas at Ypres in April for the first time, there was the chance that gas could be used by the British to make good the deficiency.

General Haig, commanding the attack, took the chance. The assault would push off on 25 September 1915, and gas would be used, as described by the man in charge of the new weapon, C.H. Foulkes:

Zero hour arrived at last at 5.50 am, and with a redoubled artillery bombardment the gas and smoke were released all along the front. The first aeroplane report that came in a few minutes later was to the effect that the gas cloud was rolling steadily over towards the German lines.[33]

The effects were variable: in some parts of the line it flowed, in others, it remained static and caused casualties amongst the British troops, who pulled off their clammy, claustrophobic and all-enveloping gas hoods as they pushed forward. The assaulting troops included two New Army divisions, both of them Scottish – the 9th and the 15th – formations that had arrived in France in May and June, together with three Regular divisions and one Territorial division.

The 15th (Scottish) Division (K2) faced Loos itself, together with the Territorial 47th (London) Division. With the gas moving in this sector, both made headway and the town was captured. The Scots pushed on to the feature behind, known as Hill 70. Not surprisingly it was all put down to dash and verve by the Scottish press:

Piper Laidlaw, who was awarded the Victoria Cross, piping the 7th (Service) Battalion King's Own Scottish Borderers from the trenches at Loos.

The first glorious charge made by our men from Vermelles trenches in the grey light of Saturday morning, which carried them right through to the village of Loos and to the summit of Hill 70 beyond it, will rank as one of the most glorious exploits of the British Army. New Army battalions played an important part in the attack. Men who had had no experience of real fighting sprang forward to the sound of officers' whistles, with a dash and gallantry that nothing could stop.[34]

Piper Laidlaw, a 40-year-old piper with the 7th (Service) Battalion King's Own Scottish Borderers, had also played his part. With his com-

rades suffering from the release of the gas, Laidlaw leaped onto the parapet and piped his comrades into action in the face of German fire. He was awarded the Victoria Cross.

Though the town was carried, the inexperience of the British divisions showed through. The Scots stalled on Hill 70, swinging to the south rather than pushing eastwards to carry the hill and move beyond it. This feature would be at the apex of the advance when the battle was finally finished, a month later.

North of Loos was one of the strongest parts of the line, a subterranean fortification known as the Hohenzollern Redoubt, described by John Hay Beith ('Ian Hay') in *The First Hundred Thousand*:

'Tower Bridge' – the distinctive mining gear faced by the men of the 15th (Scottish) Division and the Territorial 47th (London) Division at Loos.

The Hohenzollern Redoubt ... is a most inconspicuous object, but a very important factor in the present situation. It has been thrust forward from the Bosche lines to within a hundred yards of our own – a great promontory, a maze of trenches, machine gun emplacements, and barbed wire, all flush with or under the ground, and terribly difficult to cripple with shell fire.[35]

The fighting here was terrible. Again, the gas had helped in this sector, but attacking the works required bombing fights, grit and determination. The outer works would fall, but at great cost. Once more this was put down to the dynamism of the Scots, and again this involved Kitchener's Army, men of the 9th (Scottish) Division (K1). Private Stewart of the Cameron Highlanders wrote to the *Daily Record*, describing the action:

The Hohenzollern Redoubt was won by kilted regiments. This redoubt was supposed to be impregnable, but we captured it after a fierce battle. In its trenches there were regular 'room and kitchen' dugouts away under the ground, large iron girders holding up the roofs, and no wonder it was so well fortified. The Scottish regiments are fairly looked up to by the English crowd.[36]

Despite these reports, some German accounts of the Scots emphasised their 'amateur' status as Kitchener's Army men; such as that of Hauptmann Willy Lange:

All-in-all the Kitchener-Army gave a bit of a dilettante impression of itself. The initial attack with gas was planned to the last detail and as

such was quite successful. Then in the next attack unguided, unsure and in thick columns the British surged past Loos and naturally that caused them a lot of casualties. The attack that came from Loos itself did not fare much better and they seemed to be beaten before they had even started. The regiments which fought us were the same we had been facing during August in the previous year: Black Watch, Gordon Highlanders, Camerons, Royal Scots, Seaforths etc. The same and yet not the same.[37]

Nevertheless, though the Kitchener men of the

Dud Corner British cemetery at Loos, with the built-up mounds of the Double Crassier in the distance.

183

Right: Field Marshal Sir John French, commander-in-chief of the British Expeditionary Force (BEF), who would lose his position in the aftermath of Loos.

Far right: General Sir Douglas Haig, commander of the First Army at Loos, and commander-in-chief of the BEF in the battle's aftermath.

9th (K1) and the 15th (K2) Divisions had carried out their task efficiently enough, it would be the lot of two K3 divisions, the 21st and 24th (XI Corps), to be scapegoated. They were Reserves, but held too far back in reserve by Field Marshal French. On the move almost continuously since their arrival in France in early September, the movement of these divisions into the battlefront was fraught with confusion, hold-ups and congestion. Thrust into the line on 26 September, they were tired, hungry and inexperienced, yet were ordered to take on the most difficult part of the line, that between Hulluch and Hill 70.

The novice divisions were expected to assault the German second line, bristling with strongpoints, enfiladed by advanced machine-gun fire. With little in the way of artillery preparation, sleep or rations, the assault failed, the divisions broken.[38] The XI Corps commander, Major General Haking, blamed the poor march discipline of his troops, but the reality of their trials in battle would surely have challenged even the most experienced soldiers. It certainly challenged Sir John French's command. General Sir Douglas Haig would replace him as commander-in-chief of the British Expeditionary Force in the aftermath of the battle.

THE SOMME

How like drill it was the way that those human waves moved forward! But they were not waves for long ... with every man simply keeping on toward the goal till he arrived or fell ... Would England have wanted the New Army to act otherwise?[39]

It was the Battle of the Somme in 1916, the first major British offensive on the Western Front since Loos in September 1915, which would prove to be the ultimate test of Kitchener's Army in battle, and would arguably become the most hotly debated battle of the whole war. In the wake of Loos, General Sir Douglas Haig had replaced Sir John French as commander-in-chief of the British Expeditionary Force. Kitchener wrote to Haig in December 1915:

The defeat of the enemy by the combined Allied Armies must always be regarded as the primary object for which the British troops were originally sent to France, and to achieve that end the closest co-operation of French

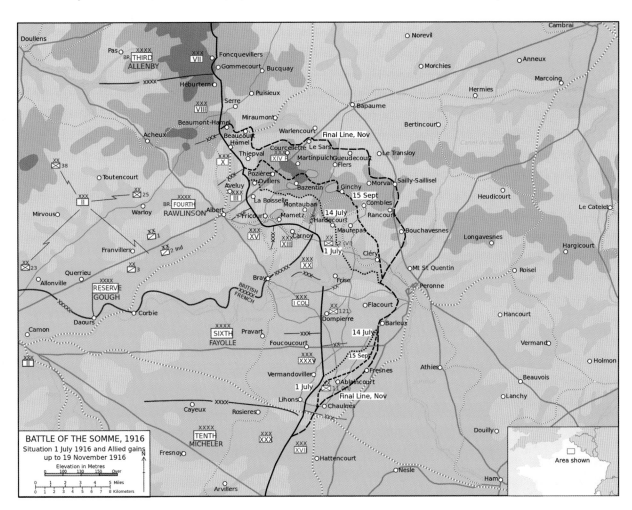

BATTLE OF THE SOMME, 1916
Situation 1 July 1916 and Allied gains up to 19 November 1916

The Somme battlefield, showing the Allied positions to the end of the battle in 1916.

and British as a united Army must be the governing policy.[40]

This memorandum emphasised the plan that had been drawn up at the Second Allied Military Conference held at Chantilly on 6 December, 'the Allied armies ought to resume the general offensive on the Franco-British, Italian and Russian fronts as soon as they were in a state to do so'.[41]

For Haig, the main area for British offensive action was always going to be Flanders. If nothing else, this would guard the flanks of the BEF and provide a chance to remove the threat to Britain of U-boat bases on the Channel coast. Joffre, the commander of the northern French armies, agreed that a British offensive could be opened in the summer, so long as there was a joint Franco-British attack astride the River Somme in the spring, thereby wearing down the German resources and their ability to withstand the main summer assault.

For the British, the risk of two offensives was too great. Instead, a single battle was planned for early July, to take place on the Somme. But if the Allies hoped for an action that would wear down their enemies, they had not expected that the German commander, Eric von Falkenhayn, was preparing to do just that at Verdun – a major French fortress town in Lorraine that jutted out belligerently towards the German border. Here, it is argued, the German commander hoped to drain the lifeblood from the French, who could be expected to defend the town with all its resources.

The Battle of Verdun opened on 21 February 1916 and the dynamics of the Battle of the Somme changed. Now it would become a predominantly British battle, supported by the French and fought to relieve pressure on the beleaguered city. As Victor

Germains put it, 'As the deep-toned baying of the German guns arose around Verdun it was clear to all that the war had reached another great crisis and that the hour of trial for the New Armies was at hand.'[42]

General Haig was now thrust into the limelight. His objectives for the battle were finalised on 16 June 1916:

The Third and Fourth Armies will undertake offensive operations on the front Maricourt–Gommecourt, in conjunction with the French Sixth Army astride the Somme with the object of relieving the pressure on the French at Verdun and inflicting loss on the enemy.[43]

The battle would be one of attrition, with the hope that a breakthrough was possible. While the Third Army would make a diversionary attack on the German Salient at Gommecourt, it would be Rawlinson's Fourth Army that would bear the brunt of the battle on its opening day. And a considerable component of this was the New Army divisions – most of them composed of locally raised Pals battalions.

The landscape of the Somme is a gently rolling chalk downland. With soft spurs and largely dry valleys – a function of the porous chalk below draining away any standing water – the topography is variable. For the most part, the Germans had occupied a ridge of higher ground that ran from the River Somme in the south-east to the village of Gommecourt in the north-west. Crossing the line was the arrow-straight Roman road that connected Albert (in British hands) to Bapaume, in German hands. North-west of the road, also crossing the line, was the River Ancre which was a low channel between the higher ground at Serre and Beaumont

Hamel, and south to Thiepval and beyond to La Boisselle, Fricourt and Mametz.

The Germans had skilfully fortified villages in their front line and had made the woods that connected them into redoubts. Poet Laureate John Masefield described the scene in his book, *The Old Front Line*, in 1917:

> The enemy had the lookout posts, with fine views over France, and the sense of domination. Our men were down below with no view of anything but of stronghold after stronghold, just up above, being made stronger daily. And if the enemy had strength of position he also had strength of equipment, of men, of guns, and explosives of all kinds.[44]

The first day of the Battle of the Somme is perhaps the most discussed of all days of the war. It figures heavily in British accounts and has become mythologised.[45] To those historians of the conflict the enduring fascination with its grim statistics – of the total casualties in even the first hour – have meant that some have considered that this day exercises a 'tyrannical hold' over the description of the British experience of the war.[46]

Nevertheless, the first day – and that very first hour – was to have a dramatic effect, pulverising the locally raised battalions that it had taken so long to assemble. In this way, the first day can be identified as the most significant 'punctuation mark' in the story of Kitchener's Army.

A BRITISH HEAVY GUN IN ACTION.

Heavy artillery take part in the opening bombardment of the German lines at the Somme. One of the *Daily Mail* 'Official War Postcard' series.

The bombardment of the German lines that opened on 24 June 1916 and lasted until 'zero hour' on 1 July 1916 became known as *Trommelfeuer* (drumfire). Intended to destroy enemy batteries, trenches, dugouts and barbed wire, the bombardment involved ceaseless shelling from almost 1,500 guns and howitzers of all types, firing some 1.7 million rounds. But even this level of fire was inadequate for a front of 18 miles. The men who went 'over the top' at 7.30 a.m. (zero hour) on 1 July 1916 climbed out of their trenches over the sandbag parapet to face the German survivors, and were ready to meet them.

With zero hour, and the bombardment reaching its height, Kitchener's men could do no more than hope that the enemy had been stunned into submission and forced to keep their heads down, rather than pouring fire into the oncoming ranks of soldiers. Sadly, that was not always the case. The chalk bedrock had proven perfect for the construction of deep dugouts, and with the Germans creating a defensive line that was meant to hold the Allies, it would take more than a simple bombardment by field guns to destroy it. John Masefield described the scene: 'The men of the first wave climbed up the parapets, in tumult, darkness and the presence of death, and having done with all pleasant things, advanced across the no-man's-land to begin the Battle of the Somme.'[47]

Stumbling forward over no-man's-land, soldiers were pushed into a maelstrom of machine-gun fire, counter-bombardment and the broken landscape of the modern battlefield. Overhead was the bombardment that was intended to protect the attackers, a moving curtain of shellfire that would

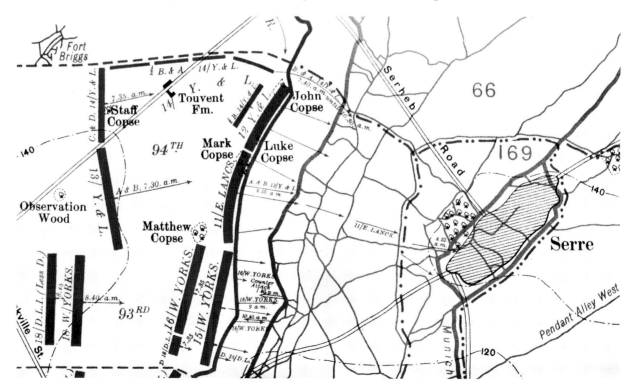

The attack of the 31st Division (94th and 93rd brigades) at Serre, 1 July 1916.

attempt to clear the trenches in front of the living wave of men. The Third Army diversionary attack by London and Midland Territorials on Gommecourt stalled; the German lines were too strong.

The New Army divisions were spread out along the line of assault and either side of them there were Regulars or Territorials. Between the 31st Division at Serre and the 36th and 32nd at Thiepval there were the Regular 4th and 29th divisions. The Regulars of the 8th Division facing Ovilliers separated the 32nd and 34th New Army divisions, and between the 21st and the 18th (Eastern) there was the 7th. The idea was a general advance on a broad front in this early stage of what became the first phase of the Battle of the Somme. The New Army divisions, a truly citizen army, were facing the challenge of the largest offensive then fought by the British.

The 31st Division was quintessentially a Pals division and faced the fortified village of Serre. In action on 1 July was the 93rd Brigade, composed of Leeds and Bradford Pals together with the 18th Durhams, and the 94th, made up of Barnsley Pals, Accrington Pals and the Sheffield City Battalion. The attack of the 31st was to form a defensive flank for the whole operation.

The bombardment had done little to subdue the defenders of Serre and as the Pals rushed forward, so the German defenders of the front line – the barrage now passing them by as it registered the support trenches – increased the intensity of their return fire.[48] They set up machine guns forward of their own line. The *Official History* recounts the story of this attack:

Only a few isolated parties of the 31st Division were able to reach the German front trench, where they were in the end either killed or taken prisoner. The extended lines started in excellent order, but gradually melted away. The magnificent gallantry, discipline and determination displayed by all ranks of this North Country division were of no avail against the concentrated fire-effect of the enemy's unshaken infantry and artillery.[49]

Farther to the south, the 36th (Ulster) and 32nd divisions faced the formidable fortifications at Thiepval, the plateau standing out 'like a great buttress' overlooking the Ancre.[50] Thiepval itself was a village with a ruined church and grand house. These had cellars that had been fortified and, once again, the German machine-gunners had escaped the attention of the opening bombardment.

There were strongpoints built into the line, similar in many respects to the Hohenzollern Redoubt near Loos. To the south and in the front line was

The front-line trench occupied by the Accrington Pals facing Serre, now preserved as part of the Sheffield Memorial Park.

Private Stott, an Accrington Pal, who fell in front of Serre on 1 July 1916. He lies in Railway Hollow Cemetery.

Railway Hollow Cemetery, Hebuterne. This cemetery has many graves of soldiers from 31st Division who faced Serre on 1 July 1916.

the Leipzig Redoubt, behind it, the *Wundt-werk* or 'wonderwork'. To the north, and in the support lines, was the Schwaben Redoubt, and there were others, all scientifically sited in order to resist any attempt at an assault.

The 32nd stood to take the line between the Leipzig Salient and Thiepval; the 36th to take the northern part of the line between the village of Thiepval and the Ancre itself. The 32nd Division had originally been the home of the three Birmingham city battalions, serving with Bristol's Own in the 95th Brigade, but in December 1915 they had been exchanged for Regular battalions.

The assault on 1 July involved the Salford Pals and Newcastle Commercials of the 96th Brigade, together with the Lonsdale and City of Glasgow battalions of the 97th. It was indeed the 17th Highland Light Infantry – the 3rd Glasgow Battalion – that proved to be the most effective. The Glasgow Commercials had crept out into no-man's-land in advance of zero hour. Waiting for the enemy wire to be cut by the bombardment, they only had 30–40 yards to cross and managed it in a rush, capturing the Germans in their deep dugouts. The Glaswegians nevertheless had to hold on like grim death. The Salford and Newcastle lads were to suffer the fate of so many other of the Pals battalions that day.

With the Leipzig Redoubt taken by Kitchener's Army, it was the Ulstermen who faced up to the

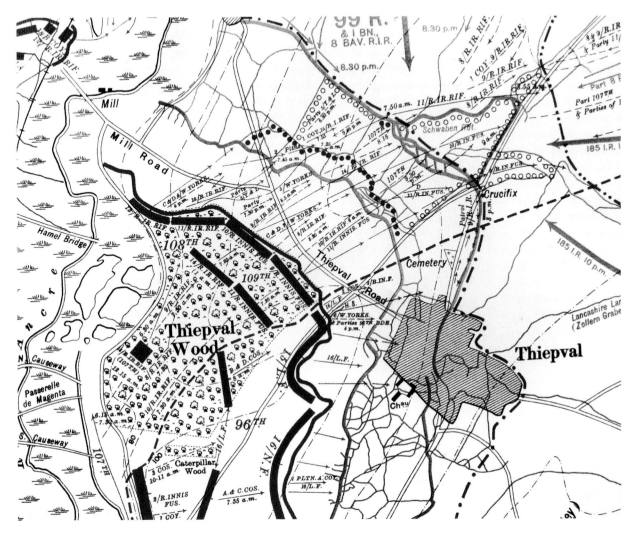

The 36th (Ulster) Division (108th and 109th Brigades) and the 32nd Division (96th Brigade) faced the formidable fortress at Thiepval on 1 July 1916.

German front line in advance of the Schwaben Redoubt. James Edmonds, the official historian, described their advance:

> At 7.30 am buglers in the front trench sounded the 'advance', and the assaulting lines rose and moved forward at a steady pace with the precision of a parade movement ... The scene with the mist clearing off and the morning sun glistening on the long rows of bayonets was brilliant and striking.[51]

The German wire had been cut effectively by the bombardment and the Ulstermen were upon the defenders before they could mount their machine guns. The former men of the Ulster Volunteer Force got as far as the Schwaben Redoubt, but with the 32nd Division held on their right flank they could move no further. Nevertheless, it was a startling success – though ultimately unsustainable. The 36th Division men would be sealed off from reinforcement by artillery fire and would be attacked in detail. They were forced to withdraw.

The Ulster Tower. A monument to the endeavours of the Ulstermen in attacking the Schwaben Redoubt on 1 July 1916.

East of Albert, along the road to Bapaume, the 34th and 21st Divisions faced the villages of La Boisselle and Contalmaison. The 34th was composed predominantly of the Tyneside Scottish and Tyneside Irish Brigades, but also featured two Edinburgh battalions, including McCrae's, serving with the Grimsby Chums (10th Lincolnshire Regiment) and the Cambridge Battalion of the Suffolk Regiment (11th Suffolks).

The 34th attacked at La Boisselle, the assault marked by the explosion of the huge mine that created the Lochnagar Crater – still a relic of the battle today – and another to the north, known as Y-Sap. The German lines at La Boisselle village – the 'glory hole' – were close to the British front but

either side of it, in the valleys christened 'Sausage' and 'Mash', where no-man's-land was at its widest. The Grimsby and Cambridge men got as far as the crater, but no further, and many would be trapped there until night fell.

The Royal Scots to the south were suffering from intense machine-gun fire that caused them some confusion. And then there was the Tyneside Scottish Brigade, which marched into a maelstrom of fire as it attempted to cross no-man's-land – casualties were exceedingly heavy. Their brigade commander described the scene:

> The attack had been pressed on with the most extraordinary heroism, but without avail. Officers and men had been literally mown down, but in rapidly diminishing numbers they had resolutely pushed on to meet their deaths close to the enemy's wire. No-Man's-Land was reported to be heaped with dead.[52]

The Tyneside Irish, attempting to follow them up, were equally decimated. The 34th Division took the heaviest casualties of all that day. To the south of La Boisselle the 21st Division, the K3 men who had taken such a mauling at Loos, attacked to the north of Fricourt. With heavy losses, they were able at least to put the memories of Loos behind them, capturing the front-line trenches in their sector.

On the first day of battle the southern sector, adjacent to the French who were astride the River Somme itself, were the 18th (Eastern) and 30th divisions, facing Montauban. The 18th Division, a K2 division, achieved almost the greatest success of the day, realising its objectives to the left of the village. The 18th was by all accounts a standard Kitchener Army division, although in Peter Simkins'

The Lochnagar Crater at
La Boisselle, and the open
expanse of no-man's-land
crossed by the Tynesiders on
1 July 1916.

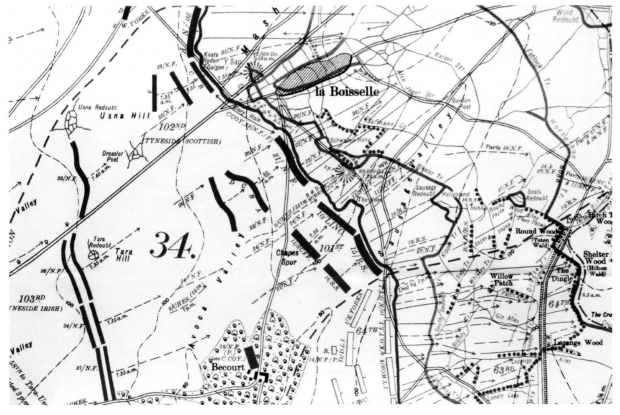

The attack of the Tyneside
brigades, components of the
34th Division, at La Boisselle.

The Tyneside Irish advance
into no-man's-land on
1 July 1916.

Right: The Tyneside Scottish
cap badge on the Tyneside
memorial seat at La Boisselle.

Far right: The Tyneside Irish
shoulder title insignia on the
memorial seat at La Boisselle.

view it had the considerable benefit of being led by Major General Ivor Maxse:

Maxse's contribution to these successes was considerable. His tactics on 1st July, when he deployed his assaulting troops in No Man's Land before Zero Hour, so that they won the race to the parapet on their first objective, proved invaluable.[53]

To the south, the 30th Division, comprising the original Pals from Liverpool and Manchester and led by Lord Derby's brother, F.C. Stanley, in the 89th Brigade, and the Manchesters in the 90th, had similar success, capturing the village of Montauban outright and attacking the works known as the Briqueterie to its right. Once again, as Stanley himself noted, the 'race to the parapet' had been won:

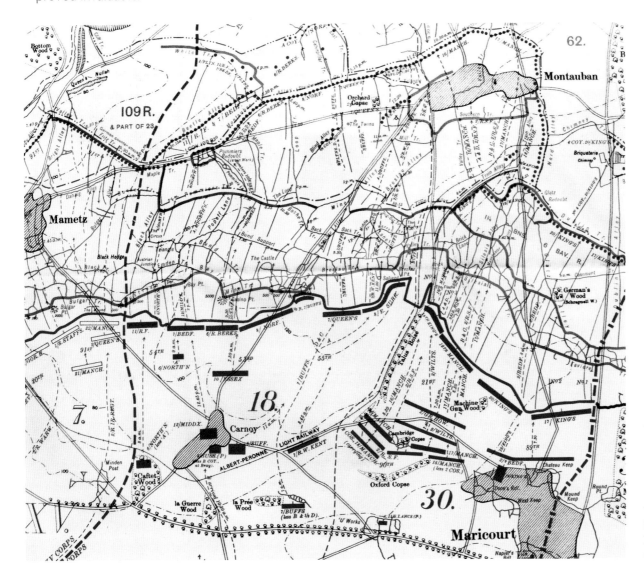

The frontage attacked by the 18th (Eastern) and 30th divisions on the first day of the Somme.

PUNCH, OR THE LONDON CHARIVARI.—JULY 12, 1916.

WELL DONE, THE NEW ARMY!

Punch recognises the efforts of Kitchener's Army on the Somme, 12 July 1916.

When the 90th Brigade had taken the village of Montauban, we were then told to go and take the Briqueterie. It had been pounded with all kinds of guns, and at the right time they lifted and in we went. Everyone who saw it said it was beautifully done.[54]

The first day of the Battle of the Somme saw Kitchener's Army in action en masse. Here the Pals battalions, those locally raised units of comrades, of men encouraged to join to be with their 'own kind', faced the deeply entrenched and fearsomely efficient German Army. The success of certain divisions and failure of others had much to do with adequate artillery preparation, adequate divisional planning and the nature of the topography as it had to do with leadership. The 'race to the parapet' was everything, and the men of the 36th, 32nd, 18th and 30th divisions – all New Army – had proven they could achieve success with the right support.

At Serre, and at La Boisselle, the tragedy of the northern Pals and the Tynesiders was all to do with the stiffness of the opposition and the roll of the dice when it came to artillery preparation and the width of no-man's-land. It had nothing to do with the valour of these men. Lord Kitchener's vision, vouchsafed in the civilian army, was intact. But the losses of the opening day were to rock the nation.

The *Official History* puts the dead of that single day at 19,420, the missing and prisoners of war at 2,737, and wounded at 35,493.[55] It was a staggering butcher's bill. And this was just the first day. The total deaths on the Somme, from all British and Commonwealth divisions, would add up to 108,724.[56]

Other New Army divisions were yet to take their place in the line and the 38th (Welsh) Division would face its task in the attack at Mametz Wood on 7 July. They would prove equal to it and, with the other divisions, would battle out the Somme until its ultimate conclusion in the mud of winter on 18 November 1916. The story of Kitchener's Army does not end with the 151 days of the Somme, but there the youthful army came of age – and it would face the challenges of 1917 head on.

The Thiepval Memorial to the Missing of the Somme, inscribed with the names of 72,253 men who have no known grave.

Monument to the 38th (Welsh) Division at Mametz. The red dragon of Wales matches that of the divisional insignia.

END OF AN EXPERIMENT

As the battle thunder of the Somme died down into the daily rumbling of the Western Front there remained of the men who joined Kitchener's Armies but enough to leaven with their own brave spirit the levies who came to fill their shattered battalions. The Volunteer Armies had played their part.[1]

Gradually voluntary recruitment ground to a halt. The heady days of the recruiting boom in the wake of the retreat from Mons in August 1914 had long since fallen away. By April 1915, conscription was being openly discussed in the House of Commons. Thomas Tickler, MP for Grimsby, put a very direct question to Lloyd George on 20 April 1915:

> Will [he] put into practice the declared intention of the Government of prosecuting the War with all the available forces of the Empire, by introducing conscription, whereby the single eligible men may be called out, and thereby saving the lives of thousands of our soldiers by bringing the War to a speedy and successful termination?[2]

Lloyd George was equally direct in his reply:

> The Government are not of the opinion that there is any ground for thinking that the War would be more successfully prosecuted by means of conscription.[3]

His reply underlined the government's reluctance to enter the arena of 'compulsion', though Lloyd George was himself supportive of the idea.[4] Certainly there was considerable opposition amongst Liberal and Labour MPs, and there was growing membership of groups such as the No-Conscription Fellowship, formed later in the year to support conscientious objectors opposed to compulsory service.

Yet time was running out, and with the falling numbers of recruits and the government labouring under the burden of 'volunteerism' that had hung over British attempts to raise a citizen army, new ideas were required. Lord Kitchener's face once again appeared on a recruiting poster – but this time with the barely veiled threat of his words in a speech to the Guildhall on 9 July 1915: 'Does the call of duty find no response in you until reinforced – let us say superseded – by the call of compulsion?'[5]

With his magnificent record of raising Pals battalions, Lord Derby was an obvious choice as

LORD KITCHENER SAYS:-

'MEN, MATERIALS & MONEY ARE THE IMMEDIATE NECESSITIES. ......

DOES THE CALL OF DUTY FIND NO RESPONSE IN YOU UNTIL REINFORCED — LET US RATHER SAY SUPERSEDED — BY THE CALL OF COMPULSION?'

Lord Kitchener Speaking at Guildhall July 9th 1915

ENLIST TO-DAY.

Using the words of Lord Kitchener, the PRC hints at the introduction of conscription in August 1915.

the new Director of Recruiting, taking the post on 5 October 1915. He was faced with a major challenge. If the country was not going to face compulsory enlistment, there would need to be a significant step up in recruitment numbers.

The first steps to compulsion had already been taken with the National Registration Act of July 1915. The act required every citizen between the ages of 15 and 65 to register their name, place of residence, nature of work and other details, and to receive a National Registration Card. By October 1915 there were 21,627,596 names on the register, of which 5,158,211 were men of military age. Of this

figure, 1,519,432 men were identified as being in reserved occupations vital to the war effort.

National Registration identified that there were at least 3.4 million men who were technically able to join the forces, but by the autumn of 1915 the numbers actually joining were falling at an alarming rate, not sufficient to fulfil the requirement of 35,000 men per week envisaged by Lord Kitchener. Lord Derby drew up a scheme that would force the issue; it would either work, or would signal conscription.

The 'Derby Scheme' entailed the voluntary attestation of all men between 18 and 40, with men of the same age and marital status being grouped together to be called to the Colours in batches. Married men would be last to go. It was a tall order. On his appointment, Lord Derby made an ominous, direct plea to the public:

War Office
Whitehall, SW
October 1915

Sir, At my request, the Parliamentary Recruiting Committee, representing all Political parties

Don't know what the Single Man's grumbling at—— Compulsion's been my lot for years

Men who had attested under the Derby Scheme wore a khaki serge armband bearing a red crown that announced to the world they were willing to serve. Single men would be compelled to go before married men. This Bamforth postcard, part of their 'Witty Armlet' series, pokes fun at 'compulsion'.

working in conjunction with the Joint Labour Recruiting Committee are organising a great recruiting campaign to induce men who can be spared, to come forward voluntarily for service in the Army. If this effort does not succeed, the Country knows that everything possible will have been done to make the voluntary system a success, and will have to decide by what method sufficient recruits can be obtained to maintain our Armies in the field at their required strength ...

May I, as Director-General of Recruiting, beg you to consider your own position? Ask yourself whether, in a country fighting as ours is for its very existence, you are doing all you can for its safety, and whether the reason you have hitherto held valid as one for not enlisting holds good at the present crisis. Lord Kitchener wants every man he can get. Will you not be one of those who respond to your Country's call?[6]

Lord Derby invited all eligible men to attest by 15 December 1915, but over 2 million of the 3.5 million men available for military service failed to attest. If it was simply an experiment, it could be deemed a failure, but with it Lord Derby paved the way to compulsory service. In the face of this pressure, the No-Conscription Fellowship sought to influence opinion through leaflets and lectures – some of which were of interest to the police through the Defence of the Realm Act:

The time has come to appeal to all those who value our traditional British freedom. A determined resistance must be made to the sinister endeavour to impose upon

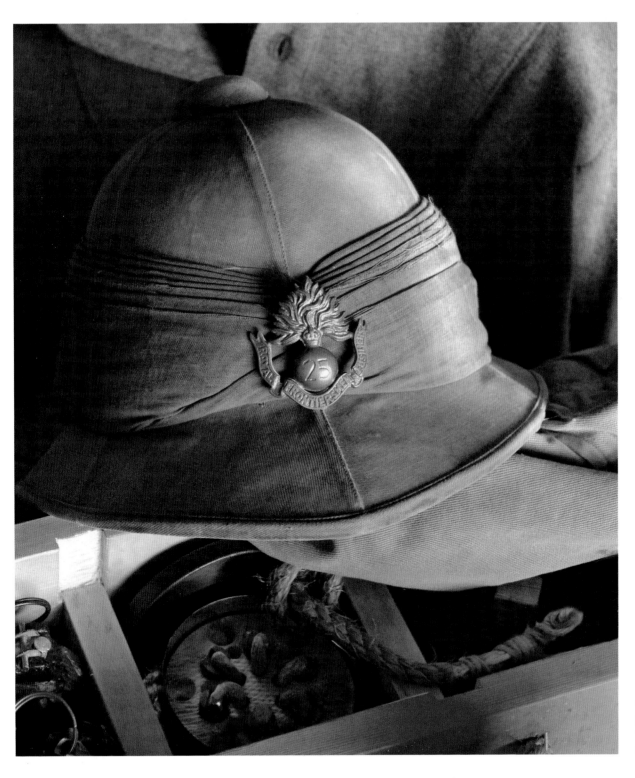

The 25th (Service) Battalion, Royal Fusiliers (Frontiersmen). The Frontiersmen served in East Africa from May 1915.

the people, under some such formula as 'compulsory attestation for single men,' the evils inherent in Conscription.[7]

But such actions were to be of no avail. The first of three Military Service Acts was introduced on 27 January 1916. All fit single men between the ages of 18 and 41 were compelled to join the Colours, married men joining them in the second Military Service Act of May 1916. Unfit men were exempted for the time being, and there would be other exemptions for those men whose work was deemed essential for the war effort, and for those who could demonstrate a 'conscientious objection' to active participation in the war. (There would be

some 16,000 conscientious objectors (COs) registered during the war, with at least a third being sent to prison at least once, their cases having been thrown out by tribunal.)

The long, hard journey predicted by Kitchener in the opening days of his service was becoming even harder as the realities of trench warfare began to bite even deeper. Three further Acts, in April 1917, January 1918 and April 1918, followed and these would find ways of 'combing-out' more men for military service (the last, reducing the recruitment age to 17, while at the same time increasing the upper limit to 55). The Kitchener divisions would be filled with conscripts.

But voluntary recruiting was not quite dead, even with the introduction of conscription. There were always men prepared to seek out adventure. True adventurers were the Legion of Frontiersmen, a paramilitary organisation that had been trained to be ready to take on the role of defenders of the frontier. Raised in 1904 by an ex-member of the Canadian Mounted Police, its mission was 'to assist the state in times of need'. The legion was offered to the War Office in 1914 as a trained body of men who were prepared to act 'behind the lines', creating havoc in occupied Belgium. But this was 1914, not 1940, and not surprisingly the offer was turned down.

Nevertheless, with the slowdown in recruiting towards the end of 1914, the legion was accepted as a Service battalion of the Royal Fusiliers on 12 February 1915, under Colonel Driscoll. They were to serve in East Africa – thoroughly acting out their role on the frontier, as the 25th (S) Battalion, Royal Fusiliers (Frontiersmen).[8] Though the Frontiersmen were recruited to the Royal Fusiliers while voluntary enlistment was the norm, the 38th, 39th and

The Jewish battalions were volunteers who served as Service battalions with the 38th, 39th and 40th Royal Fusiliers in the Holy Land. They were granted the use of the Menorah as a cap insignia in 1919.

40th (Service) Battalions, the Royal Fusiliers were not. They were Jewish battalions, recruited from volunteers to serve in the Holy Land. They served with distinction, and in 1919 were granted the right to wear a holy symbol, the Jewish Menorah, bearing the Hebrew motto, *Kadimah* (eastwards), in recognition of their service.[9]

Kitchener's Army had been a bold experiment. Born out of the impatience and imperiousness of one man – Field Marshal Lord Horatio Herbert Kitchener of Khartoum – it had been slow to ignite into a burning brand, a bright torch that was carried through the commercial cities of the Empire, the manufacturing giants, the cities of pride and of civic duty. The posters and recruiting campaigns had persuaded the earnest and had cajoled, even bullied, the timid into joining. It had demanded of the average citizen that he did the right thing, that he serve his country and earn the right of citizenship.

With so many years passed, and with the benefit of reflection and analysis, it is for us to balance whether the sacrifice made by these men was worth the outcome, particularly on the Somme. The New Armies were raised to match the threat of the German war machine that had been roused and which massed on the soil of France and Belgium. Citizens of town and country, the men of the first 300,000 called to the Colours by their originator, joined the ever expanding army and were forced to make do with indifferent uniforms and drill-purpose rifles.

Hastily constructed camps were distributed across Britain, camps that were soon transformed by the tramp of feet into a sea of mud that was trying for the new soldiers unused to field conditions. It took time to equip and train these new men, and an absence of suitably experienced NCOs and junior officers meant that in some cases the carefully laid out training manuals were inadequately used, as noted by Major Ewing of the 6th King's Own Scottish Borderers:

> The training was on lines identical with those of the old army and a similar syllabus was carried out with satisfactory results. The hardest lot fell to the young recently commissioned officers; they went through exactly the same routine as the men but they were also obliged to spend their spare time learning their particular duties as officers ...

LORD KITCHENER.

Lord Kitchener – a postcard based on the famous Bassano image.

The manual dealing with tactics and strategy, *Field Service Regulations*, was excellent in its statement of general principles but it did not give a young officer, unfamiliar with military terms, much assistance in such a matter as the handling of a platoon.[10]

When Kitchener's men finally left for France to take up the flaming brand from the Regular soldiers of the original British Expeditionary Force, they were well equipped physically. But the inadequacies of their training and the inexperience of their leadership – at all levels – would take time to resolve themselves, and this would have ramifications when the men were first committed to battle. In Gallipoli, or at Loos in 1915, there were criticisms, not always warranted, of the standard of the men and their leaders. In both cases, the divisions criticised were fresh to the battlefront and committed in haste, without adequate preparation or acclimatisation. And where senior leadership was up to the mark – as with Major General Ivor Maxse, commanding the 18th (Eastern) Division (K2) – great results could be achieved.[11]

It was on the Somme that the social experiment of locally raised battalions of pals, raised and equipped from subscription, municipal purse or rich benefactor, met the reality of modern warfare. Like the first three Kitchener Armies, which were composed of battalions of men from the same social background and the commercial houses of Britain's great towns and cities, they would eventually be well equipped, clothed and shod.

Arriving in France in time for the 'Great Push', most became acclimatised to trench warfare in the weeks before the battle, but would suffer most in its opening stages from the inability to win the 'race to the parapet' across no-man's-land. In this patch of earth many would lie forever, on the once quiet downlands of France, now transformed into the murderous landscape of modern battle. The losses of the first day can be linked to the same inadequacies that bedevilled their forebears at Loos and Gallipoli: the lack of experience of men and their leaders.[12]

The impact on Britain was profound. The film *The Battle of the Somme*, released on 11 August 1916 (while the battle still raged) was watched by a record 20 million people across the country. Hushed audiences observed men fall in battle – the very men they had supported in the heady days of the late summer and autumn of 1914, and the men to whom they had bidden farewell and wished 'Godspeed' in the spring of 1916.

The Somme would run its course until November and Kitchener's men would take their part, now battle hardened. It would be one of the most costly battles in history. But the question remains: without the Somme, could the British Army under Haig have faced the challenges that lay before it and go on to learn the art of winning wars in 1918? This question, so open to interpretation, is still hotly debated.

Without Kitchener's vision, and Kitchener's Mob, would Britain have been in a position to create the mass army that would consist of the remnants of the Regulars of 1914, the Territorials who followed, and the Kitchener divisions that came after – seventy-four whole divisions in total? Though volunteerism turned to compulsion by the end of 1915, the weapon was forged. And one thing is clear: the road to the Somme paved by Kitchener's Army continued on to the victory of the citizen army in November 1918.

Kitchener's Man – Charlie Branston was a volunteer, one of Tunstill's Men, who served with the 10th (Service) Battalion, Duke of Wellington's Regiment. Wounded by shellfire in the trenches at Contalmaison on 10 July 1916, he was later posted to the 2nd Battalion, and was killed in action on 12 October 1916 near Lesboeufs. He has no known grave, and his name is one of the thousands marked on the immense memorial to the missing of the Somme at Thiepval.

BIBLIOGRAPHY

DOCUMENTARY SOURCES

Kitchener Papers

The National Archives (TNA), London, PRO
  30/57/76
TNA PRO 30/57/73
TNA 162/32 'Approximate Number of Recruits
  Raised Day-by-Day'
TNA ACD/43896, 'Sealed Pattern 8365'

War Office Papers

TNA WO 162/3 'New Armies, Organisation'

Committee of Imperial Defence

TNA CAB 42/5/23, 'C.I.D. Paper G-25'

Army Clothing Department

TNA ACD/43896, 'Sealed Pattern 8365'

Welsh Army Corps Papers

National Library of Wales (NLW), MS 13925D,
  'Minute Book of the London Welsh Battalion
  Committee'

Private Papers

Sergeant Oswald Blencowe letter, www.europe-
  ana.eu, CC-A-SA 3.0
Private H. Mason papers, private collection
Private Robert Price letters, www.europeana.eu,
  CC-A-SA 3.0 (courtesy Michael Payne)

Others

*Advice to NCOs and Men of the 1st Birmingham
  Battalion*, pamphlet, 1914
'No-Conscription Fellowship Papers', TNA, HO 45
  10801/307402/57
'Ulster's Solemn League and Covenant',
  28 September 1912
1911 Census, 'General Reports with Appendices',
  Report Cd.8491, 1917–18
R. King Brown, 'Report on the Sanitary Condition
  of the Borough of Bermondsey for the Year
  1914', Bermondsey, 1915

NEWSPAPERS AND JOURNALS

Aberdeen Evening Express
Aberdeen Journal
Auckland Star
Birmingham Daily Mail
Birmingham Daily Post
The Boot & Shoe Retailer
Bristol Times and Mirror
Burnley Express
Cheshire Observer
Chester Chronicle
Craven Herald
Daily Herald
Daily Mail
Daily Record
Daily Sketch
The Daily Telegraph
Derby Daily Telegraph
Dumfries & Galloway Standard
Dundee Courier
Edinburgh Evening News
Exeter & Plymouth Gazette

Falkirk Herald
Gloucestershire Echo
The Great War, I Was There
The Illustrated War News
Liverpool Daily Post
Manchester Courier & Lancashire General
   Advertiser
Manchester Evening News
Newcastle Journal
The Pow-Wow
Punch
Tailor & Cutter
The Times
The War Budget
The War Illustrated
Western Daily Press
The Western Mail
Western Times
Yorkshire Evening Post
Yorkshire Post & Leeds Intelligencer

HANSARD

House of Lords Debate, 25 August 1914, vol. 17
   cc.501-3

House of Commons Debate, 26 November 1914,
   vol. 68, col. 1305

WAR OFFICE MANUALS

'Appendix to Training Manuals', 1905
Bayonet Fighting (1916), reprinted with amendments 1918
Field Service Pocket Book, 1914

Infantry Training (4 – Company Organisation),
   1914
Manual of Military Hygiene (1912), reprinted 1914
Manual of Military Law, 1914.

Manual of Physical Training (1908), reprinted with amendments 1914.

Musketry Regulations Part 1 (1909), reprinted with amendments 1914.

The Pattern 1908 Web Infantry Equipment, London, 1913.

The Pattern 1914 Leather Infantry Equipment, London, 1914.

PRIMARY AND CONTEMPORARY SOURCES AND REGIMENTAL HISTORIES

Anon, *The History of the Royal Fusiliers 'U.P.S.', University and Public Schools Brigade (Formation and Training)* (London: 1917)

Anon, *Sixteenth, Seventeenth, Eighteenth, Nineteenth Battalions the Manchester Regiment: A Record, 1914–1919* (Manchester: 1923)

Anon, *Snapshots of the 15th Battalion the Prince of Wales's Own (West Yorkshire Regiment)* (Leeds: 1917)

Asquith, Herbert Henry, *Memories and Reflections*, vol. 2 (London: 1928)

Aston, John, & L.M. Duggan, *The History of the 12th (Bermondsey) Battalion, East Surrey Regiment* (London: 1936)

Atteridge, Captain A.H., *The Army Shown to the Children* (London: 1915)

Atteridge, Captain A.H., *The British Army of Today* (London: 1915)

Birkenhead News, 'Victory Souvenir of the Great War 1914–1919' (Birkenhead: 1919)

Bryce, Viscount, 'Report of the Committee on Alleged German Outrages' (London: 1915)

Churchill, Winston S., *The World Crisis 1911–1918* (London: 1931)

Clayton, John T., *Craven's Part in the Great War* (London: 1919)

Clifford, W.G., *The British Army* (London: 1915)

Cooper, Bryan, *The Tenth (Irish) Division in Gallipoli* (Dublin: 1993. First printed in London, 1918)

Crookenden, Arthur, *The History of the Cheshire Regiment in the Great War* (Chester: 1925)

Crozier, Brigadier General F.P., *A Brass Hat in No Man's Land* (London: 1930)

Danby, Paul & Lieutenant Colonel Cyril Field, *The British Army Book* (London: 1915)

Edwards, Major T.J., *Regimental Badges* (Aldershot: 1951)

Empey, Arthur Guy, *Over the Top* (New York: 1917)

Ewing, Major John, *The History of the 9th (Scottish) Division 1914–1919* (London: 1921)

Falls, Cyril, *The History of the 36th (Ulster) Division* (London: 1996, reprint of 1922 original), p.3

Foulkes, Major General C.H., *Gas! The Story of the Special Brigade* (Edinburgh: 1934)

Germains, Victor Wallace, *The Kitchener Armies: The Story of a National Achievement* (London: 1930)

Gibbs, Philip, *Realities of War* (London: 1920)

Hall, James Norman, *Kitchener's Mob* (London: 1916)

Hamilton, General Sir Ian, *General Sir Ian Hamilton's Despatches from the Dardanelles, etc.* (London: 1917)

Hanna, Henry, *The Pals at Suvla Bay* (Dublin: 1920)

Hargrave, John, *At Suvla Bay* (London: 1916)

Hay, Ian (John Hay Beith), *The First Hundred Thousand* (Edinburgh and London: 1915)

Illustrated London News, 'Special Memorial: Lord Kitchener' (13 June 1915, London)

Inglefield, Captain V.E., *The History of the Twentieth (Light) Division* (London: 1921)

Institution of Royal Engineers, *History of the Corps of Royal Engineers*, vol. V (Chatham: 1952)

Jeffery, Jeffrey E. (ed.), '1918 Souvenir of the Welsh Division', *Western Mail* (Cardiff: 1918)

Kempster, Brigadier General F. & Brigadier General H.C.E. Westropp (eds), *Manchester City Battalions Book of Honour* (London & Manchester: 1916)

Lloyd George, David, *War Memoirs of David Lloyd George* (London: 1938)

Lyons, A. Neil, *Kitchener Chaps* (London: 1915)

Malins, Geoffrey H., *How I Filmed the War* (London: 1920)

Masefield, John, *The Old Front Line* (London: 1917)

O'Neill, H.C., *The Royal Fusiliers in the Great War* (London: 1922)

O'Toole, Thomas, *The Way They Have in the Army* (London: 1916)

Osborne, E.B., *The Muse in Arms* (London: 1918)

Palmer, Frederick, *With the New Army on the Somme* (London: 1917)

Parker, Ernest, *Into Battle 1914–18* (London: 1964)

Purdom, C.B. (ed.), *Everyman at War. Sixty Personal Narratives of the War* (London: 1930)

Read, I.L. 'Dick', *Of Those We Loved* (Barnsley: 2013)

Rogerson, Sidney, *Twelve Days on the Somme: A Memoir of the Trenches, 1916* (London: 2006, originally published 1933)

Stanley, Brigadier General F.C., *The History of the 89th Brigade 1914–1918* (Liverpool: 1919)

Ternan, Brigadier General Trevor, *The Story of the Tyneside Scottish* (Newcastle-upon-Tyne: 1919)

Wallace, Edgar, *Kitchener's Army and the Territorial Forces* (London: 1915)

War Office, *Statistics of the Military Effort of the British Empire during the Great War 1914–1920* (London: 1922)

Ward, Fred. W., *The 23rd (Service) Battalion Royal Fusiliers (First Sportsman's), A Record of its Services in the Great War, 1914–1919* (London: 1920)

Watkins, Owen Spencer, *With Kitchener's Army* (London: 1899)

Welsh Army Corps, 'Report of the Executive Committee' (Cardiff: 1921)

Wheeler-Holohan, V., *Divisional and Other Signs* (London: 1920)

Williams, Captain Basil, *Raising and Training the New Armies* (London: 1918) Wyrall, Everard, *The Die Hards in the Great War*, vol. 1, 1914–1916 (London: 2002)

SECONDARY SOURCES

Alexander, Jack, *McCrae's Battalion: The Story of the 16th Royal Scots* (Edinburgh: 2004)

Aspinall-Oglander, Brigadier General C.F., *Official History of the Great War. Military Operations, Gallipoli, 1915*, vol. 1 (London: 1929)

Aspinall-Oglander, Brigadier General C.F., *Official History of the Great War. Military Operations, Gallipoli, 1915*, vol. 2 (London: 1932)

Ballard, Brigadier General C.R., *Kitchener* (London: 1930)

Bardgett, Colin, *The 'Lonsdale Battalion' 1914–1918* (Wigtown: 1993)

Barlow, Robin, *Wales and World War One* (Ceredigion: 2014)

Barnes, Major R. Money, *The British Army of 1914* (London: 1968)

Bean, C.E.W, *The Story of Anzac* (Sydney: 1924)

Bilton, David, *The Trench: The Full Story of the 1st Hull Pals* (Barnsley: 2002)

Bodsworth, John, *British Uniforms and Equipment of the Great War, 1914–18* (MLRS: 2010)

Brown, Malcolm, *Tommy Goes to War* (London: 1978)

Caradice, Phil, *Cardiff & the Vale in the First World War* (Stroud: 2014)

Carter, Terry, *Birmingham Pals* (Barnsley: 1997)

Cherry, Niall, *Most Unfavourable Ground: The Battle of Loos 1915* (Birmingham: 2005)

Churchill, Colin, *History of the British Army Infantry Collar Badge* (Uckfield: 2002)

Corrigan, Gordon, *Loos 1915* (Staplehurst: 2005)

Corrigan, Gordon, *Mud, Blood and Poppycock* (London: 2003)

Darracott, Joseph & Belinda Loftus, *First World War Posters* (London: 1981)

Davison, John, *Durham Men in the Great War* (History of Education Project: 2000)

Denman, Terence, *Ireland's Unknown Soldiers: The 16th (Irish) Division in the Great War* (Dublin: 1992)

Doyle, Peter, *Gallipoli 1915* (Stroud: 2011)

Doyle, Peter, *Loos 1915* (Stroud: 2012)

Doyle, Peter & Chris Foster, *British Army Cap Badges of the First World War* (Oxford: 2010)

Doyle, Peter & Chris Foster, *Remembering Tommy: The British Soldier in the First World War* (Stroud: 2013)

Dungan, Myles, *They Shall Grow Not Old: Irish Soldiers and the Great War* (Dublin: 1997)

Edmonds, Brigadier General Sir James, *Official History of the Great War: Military Operations, France and Belgium, 1914* (London: 1926)

Edmonds, Brigadier General Sir James, *Official History of the Great War: Military Operations, France and Belgium, 1915* (London: 1928)

Edmonds, Brigadier General Sir James, *Official History of the Great War: Military Operations, France and Belgium, 1916* (London: 1932)

Edmonds, Brigadier General Sir James, *Appendices, History of the Great War: Military Operations, France and Belgium, 1916* (London: 1932)

Edwards, Major T.J., *Regimental Badges* (Aldershot: 1951)

Falls, Captain Cyril, *Official History of the Great War: Military Operations, Macedonia* (London: 1933)

French, David, *British Economic and Strategic Planning 1905–1915* (London: 1982)

French, David, *Military Identities: The Regimental System, the British Army, & the British People, c.1870–2000* (Oxford: 2005)

Garwood, John H., *Chorley Pals* (Manchester: 1989)

Grayson, Richard E., *Belfast Boys: How Unionists and Nationalists Fought and Died Together in the First World War* (London: 2010)

Holmes Richard, *The Little Field Marshal, Sir John French* (London: 1981)

Holmes, Richard, *Tommy. The British Soldier on the Western Front 1914–1918* (London: 2004)

James, Brigadier General E.A., *British Regiments 1914–18* (London: 1976)

James, Robert Rhodes, *Gallipoli* (London: 1965)

Kipling, Arthur L. & Hugh L. King, *Headdress Badges of the British Army*, vol. 1 (Uckfield: 2006)

Lethern, Albert A., *The Development of the Mills Woven Cartridge Belt 1877–1956* (London: 1986 (reprint edition))

Lewis, Bernard, *Swansea Pals* (Barnsley: 2004)

Mace, Martin & John Grehan, *Slaughter on the Somme, 1 July 1916: The Complete War Diaries of the British Army's Worst Day* (Barnsley: 2013)

McGreal, Stephen, *The Cheshire Bantams* (Barnsley: 2006)

MacMunn, Lieutenant General Sir George & Captain Cyril Falls, *Official History of the Great War, Military Operations Egypt & Palestine* (London: 1928)

Maddocks, Graham, *Liverpool Pals* (Barnsley: 1991)

Marks, Dean, *'Bristol's Own' 12th Battalion Gloucestershire Regiment* (Bristol: 2011)

Messenger, Charles, *Call to Arms: The British Army 1914–18* (London: 2005)

Middlebrook, Martin, *The First Day of the Battle of the Somme* (London: 1971)

Middlebrook, Martin, *Your Country Needs You* (Barnsley: 2000)

Milner, Laurie, *Leeds Pals* (Barnsley: 1991)

Mitchinson, K.W., *Pioneer Battalions in the Great War* (London: 1997)

Mitchinson, K.W. & I. McInnes, *Cotton Town Comrades* (self-published, 1993)

Philpott, William, *Three Armies on the Somme: The First Battle of the Twentieth Century* (New York: 2010)

Pollock, John, *Kitchener* (London: 2001)

Prior, Robin, *Gallipoli: The End of the Myth* (New Haven and London: 2009)

Raw, David, *Bradford Pals* (Barnsley: 2005)

Richardson, Matthew, *The Tigers, 6th, 7th, 8th & 9th Battalions of the Leicestershire Regiment* (Barnsley: 2000)

Riddoch, Andrew & John Kemp, *When the Whistle Blows* (Yeovil: 2008)

Sheffield, Gary, *The Chief, Douglas Haig and the British Army* (London: 2011)

Sheffield, Gary, *The Somme* (London: 2003)

Simkins, Peter, *Kitchener's Army* (Manchester: 1988)

Stanley, Jeremy, *Ireland's Forgotten 10th* (self-published: 2003)

Stedman, Michael, *Salford Pals* (Barnsley: 1993)

Stewart, Graham & John Sheen, *Tyneside Scottish* (Barnsley: 1999)

Taylor, Elliot, *'Up the Hammers': The West Ham Battalion in the Great War* (self-published, 2012)

Taylor, James, *'Your Country Needs You': The Secret History of the Propaganda Poster* (Glasgow: 2013)

Terraine, John, *Mons, Defeat to Victory* (London: 1960)

Turner, Pierre, *Soldiers' Accoutrements of the British Army 1750–1900* (Marlborough: 2006)

Turner, William, *Accrington Pals* (Barnsley: 1987)

Ulster-Scots Community Network, *Young Citizen Volunteers* (Belfast: 2012)

Van Emden, Richard, *Boy Soldiers of the Great War* (London: 2005)

Westlake, Ray, *Collecting Metal Shoulder Titles* (Barnsley: 1996)

Westlake, Ray, *Kitchener's Army* (Tunbridge Wells: 1989)

Wood, Denis, *The Fifth Fusiliers and its Badges* (London: 2014)

Young, Michael, *Army Service Corps 1902–1918* (Barnsley: 2000)

ARTICLES AND CHAPTERS

Douglas, Roy, 'Voluntary Enlistment in the First World War and the work of the Parliamentary Recruiting Committee', *The Journal of Modern History*, vol. 42, 1970, p.566

Hatton, T.J. & E. Bray, 'Long Run Trends in the Heights of European Men, 19th and 20th Centuries', *Economics and Human Biology*, vol. 8, 2010, pp.405–13

Hughes, Clive, 'The Welsh Army Corps 1914–15: Shortages of Equipment Promote a "National" Uniform', *Imperial War Museum Review*, No. 1, 1986, p.93

Martin, Ernest J., 'Badges of Kitchener's Army', *Journal of the Society of Army Historical Research*, vol. 21, 1942, p.127

Martin, Ernest J., 'Badges of Kitchener's Army', *Journal of the Society of Army Historical Research*, vol. 25, 1957, p.35

Simkins, Peter, 'The War Experience of a Typical Kitchener Division – the 18th Division' in Hugh Cecil & Peter H. Liddle (eds), *Facing Armageddon* (London: 1996)

Simkins, Peter, 'Each One a Pocket Hercules: The Bantam Experiment and the Case of the Thirty-fifth Divison' in Sanders Marble (ed.), *Scraping the Barrel* (New York: 2012)

Werner, Bernard, *Das Königlich Preußische Inf-Rgt Prinz Louis Ferdinand von Preußen (2. Magdeb.) Nr. 27 im Weltkriege 1914–1918*, Deutsche Tat im Weltkrieg, Band 5, (Berlin: 1933)

NOTES

CHAPTER 1

1   A. Neil Lyons, *Kitchener Chaps*, London, 1915, p.47.

2   'A General' from E.B. Osborne, *The Muse in Arms*, London, 1918, p.vi.

3   There are many biographies of Kitchener. Of use here was John Pollock's *Kitchener*, London, 2001.

4   Owen Spencer Watkins, *With Kitchener's Army*, London, 1899, p.42.

5   Although some contemporaries wrote that 'he hated organisations' (Ian Hamilton, quoted in John Terraine, *Mons, Retreat to Victory*, London, 1960, p.41), Kitchener's low regard for established methods is discussed in Peter Simkins, *Kitchener's Army*, Manchester, 1988, pp.36–7.

6   Correspondence in Kitchener Papers, National Archives (TNA) PRO 30/57/76.

7   See Richard Holmes, *The Little Field Marshal, Sir John French*, London, 1981.

8   Herbert Henry Asquith, *Memories and Reflections*, vol. 2, p.24, London, 1928.

9   Terraine, op. cit., p.41.

10 Brigadier General C.R. Ballard, *Kitchener*, London, 1930, pp.165–6.

11 G.R. Steevens, *Daily Mail*, 1897.

12 Winston S. Churchill, *The World Crisis 1911–1918*, London, 1931, p.140.

13 *Ibid.*, p.141.

14 Victor Wallace Germains, *The Kitchener Armies: The Story of a National Achievement*, London, 1930, p.37.

15 The atrocities were examined in a controversial report by Viscount Bryce, 'Report of the Committee on Alleged German Outrages', London, 1915. The report helped fuel the propaganda, though much of it was overexpressed.

16 See David French, *Military Identities: The Regimental System, the British Army & the British People, c. 1870–2000*, Oxford, 2005.

17 W.G. Clifford, *The British Army*, London, 1915, pp.17–18.

18 *The Times*, 13 July 1914, p.6.

19 *Ibid.*

20 Paul Danby & Lieutenant Colonel Cyril Field, *The British Army Book*, London, 1915, p.125.

21 Danby & Field, op. cit., pp.125–6.

22 This rejection of the Territorial Army has been discussed by Peter Simkins in his masterful account *Kitchener's Army*, Manchester, 1988, pp.40–2. Churchill had claimed, 'It would have been far better to have formed the new volunteers upon the cadres of the Territorial Army, each of which could have been duplicated or quadruplicated in successive stages. But the new Secretary of State had little knowledge of and no faith in the British territorial system.' Churchill, op. cit., p.140.

23 Germains, op. cit., p.44.

24 *Ibid.*, p.44.

25 David French, *British Economic and Strategic Planning 1905–1915*, London, 1982, p.127.

26 The fact that the call was about to be issued by the press was also announced. The *Birmingham Daily Post* for Friday 7 August carried a short article on its front page: 'Call to Arms. An appeal for Recruits to the Regular Army', with the text of the poster to be released the next day.

27 For example, the *Liverpool Echo*, Saturday 8 August 1914, carried the advertisement as a column-width blocked out advertisement – as would so many other regional papers.

28 *The Times*, 8 August 1914, p.5.

29 Germains, op. cit., p.37.

30 Thomas O'Toole, *The Way They Have in the Army*, London, 1916, p.20.

31 Germains, op. cit., p.38.

32 *The Times*, 8 August 1914, p.4.

33 Edgar Wallace was working for the *Daily Mail* and the Harmondsworth Press at this point; his account appeared in many guises in 1915.

34 Edgar Wallace, *Kitchener's Army and the Territorial Forces*, London, 1915, p.17.

35 Philip Gibbs, *Realities of War*, London, 1920, p.57.

36 See discussion in James Taylor, *'Your Country Needs You': The Secret History of the Propaganda Poster*, Glasgow, 2013. See also, Joseph Darracott & Belinda Loftus, *First World War Posters*, London, 1981.

37 Captain Basil Williams, *Raising and Training the New Armies*, London, 1918, pp.15–16.

38 The famous Kitchener poster is discussed at length in the book by James Taylor, op. cit.

39 Arthur Guy Empey, *Over the Top*, New York, 1917, pp.4–5. Empey, like Hall, enlisted in the Royal Fusiliers and was later discharged as a 'foreign citizen'.

40 Roy Douglas, 1970, 'Voluntary Enlistment in the First World War and the Work of the Parliamentary Recruiting Committee' in *The Journal of Modern History*, vol. 42, p.566.

41 TNA 162/32, 'Approximate Number of Recruits Raised Day-by-Day'.

42 Edgar Wallace, *ibid.*, pp.16–17.

43 Captain A.H. Atteridge, *The British Army of Today*, London, 1915, p.39.

44 The pattern was repetitive: 2,843 men on Sunday 9 August; 4,823 men on Monday 10 August; 3,215 on Sunday 16 August, 7,934 on Monday 17 August; 2,571 on Sunday 18 August; 8,011 on Monday 19 August. TNA 162/32 op. cit.

45 Parliamentary Recruiting Committee (PRC) Poster 86.

46 TNA 162/32 op. cit.

47 *The Times*, 29 August 1914, p.3.

48 TNA 162/32 op. cit.

49 Edgar Wallace, op. cit., p.19.

50 Roy Douglas, op. cit., p.568.

51 *Daily Record*, Monday 10 August 1914; this public notice appears on the front page with Kitchener's Call to Arms.

52 Edgar Wallace, op. cit., pp.9–10.

53 James Norman Hall, *Kitchener's Mob*, London, 1916, p.9.

54 See Richard van Emden, *Boy Soldiers of the Great War*, London, 2005.

55 Ernest Parker, *Into Battle 1914–18*, London, 1964, p.1.

56 Edgar Wallace, op. cit., p.9.

57 *Ibid.*, pp.11–12.

58 From 1 May 1916, with the instigation of the Military Service Act, a more stringent approach was taken. Here men would be classified with grades that would go from A1 (general service) to C3 (garrison service at home).

59 James Norman Hall, op. cit., p.7.

60 *Ibid.*, p.10.

61 *Manual of Military Law*, War Office, 1914, Chapter X, para. 18, p.189.

62 Edgar Wallace, op. cit., p.12.

63 *Manual of Military Law*, op. cit., Chapter X, para. 21.

64 *Ibid.*

65 Germains, op. cit., p.52.

66 *Yorkshire Evening Post*, Monday 10 August 1914; a prominent front-page advertisement, or *Daily Mirror*, same date, which carried the advertisement adjacent to a map of the Western Front as it was then, on p.4.

67 Spencer Jones, unpublished PhD thesis, University of Wolverhampton.

68 Anon, *The History of the Royal Fusiliers 'U.P.S.' University and Public Schools Brigade (Formation and Training)*, London, 1917, p.14.

69 Captain A.H. Atteridge, *The Army Shown to the Children*, London, 1915, p.73.

70 Germains, op. cit., p.65.

71 Army Order 324, quoted in Brigadier General E.A. James' book, *British Regiments 1914–18*, London, 1976, p.38.

72 See Major T.J. Edwards, *Regimental Badges*, Aldershot, 1951; also discussed the authors' book *British Army Cap Badges 1914–1918*, Oxford, 2010.

73 James, op. cit., p.128.

74 Institution of Royal Engineers, *History of the Corps of Royal Engineers*, vol. V, Chatham, 1952, p.43.

75 *Ibid.*, pp.141–2.

76 Germains, op. cit., p.65.

77 Simkins, op. cit., p.66.

78 Germains, op. cit., p.108.

79 *Ibid.*, p.67.

80 Hansard, House of Lords Debate, 25 August 1914, vol. 17 cc.501–2.

81 *Ibid.*, cc.504.

82 James Norman Hall, op. cit., p.21.

83 Ian Hay, *The First Hundred Thousand*, Blackwood, Edinburgh and London, 1915.

84 Poem 'K1' published at the opening of Hay's book.

85 Ian Hay, *Ibid.*, p.5.

86 Major John Ewing, *The History of the 9th (Scottish) Division 1914–1919*, London, 1921, p.9.

87 Germains, op. cit., p.66.

88 Ian Hay, *Ibid.*, pp.67–8.

89 *Manchester Evening News*, Friday 28 August 1914.

90 Private H. Mason papers, private collection.

91 Germains, op. cit., p.112.

92 *Ibid.*

93 Ian Hay, op. cit., p.69.

94 *Ibid.*, p.70.

95 Germains, op. cit., pp.87–8.

96 Martin Middlebrook, *Your Country Needs You*, Barnsley, 2000, pp.66–7.

97 The story of Tunstill's 'Craven Legion' is reported in the memorial book, *Craven's Part in the Great War*, published locally and edited by John T. Clayton. Dr Bill Smith kindly provided further information on Tunstill's Men.

98 *Ibid.*, p.49.

CHAPTER 2

1 Edgar Wallace, op. cit., p.8.

2 Asquith, op. cit., p.31.

3 War Office, *Statistics of the Military Effort of the British Empire during the Great War 1914–1920*, London, 1922, p.868.

4 Williams, op. cit., p.51.

5 *Ibid.*, p.868.

6 *Ibid.*, p.868. 'Quantities of the former [blue material] were obtained from the Post Office from stocks which that department had in hand.'

7 *The Tailor & Cutter*, 5 November 1914, p.877.

8 Rudyard Kipling, 'The New Army in Training', the first of several articles in *The Daily Telegraph*, 1914.

9 Including the 'sealed pattern' currently on display in the Imperial War Museum's new First World War Gallery.

10 *The Pow-Wow*, No. 1, November 1914 – the newspaper of the UPS.

11 Taff Gillingham, personal correspondence. His extensive research into the uniforms of the Great War has so far drawn a blank on the official pattern, and no surviving example of this first pattern has, as yet, been unearthed.

12 Kipling, op. cit.

13 Illustrated by Ray Westlake, *Kitchener's Army*, Tunbridge Wells, 1989, p.21, with the 9th Battalion Suffolk Regiment, formed in September 1914 as part of the Third New Army (K3).

14 Lyons, op. cit., p.29.

15 James Norman Hall, op. cit., p.20.

16 *Ibid.*, p.21.

17 *Statistics of the Military Effort*, op. cit., p.870.

18 *The Boot and Shoe Retailer*, 23 October 1914.

19 *Ibid.*

20 *Ibid.*, p.21.

21 *The Tailor & Cutter*, supplement, October 1914; an advertisement for the supplier Hunter & Nesbit, Newcastle upon Tyne. Clearly khaki cloth was there for those who wished to seek it out – no doubt at competitive prices.

22 A 'sealed pattern', i.e. standard for this uniform jacket, is on display in the Imperial War Museum, sealed on 8 February 1915. According to John Bodsworth, *British Uniforms and Equipment of the Great War, 1914–18*, MLRS, 2010, p.43, there was also a 'simplified pattern' which may have led to the making up of this type of jacket as a simplified uniform in khaki serge.

23 Williams, op. cit., p.52.

24 Brigadier General F.C. Stanley, *The History of the 89th Brigade 1914–1918*, Liverpool, 1919, p.27.

25 'Report of the Executive Committee', Welsh Army Corps, Cardiff, 1921, p.18.

26 Clive Hughes, 'The Welsh Army Corps 1914–15: Shortages of Equipment Promote a "National" Uniform', *Imperial War Museum Review*, No. 1, 1986, p.93.

27 *Western Mail*, Wednesday 11 November 1914.

28 Hughes, op. cit., p.93.

29 *Ibid.*

30 Germains, op. cit., p.59.

31 War Office, *The Pattern 1908 Web Infantry Equipment*, London, 1913.

32 *Ibid.*

33 *Statistics of the Military Effort*, op. cit., p.870.

34 See Pierre Turner, *Soldiers' Accoutrements of the British Army 1750–1900*, Marlborough, 2006, pp.83 and 86.

35 *The Boot & Shoe Retailer and Leather Trades' Gazette*, 2 October 1914, p.30.

36 War Office, *Pattern 1914 Leather Infantry Equipment*, London.

37 Sidney Rogerson, *Twelve Days on the Somme: A Memoir of the Trenches, 1916*, London, 2006 (originally published 1933), p.160. Rogerson was a subaltern in a Regular battalion of the West Yorkshire Regiment.

38 Lethern, Albert A., *The Development of the Mills Woven Cartridge Belt 1877–1956*, London, reprinted 1986.

39 War Office, *Pattern 1914 Leather Infantry Equipment*, London.

40 War Office, *Field Service Pocket Book*, 1914.

41 Whose kilt was that much heavier than standard uniform trousers.

42 Captain A.H. Atteridge, *The Army Shown to the Children*, London, 1915, p.76.

43 Brigadier General Sir James Edmonds, *Official History of the Great War: Military Operations, France and Belgium, 1916*, London, 1932, p.314.

44 War Office, *Appendix to Training Manuals*, 1905.

45 Simkins, op. cit., p.279.

46 Captain V.E. Inglefield, *The History of the Twentieth (Light) Division*, London, 1921, pp.4–5.

47 James Norman Hall, op. cit., pp.39–40.

48 Williams, op. cit., p.54.

49 Simkins, op. cit., p.270, notes that full sets of 1914 leather equipment would, in some cases, only be available a month or so before the battalion left for France.

50 Williams, op. cit., p.75.

51 *Ibid.*, p.24.

52 Hall, op. cit., pp.26–7.

53 Institution of Royal Engineers, *The History of the Corps of Royal Engineers*, vol. V, Chatham, 1952, pp.69–70.

54 *Ibid.*, pp.70 and 75.

55 Postcards were produced for the soldier market that invariably parodied the routine and the hard work. These were eagerly snapped up and sent home by soldiers.

56 *Manchester Courier & Lancashire General Advertiser*, Thursday 10 September 1914.

57 Stanley, op. cit., p.23.

58 H.C. O'Neill, *The Royal Fusiliers in the Great War*, London, 1922, p.5.

59 War Office, *Infantry Training (4 – Company Organisation)*, 1914.

60 Edgar Wallace, op. cit., p.13.

61 Captain A.H. Atteridge, op. cit., p.75.

62 *Drill and Field Training* (1914).

63 Williams, op. cit., p.43.

64 War Office, *Manual of Physical Training 1908* (reprinted with amendments, 1914).

65 *Ibid.*

66 Hall, op. cit., p.27.

67 War Office, *Infantry Training (4 – Company Organisation)*, 1914.

68 *Ibid.*

69 War Office, *Musketry Regulations Part 1 1909* (reprinted with amendments, 1914).

70 Hall, op. cit., p.27.

71 War Office, *Manual of Military Hygiene 1912* (reprinted 1914).

72 Hall, op. cit., p.28.

73 Lance Corporal Norman Roberts, letter to the *Craven Herald*, 31 March 1916.

74 War Office, *Bayonet Fighting 1916* (reprinted with amendments, 1918), p.1.

CHAPTER 3

1 Stanley, op. cit., p.16.

2 *Birmingham Daily Post*, Thursday 27 August 1914.

3 *Aberdeen Evening Express*, Thursday 27 August 1914.

4 Simkins, op. cit., p.79.

5 O'Neill, op. cit., p.10.

6 *Ibid.*

7 Edgar Wallace, op. cit., p.17.

8 *Ibid.*, p.22.

9 *Liverpool Daily Post*, Thursday 27 August 1914.

10 *Burnley Express*, Saturday 5 September 1914.

11 Stanley, op. cit., p.8.

12 *Ibid.*, p.8.

13 *Ibid.*, p.51.

14 Stanley, op. cit., p.53. The first three city battalions certainly received one; the fourth, raised later in the year, may also have done; see Graham Maddocks, *Liverpool Pals*, Barnsley, 1991, p.33.

15 Maddocks, op. cit., p.33.

16 Colin Bardgett, *The 'Lonsdale Battalion' 1914–1918*, Wigtown, 1993, p.8.

17 Recruiting poster, printed in Penrith and signed 'Lonsdale, Lowther Castle'. The poster was intended to 'stimulate' recruiting for the whole of Kitchener's Army.

18 *Yorkshire Post & Leeds Intelligencer*, Wednesday 23 September 1914.

19 *Newcastle Journal*, Thursday 17 September 1914.

20 Williams, op. cit., p.7.

21 *Ibid.*, p.8.

22 Brigadier General F. Kempster & Brigadier General H.C.E. Westropp (eds), *Manchester City Battalions Book of Honour*, London & Manchester, 1916, p.xii.

23 *Manchester Evening News*, Saturday 29 August 1914.

24 *Ibid.*

25 Kempster & Westropp, op. cit., p.xvi.

26 *Ibid.*

27 *Ibid.*

28 *Manchester Courier & Lancashire General Advertiser*, Thursday 10 September 1914.

29 V. Wheeler-Holohan, *Divisional and Other Signs*, London, 1920, p.63.

30 *Manchester Courier & Lancashire General Advertiser*, Thursday 10 September 1914.

31 Michael Stedman, *Salford Pals*, Barnsley, 1993.

32 William Turner, *Accrington Pals*, Barnsley, 1987, p.19.

33 *Ibid.*, p.21; John H. Garwood, *Chorley Pals*, Manchester, 1989, p.3.

34 Simkins, op. cit., p.82.

35 1911 Census, 'General Reports with Appendices', Report Cd.8491, 1917–18, accessible through www.visionofbritain.org.uk.

36 Terry Carter, *Birmingham Pals*, Barnsley, 1997, pp.27–8.

37 *Birmingham Daily Post*, Friday 28 August 1914.

38 Carter, op. cit., p.36.

39 *Yorkshire Evening Post*, Tuesday 8 September 1914.

40 *Western Daily Press*, Wednesday 9 September 1914.

41 Carter, op. cit., p.66.

42 'Advice to NCO's and Men of the 1st Birmingham Battalion', pamphlet, 1914.

43 *Daily Record*, Tuesday 8 September 1914.

44 *Daily Record*, Sunday 6 September 1914.

45 Laurie Milner, *Leeds Pals*, Barnsley, 1991, p.16.

46 *Yorkshire Evening Post*, Friday 4 September 1914.

47 *Yorkshire Evening Post*, Monday 31 August 1914.

48 *Yorkshire Evening Post*, Tuesday 1 September 1914.

49 *Yorkshire Evening Post*, Thursday 3 September 1914; Milner, op. cit., p.20.

50 *Yorkshire Evening Post*, Tuesday 8 September 1914.

51 *Yorkshire Post & Leeds Intelligencer*, Wednesday 23 September 1914.

52 David Raw, *Bradford Pals*, Barnsley, 2005, p.30.

53 *Yorkshire Evening Post*, Tuesday 8 September 1914.

54 Raw, op. cit., p.40.

55 *Ibid.*, pp.50–1.

56 *Newcastle Journal*, Tuesday 8 September 1914.

57 David Bilton, *The Trench: The Full Story of the 1st Hull Pals*, Barnsley, 2002, p.27. Nicknames for the Hull Pals were: the Commercials (1st Hull); the Tradesmen (2nd Hull); the Sportsmen (3rd Hull), and 'T'others' (4th Hull).

58 V. Wheeler-Holohan, *Divisional and Other Signs*, London, 1920.

59 See Martin Middlebrook, *Your Country Needs You*, op. cit. The 26th–29th Divisions were formed by assembling Regular battalions returning from overseas' service – their places on garrison duty were invariably taken by Territorials.

60 *The Times*, 26 August 1914; *The History of the Royal Fusiliers 'U.P.S.' University and Public Schools Brigade*, p.15.

61 *The History of the Royal Fusiliers 'U.P.S.' ...*, p.16.

62 *Ibid.*, p.19; O'Neill, op. cit., p.15.

63 *The History of the Royal Fusiliers 'U.P.S.' ...*, p.29; *The Morning Post*, 8 September 1914.

64 *The History of the Royal Fusiliers 'U.P.S.' ...*, p.30.

65 O'Neill, op. cit., p.19.

66 *Gloucestershire Echo*, Wednesday 16 September 1914: 'Lord Kitchener has sanctioned the enrolment of a battalion of 1,300 sportsmen up to the age of 45 for service with the army.'

67 O'Neill, op. cit., p.19.

68 Fred W. Ward, *The 23rd (Service) Battalion, Royal Fusiliers (First Sportsmen's)*, London, 1920.

69 *Exeter & Plymouth Gazette*, Monday 5 October 1914.

70 *Edinburgh Evening News*, Wednesday 2 September 1914.

71 Andrew Riddoch & John Kemp, *When the Whistle Blows*, Yeovil, 2008, p.23.

72 *Punch*, 21 October 1914; subsequently produced as a poster under the title 'The Greater Game'.

73 Hansard, HC Debate, 26 November 1914, vol. 68, col. 1305.

74 *Ibid.*

75 Alexander, Jack, *McCrae's Battalion: The Story of the 16th Royal Scots*, 2004.

76 *Birmingham Daily Mail*, Tuesday 8 December 1914.

77 Riddoch & Kemp, op. cit., p.33.

78 *Western Times*, Friday 18 December 1914.

79 See Elliot Taylor, *Up the Hammers': The West Ham Battalion in the Great War*, 2012.

80 Dean Marks, *'Bristol's Own' 12th Battalion Gloucestershire Regiment*, Bristol, 2011, p.9.

81 *Western Daily Press*, Saturday 5 September 1914.

82 *Bristol Times and Mirror*, Saturday 5 September 1915; Marks, op. cit., p.10.

83 *Western Daily Press*, Wednesday 9 September 1914.

84 An article in the *Western Daily Press* for 26 September 1914 then put the recruitment figures at 878, much below the usual target figure of 1,200.

85 *Western Daily Press*, Tuesday 22 September 1914.

86 James, op. cit., pp.46–8. James lists thirty-seven battalions in total, plus three additional Garrison battalions, as well as two late-war Graduated and one Young Soldier battalion.

87 *Newcastle Journal*, Wednesday 9 September 1914.

88 *Newcastle Journal*, Tuesday 8 September 1914.

89 Graham Stewart and John Sheen, *Tyneside Scottish*, Barnsley, 1999, p.26.

90 *Newcastle Journal*, Tuesday 15 September 1914.

91 Simkins, op. cit., p.99.

92 *Newcastle Journal*, Thursday 15 October 1914; Brigadier General Trevor Ternan, *The Story of the Tyneside Scottish*, p.12.

93 *Newcastle Journal*, Thursday 15 October 1914.

94 *Newcastle Journal*, Monday 19 October 1914.

95 Denis Wood, *The Fifth Fusiliers and its Badges*, London, 2014, pp.156–7.

96 *Ibid.*, pp.148–50; the first pattern, produced in November 1914 was rather small; there were three separate and more overtly Scottish replacement badges from early 1915 onwards.

97 Wood, op. cit., pp.144 and 156.

98 *Newcastle Journal*, Thursday 19 November 1914.

99 Wood, op. cit., p.160.

100 Ternan, op. cit., p.12.

101 *Daily Herald*, Saturday 12 September 1914: 'The War Office, through the Press Bureau, announces that until further orders the minimum height for all men, other than ex-soldiers, who enlist in the Infantry of the Line, will be raised to 5ft 6in'. For height averages see T.J. Hatton and E. Bray, 'Long-run trends in the heights of European men, 19th and 20th centuries' in *Economics and Human Biology*, vol. 8, pp.405–13.

102 Arthur Crookenden, *The History of the Cheshire Regiment in the Great War*, Chester, 1925, p.347; see also Peter Simkins, '"Each One a Pocket Hercules": The Bantam Experiment and the Case of the Thirty-fifth Division' in Sanders Marble (ed.), *Scraping the Barrel* (New York: 2012), p.80.

103 Stephen McGreal, *The Cheshire Bantams*, Barnsley, 2006.

104 *Cheshire Observer*, Saturday 5 December 1914.

105 Crookenden, op. cit.; *Birkenhead News*, 'Victory Souvenir of the Great War 1914–1919', Birkenhead, 1919, pp.10–11.

106 *Chester Chronicle*, Saturday 5 December 1914.

107 *Daily Sketch*, Tuesday 1 December 1914.

108 McGreal, op. cit., p.30.

109 Crookenden, op. cit., p.346.

110 Ernest J. Martin, 'Badges of Kitchener's Army' in *Journal of the Society of Army Historical Research*, vol. 21, 1942, p.127.

111 Ernest J. Martin, 'Badges of Kitchener's Army' in *Journal of the Society of Army Historical Research*, vol. 25, 1957, p.35.

112 *Daily Record*, Monday 1 February 1915.

113 *Falkirk Herald*, Saturday 30 January 1915.

114 Simkins, 'Each One a Pocket Hercules' ..., op. cit.

115 Simkins, *Kitchener's Army*, p.120.

116 R. King Brown, 'Report on the Sanitary Condition of the Borough of Bermondsey for the Year 1914', Bermondsey, 1915.

117 John Aston & L.M. Duggan, *The History of the 12th (Bermondsey) Battalion, East Surrey Regiment*, London, 1936, p.3.

118 *Ibid.*, p.3.

119 *Ibid.*, p.4.

120 *Ibid.*, p.4.

121 *Ibid.*, p.4.

122 *Ibid.*, p.7.

123 Myles Dungan, *They Shall Grow Not Old: Irish Soldiers and the Great War*, Dublin, 1997, p.15.

124 Bryan Cooper, *The Tenth (Irish) Division in Gallipoli*, Dublin, 1993 (first printed London, 1918), p.24.

125 *Ibid.*, p.24.

126 Terence Denman, *Ireland's Unknown Soldiers: The 16th (Irish) Division in the Great War*, Dublin, 1992, p.23 *et seq.*

127 In 1966, a loyalist paramilitary group was raised under the same name 'Ulster Volunteer Force'. There was no direct link with the organisation of the early twentieth century.

128 Text of 'Ulster's Solemn League and Covenant', 28 September 1912.

129 Discussed by Richard E. Grayson, *Belfast Boys: How Unionists and Nationalists Fought and Died Together in the First World War*, London, 2010.

130 *Ibid.*

131 Cyril Falls, *The History of the 36th (Ulster) Division*, London, 1996 (reprint of 1922 original), p.3.

132 Grayson, op. cit.

133 Falls, op. cit., p.10.

134 Brigadier General F.P. Crozier, *A Brass Hat in No Man's Land*, London, 1930, p.45.

135 See Ulster-Scots Community Network, *Young Citizen Volunteers*, Belfast, 2012.

136 *Dundee Courier*, Wednesday 11 September 1912.

137 Westlake, op. cit.; Ray Westlake, *Collecting Metal Shoulder Titles*, Barnsley, 1996, p.124; Martin, op. cit., p.128.

138 *The Times*, 17 September 1914, p.8.

139 *Ibid.*, 18 September 1914, p.5.

140 Denman, op. cit., p.40.

141 *The Times*, 12 October 1914, p.5.

142 David Lloyd George, reported in the 'Report of the Executive Committee', Welsh Army Corps, Cardiff, 1921, p.3.

143 Discussed in Robin Barlow, *Wales and World War One*, Ceredigion, 2014, p.42 *et seq.*

144 *Derby Daily Telegraph*, Monday 21 September 1914.

145 *Birmingham Daily Post*, Monday 21 September 1914.

146 Welsh Army Corps, op. cit., p.3.

147 *Western Mail*, Tuesday 22 September 1914.

148 David Lloyd George, *War Memoirs of David Lloyd George*, London, 1938, p.452.

149 Welsh Army Corps, op. cit., p.6.

150 *Ibid.*, p.5.

151 *Ibid.*, p.6.

152 *Ibid.*, p.10.

153 *Ibid.*, p.16.

154 Barlow, op. cit., p.50.

155 Welsh Army Corps, op. cit., pp.18, 32 *et seq*; James, op. cit. pp.67 and 83; Bernard Lewis, *Swansea Pals*, Barnsley, 2004.

156 Welsh Army Corps, op. cit., p.23 *et seq.*

157 Jeffrey E. Jeffery (ed.) '1918 Souvenir of The Welsh Division', *Western Mail*, Cardiff, 1918, p.15.

158 *Western Mail*, Monday 7 September 1914.

159 *Minute Book of the London Welsh Battalion Committee*, National Library of Wales (NLW MS 13925D).

160 Footage of the London Welsh exists in the archive of the British Pathé news, URN 74750, ID 2322.22.

161 Ray Westlake, *Collecting Metal Shoulder Titles*, Barnsley, 1996, p.84; Martin, 1942, op. cit., p.127.

162 *Western Mail*, Tuesday 5 September 1914.

163 Phil Caradice, *Cardiff & the Vale in the First World War*, Stroud, 2014.

164 *Brief News of the Cardiff (Pals) Commercial Battalion*, No. 9, August 1916.

165 *Ibid.*

166 Welsh Army Corps, op. cit., p.35.

167 Caradice, op. cit.

168 Colin Churchill, *History of the British Army Infantry Collar Badge*, Uckfield, 2002, p.185.

169 Kevin Thomas, personal communication, 2015.

CHAPTER 4

1 E.B. Osborne, op. cit., p.viii.

2 Gibbs, op. cit., p.59.

3 Ewing, op. cit., p.11.

4 *Ibid.*, p.17.

5 Parker, op. cit., p.19.

6 I.L. 'Dick' Read, *Of Those We Loved*, Barnsley, 2013, p.17.

7 Private Irvine Clark, letter to the *Craven Herald*, 31 March 1916.

8 Lance Corporal Norman Roberts, letter to the *Craven Herald*, 25 November 1915.

9 Read, op. cit., p.18.

10 Captain Geoffrey Mainwaring Brown ('G.B. Mainwaring'), *If We Return: Letters of a Soldier of Kitchener's Army*, London, 1918, p.98.

11 *Field Service Pocket Book*, 1914.

12 ACD/43896, Sealed Pattern 8365; see Churchill, *Collar Badges*, op. cit.

13 War Office 162/3 'New Armies, Organisation'; see also K.W. Mitchinson, *Pioneer Battalions in the Great War*, London, 1997.

14 See K.W. Mitchinson & I. McInnes, *Cotton Town Comrades*, 1993.

15 Mitchinson, op. cit., p.7.

16 *Auckland Star*, 23 April 1915.

17 Everard Wyrall, *The Die Hards in the Great War*, Vol. 1, 1914–1916.

18 Lance Corporal Norman Roberts' letter to the *Craven Herald*, 26 November 1915.

19 Private Robert Price's letters, www.europeana.eu, CC-A-SA 3.0 (courtesy Michael Payne).

20 Sergeant Oswald Blencowe letter, www.europeana.eu, CC-A-SA 3.0.

21 Private Humphrey Mason papers, private collection.

22 Parker, op. cit., p.25.

23 Lance Corporal Norman Roberts, letter to the *Craven Herald*, 26 November 1915.

24 Ballard, op. cit., p.310.

25 John Hargrave, *At Suvla Bay*, London, 1916, p.59.

26 General Sir Ian Hamilton, *General Sir Ian Hamilton's Despatches from the Dardanelles, etc.* London, 1917, p.235.

27 C.E.W. Bean, *The Story of Anzac*, Sydney, 1924, p.716.

28 TNA CAB 42/5/23, Committee of Imperial Defence (C.I.D. Paper G-25).

29 *Ibid.*

30 Lieutenant General Sir George MacMunn and Captain Cyril Falls, *Official History of the Great War, Military Operations Egypt & Palestine*, London, 1928, p.88.

31 *Snapshots of the 15th Battalion the Prince of Wales's Own (West Yorkshire Regiment)*, Leeds, 1917.

32 Soldier's letter, *Dumfries & Galloway Standard*, Wednesday 20 October 1915.

33 Major General C.H. Foulkes, *Gas! The Story of the Special Brigade*, Edinburgh, 1934, p.69.

34 *Aberdeen Journal*, Thursday 30 September 1915.

35 Ian Hay (John Hay Beith), op. cit.

36 Letter from Private Robert H. Stewart, 5th (S) Battalion, Cameron Highlanders, *Daily Record*, Friday 29 October 1915.

37 Letter, Hauptmann Willy Lange, *Infanterie-Regiment Nr. 2*, in Bernard Werner, *Das Königlich Preußische Inf.-Rgt. Prinz Louis Ferdinand von Preußen (2. Magdeb.) Nr. 27 im Weltkriege 1914–1918*. Deutsche Tat im Weltkrieg, Band 5, Berlin, 1933.

38 See Edmonds, op. cit., p.287 *et seq.*

39 Frederick Palmer, *With the New Army on the Somme*, London, 1917, p.76.

40 Instructions for General Sir D. Haig, 28 December 1915; 'Appendices', *History of the Great War, Military Operations, France and Belgium 1916*, London, 1932, p.40.

41 'Appendices', op. cit., p.1.

42 Germains, op. cit., p.223.

43 Letter to General Sir H. Rawlinson, commanding the Fourth Army; 'Appendices', op. cit., p.86.

44 John Masefield, *The Old Frontline*, London, 1917, p.13.

45 The 1971 account by Martin Middlebrook, *The First Day of the Battle of the Somme*, describes this day and has done much to shape later considerations of the battle as part of social history.

46 Peter Simkins, quoted in Gary Sheffield, *The Somme*, London, 2003, p.73.

47 Masefield, op. cit., p.128.

48 Brigadier General Sir James Edmonds, *History of the Great War: Military Operations, France and Belgium 1916*, London, 1932, p.442.

49 *Ibid.*

50 *Ibid.*, p.394.

51 *Ibid.*, p.404.

52 Brigadier General Trevor Ternan, *The Story of the Tyneside Scottish*, Newcastle-upon-Tyne, 1919, p.107.

53 Peter Simkins, 'The War Experience of a Typical Kitchener Division – the 18th Division' in Hugh Cecil and Peter H. Liddle, *Facing Armageddon*, London, 1996, p.301.

54 Stanley, op. cit., p.131.

55 Edmonds, 1932, op. cit., p.483.

56 *Statistics of the Military Effort of the British Empire*, op. cit., p.324.

CHAPTER 5

1 Germains, op. cit., p.294.

2 Hansard, House of Commons Debate, 20 April 1915, vol. 71, cc.172–3.

3 *Ibid.*

4 The introduction of conscription is discussed in greater depth by Simkins, op. cit., p.138 *et seq.*

5 PRC poster No. 113, issued August 1915.

6 Kitchener Papers, TNA PRO 30/57/73.

7 No-Conscription Fellowship leaflet, 'Shall Britons Be Conscripts', TNA HO 45 10801/307402.

8 O'Neill, op. cit., p.22.

9 *Ibid.*, p.26 *et seq.*

10 Ewing, op. cit., p.9.

11 Discussed by Simkins, in Hugh Cecil and Peter H. Liddle, *Facing Armageddon*, London, 1996, p.297 *et seq.*

12 'The reason that 1 July saw more British deaths than any other day in British military history is a combination of there never before or since having been a British offensive of such ferocity, against the main enemy in the main theatre of war, and the lack of experience of the troops and their leaders at battalion level'. Gordon Corrigan, *Mud, Blood and Poppycock*, London, 2003, p.276.

INDEX

Accrington 106, 107, 110, 121, 179, 190
Albert 186, 192
Aldershot 44, 52, 63, 75, 87
Arms and Services
 Army Service Corps 42
 Corps of Royal Engineers 7, 42, 43, 62, 79, 81, 154, 155, 169
 Royal Army Medical Corps 7, 42
 Royal Field Artillery 7, 21, 42, 43, 74, 85, 154
Artillery 7, 21, 42, 43, 74, 85, 154, 165, 180, 181, 187, 189, 191, 196
Atteridge, Captain A.H. 30, 39, 72, 83

Badges 40, 56, 59, 97, 98, 99, 101, 102, 105, 106, 110, 111–12, 113, 114, 115, 117, 119, 123, 124, 125, 127, 130, 131, 133, 134, 135, 139, 140, 143, 144, 146, 151, 158, 159, 160, 161, 169, 170, 194
Bantam Battalions 108, 109, 115, 121, 137–141
 Bigland's Birkenhead Bantams 137–141
 Rosebery Battalion 139, 140, 141
 Salford Bantams 109, 141
Bapaume 186, 192
Barlow, Montague MP 106, 141
Barnsley 121, 179, 189
Bassano 14, 203
Battle of the Somme, The 204
Bean, Charles 178, 179
Belfast 146, 150, 151
Belle Vue Barracks 119
Bermondsey 141–4
Bigland, Arthur MP, 137, 138, 139
Birkenhead 137–41
Birmingham 65, 83, 87, 107, 109, 109–14, 116, 119, 190
Birmingham Battalion Equipment Fund Committee 111, 112
Boots 48, 55, 61, 62, 63, 64, 68, 72, 105, 113, 118
Bradford 65, 113–20, 121, 179, 189
Bradford Citizens Army League 118, 119

Brethyn llwyd 66
Brotherton, Edward 117
Bristol 111, 129–31, 131, 133, 190
Bristol Citizens' Recruiting Committee 129–30
Bulford Camp 42

'Call to Arms', The 22, 23, 24, 38, 50, 77, 115, 129, 137, 163
Camps 21, 25, 42, 77–81, 83, 84, 117, 131
Cannock Chase 81
Cardiff 66, 83, 153, 156–61
Cardwell–Childers Reforms 19
Carson, Sir Edward MP 145, 149, 151
Charrington, F.N. 126
Chocolate Hill 177
Chorley 107
Chunuk Bair 177, 178
Clipstone Camp 81
Colston Hall 129, 130
Commissions 39, 122, 124
Conscription 7, 198, 199, 200, 202
Contalmasion 192, 204
'County patriotism' 154
Cunliffe-Owen, Mrs Emma 125, 126, 127
Curragh Incident 12, 44, 145

Derby, Lord 65, 85, 91, 95, 96, 99, 103, 106, 110, 113, 115, 129, 131, 142, 195, 198, 199, 200
Derby scheme 199, 200
Divisions 9, 13, 14, 20, 21, 42, 44, 46, 47, 48, 49, 50, 55, 74, 77, 96, 106, 107, 109, 115, 121, 124, 126, 128, 137, 139, 141, 145, 149, 151, 152, 154, 157, 158, 159, 162, 163, 164, 165, 168, 169, 170, 171, 172, 173, 176, 177, 178, 180, 181, 182, 183, 184, 186, 188, 189, 190, 191, 192, 193, 195, 196, 197
 6th Division 164
 7th Division 189
 8th Division 189

9th (Scottish) 44, 46, 162, 163, 164, 181, 183
10th (Irish) 44, 145, 176, 177, 178
11th (Northern) 44, 157, 176, 177, 178, 179
12th (Eastern) 44
13th (Western) 44, 107, 176, 177, 178
14th (Light) 42, 44, 162, 165, 179
15th (Scottish) 48, 181, 183
16th (Irish) 145, 151, 152
18th (Eastern) 198
20th (Light) 47, 172, 173
21st Division 184, 189, 192
22nd Division 158
23rd Division 165
24th Division 107, 168, 184
29th Division 175, 176, 189
30th Division 96, 106, 109, 121, 192, 195, 196
31st Division 121, 179, 188, 189, 190
32nd Division 106, 115, 121, 137, 176, 189, 190, 191, 196
33rd Division 121, 124, 126, 128, 172
35th (Bantam) 121, 139
36th (Ulster) 141, 145, 146, 149, 151, 154, 161, 189, 191, 196
37th Division 107, 141, 165
38th (Welsh) 154, 155, 157, 159, 161, 171, 197
39th Division 141
40th Division 141
41st Division 141, 170
46th (North Midland) 179
47th (London) 181, 182
Dublin 12, 44, 146
Durham 119, 137, 165, 173, 189

Edinburgh 126, 127, 192
Egypt 11, 12, 66, 85, 117, 162, 175, 179
Empey, Arthur Guy 25
Equipment
 1882 Pattern Valise Equipment 68, 69

1888 Pattern Slade Wallace 67, 68
1903 Pattern Bandolier 88
1908 Pattern webbing 66–8, 70
1914 Infantry Pattern leather 68–72, 98
Equipment supply 48, 57, 62, 64, 66, 67, 68, 73, 74, 76, 77, 85, 87, 91, 121

First Hundred Thousand, The 45, 182
Football Association 126, 127
French, Field Marshal Sir John 12, 54, 180, 184, 185
Fricourt 187, 192

Gallipoli (Dardanelles) 85, 162, 174, 175–9, 204
Gas 181–183
Germains, Victor 21, 23, 37, 48, 49, 66, 186
Glasgow 34, 107, 113, 115, 190
Glasgow tramways 113, 115
Green Hill 177
Grimsby 192, 198
Guildford 143, 144
Guillemont 167

Haig, General (later Field Marshal) Sir Douglas 180, 181, 184, 185, 186, 204
Haking, Major General 184
Haldane, Lord 16, 133, 134
Haldane Reforms 13, 16, 19, 20, 39, 40, 77, 121
Hall, James Norman 4, 35, 37, 46, 61, 62, 86, 87
Hamilton, General Sir Ian 175, 176, 177, 179
Hampshire, HMS 174, 175
'Hay, Ian' (John Hay Beith) 46, 182
Heart of Midlothian FC 126, 127
Hebuterne 190
Hickman, Colonel T.C. 146, 149
Hill 10 177
Hill 70 181, 182, 184
Hohenzollern Redoubt 181, 182, 183, 189
Hull 121, 161, 179
Hulluch 184
Hundred Thousand
    First (K1) 14, 22, 23, 39–47, 48, 63, 94, 104, 145, 203
    Second (K2) 47–9, 203
    Third (K3) 49–53, 203
Huts 62, 77, 79–81

Ireland 12, 19, 49, 70, 141, 145, 146, 151, 152
Irish Home Rule 12, 145, 146, 149
Irish National Volunteers 146, 151–2
Irish regiments 19, 49, 145–52
Isle of Man Service Company 139, 140

Jowitt, Fred MP 118

Khaki uniforms, supply of 57, 58, 65, 66, 104, 112, 118, 129, 133
Kinmel Park Camp 81
'Kitchener blue' 40, 45, 48, 52, 53, 57–61, 62, 63, 65, 66, 67, 68, 69, 74, 80, 98, 104, 105, 106, 109, 112, 113, 119, 129, 131, 133, 157
Kitchener, Field Marshal Lord Horatio Herbert 7, 11–14, 22–6, 30, 37, 38, 39, 44, 40, 46, 47, 49, 77, 81, 91, 101, 103, 107, 113, 115, 121, 122, 123, 125, 129, 132, 133, 141, 145, 146, 149, 153, 157, 174, 175, 179, 180, 185, 195, 198, 200, 202, 203, 204
Kitchener poster 25, 29, 148, 198, 199
'Kitchener's Man' 50–2, 54, 204
'Kitchener's Mob' 4, 35

La Boisselle 187, 192, 193, 194, 196
Laidlaw, Piper VC 182
Lala Baba 176, 177
Leeds 27, 111, 115, 117, 118, 119, 121, 179, 189
Legion of Frontiersmen 107, 201, 202
Leipzig Salient 190
Liverpool 65, 82, 91, 95–9, 101, 103, 106, 107, 109, 110, 115, 116, 126, 129, 131, 132, 156, 195
Lloyd George, David MP 66, 152, 153, 156, 198
Lochnagar crater 192, 193
London 4, 24, 93, 94, 107, 123, 124, 125, 127, 128, 141, 142, 152, 154, 156, 170, 181, 182, 189
London Welsh RFC 155, 156
Lonsdale, Lord 99, 100, 101, 102, 115, 190
Lonsdale, Sir John MP 127
Loos, Battle of 168, 171, 179, 180–4, 185, 189, 192, 204
Lyons, A. Neil 61

Mahon, General Sir Bryan 44
Mametz 187, 192, 197
Manchester 65, 81, 83, 95, 103, 104–7, 112, 124, 132, 156, 169, 177, 195
'Mash' valley 192
Maxse, Major General Ivor 195, 204
Maxwell, Lieutenant General Sir John 179
McCrae, Sir George 127, 128, 192
McGill, Donald 72, 83
Messines, Battle of 152
Military Service Acts 202
Mons, Retreat from 31, 33, 35, 47, 54, 91, 94, 162, 198
Montauban 192, 195, 196
Murdoch, Keith 178, 179

'Navvies' Battalion' 170
Newcastle upon Tyne 83, 131, 132, 133, 137, 190

Officer Training Corps (OTC) 39, 121
Officers 34, 38, 39, 46, 47, 48, 73, 88, 122, 135, 146, 182, 192, 203
Old Public School and University Men's Committee 122, 123
Oldham 169
Oliver, Sir Thomas 132
Ovilliers 189

'Pals' battalions 81, 82, 91–161
    Accrington Pals 107, 110, 179, 189, 190
    Barnsley Pals 121, 179, 189
    Bermondsey Battalion 141, 142–3, 144
    Birmingham Pals 107–14, 116, 119, 190
    Bradford Pals 115, 118–21, 179, 189
    Bristol's Own 129–31, 190
    Cambridge Battalion 192
    Cardiff City Battalion 158–61
    Cardiff Commercial Battalion ('Pals') 157–9
    Chorley Pals 107
    Footballers' Battalion 126, 128
    Frontiersmen 201, 202
    Grimsby Chums 192
    Hull Pals 121, 164, 179
    Jewish battalions 202, 203
    Liverpool Pals 65, 82, 91, 95–9, 101, 103, 106, 108, 109, 115, 116, 126, 129, 131, 156, 195
    Leeds Pals 115–18, 119, 121, 179, 189
    London Welsh 156–7
    Lonsdale Battalion 99–102, 115, 190
    Manchester Pals 65, 95, 103–6, 156, 195
    McCrae's Battalion 127–8, 192
    Oldham Comrades 169
    Public Schools' Battalion 123, 124, 172
    Public Works Pioneers 170
    Salford Pals 105–6, 109, 141, 190
    Sheffield City Battalion 121, 122, 179, 189
    Sportsmen's Battalion 125–6
    Stockbrokers' Battalion 93–4
    Tyneside Commercials 132, 133
    Tyneside Irish 136, 192, 193, 194
    Tyneside Scottish 131–6, 192, 194
    Wandsworth Battalion 193, 194
    Young Citizen's Volunteers (YCV) 150
Pals magazine 159

Parliamentary Recruiting Committee (PRC) 24, 25, 29, 91, 103, 200
Pioneer battalions 121, 155, 169–70
Pipers 134, 135, 182
Pow-Wow, The 125
Priestly, Sir William MP 119
Punch 126, 162, 196

Recruiting
    Committees 8, 66, 81, 82, 91, 99, 103, 111, 112, 117, 122, 123, 129, 130, 132, 133, 134, 153, 154, 156, 158, 200
    Officers 34, 36, 37, 91, 111, 153
    Offices 24, 27, 30, 33–6, 37, 47, 83, 92, 94, 101, 105, 110, 114, 115, 116, 125, 129, 130, 137
    Posters 16, 24, 25, 27, 28, 29, 30, 32, 33, 99, 100, 103, 122, 125, 126, 145, 148, 198, 199, 203
    Statistics 30, 31, 33
    Trams 24, 27, 116, 139, 148, 169
Redmond, John MP 146, 151, 152
Redmond, Major William 152
Regimental depots 16, 19, 20, 39, 44, 47, 50, 77, 79, 82, 94, 103
Regimental system 19–20
Regiments
    Argyll & Sutherland Highlanders 46
    Black Watch 49, 183
    Border Regiment 101
    Cameron Highlanders 44, 183
    Cheshire Regiment 138, 139, 140
    Connaught Rangers 19, 146
    Duke of Wellington's Regiment 52, 53, 88, 94, 165, 166, 171, 174, 205
    Duke of Cornwall's Light Infantry 173
    Durham Light Infantry 119, 165, 173
    East Lancashire Regiment 107, 110
    East Surrey Regiment 142–4
    East Yorkshire Regiment 164
    Essex Regiment 128
    Gloucestershire Regiment 88, 129, 130, 131, 177
    Gordon Highlanders 18, 49, 164, 183
    Highland Light Infantry 113, 115, 190
    Inniskilling Fusiliers 150
    King's (Liverpool) Regiment 44, 96, 98, 140, 195
    King's Own Scottish Borderers 182, 203
    Lancashire Fusiliers 106, 109, 141, 177
    Leinster Regiment 146
    Lincolnshire Regiment 192

Loyal North Lancashire Regiment 178
Manchester Regiment 104, 105, 106, 107, 169, 177, 195
Middlesex Regiment 124, 128, 168, 170
Northumberland Fusiliers 131
Oxfordshire & Buckinghamshire Light Infantry 40, 47, 49, 88, 172
Royal Dublin Fusiliers 146
Royal Fusiliers 4, 62, 73, 75, 82, 86, 93–4, 123, 124, 125, 126, 127, 172, 201, 202, 203
Royal Irish Fusiliers 146
Royal Irish Rifles 150
Royal Munster Fusiliers 146
Royal Scots 128, 139, 140, 183, 192
Royal Warwickshire Regiment 107, 113, 114
Royal Welsh Fusiliers 153, 154, 155, 156, 157
South Wales Borderers 153, 155
Suffolk Regiment 52, 168, 192
Welsh Regiment 153, 154, 155
West Yorkshire Regiment 115, 118, 119, 121
York & Lancaster Regiment 121, 122
Yorkshire Regiment 176, 178
Rifle supply 48, 77, 87
Rifles
    Arisaka 87
    Drill Purpose (DP) 48, 74, 203
    Magazine Lee–Enfield (MLE, 'Long Lee') 68, 73–4, 76, 87, 98
    Ross 87
    Short, Magazine, Lee–Enfield (SMLE) 73–5, 86, 87, 88
Rosebery, Lord 139–41

Salisbury Plain 40, 44, 78, 81
Salonika 158
'Sausage' valley 192
Schwaben Redoubt 190, 191, 192
Serre 186, 188, 189, 190, 196
Service Battalions 7, 8, 40, 44, 46, 47, 50, 67, 68, 86, 93, 94, 96, 104, 107, 109, 113, 115, 119, 121, 123, 124, 126, 129, 137, 139, 141, 150, 151, 154, 157, 158, 160, 165, 170, 172, 182, 202, 203
Sheffield 121, 122, 179, 189
Simkins, Peter 5–9, 47, 107, 141, 192
Smith-Dorrien, General Sir H.L. 44
Somme, Battle of 9, 73, 96, 119, 161, 162, 167, 168, 175, 179, 180, 185–97, 198, 203, 204, 205

Special Reserve 39, 40, 47, 49, 77, 94, 153
Stanley, Brigadier General F.C. 65, 95, 195
Stanley Crest 96, 97, 106, 109
Stopford, General 176, 177
Suvla Bay 175, 176, 177, 179
'Swedish drill' 84–6
'Sweetheart brooches' 99, 101, 102, 161

'Terms of Service' 23, 39, 44
Territorial Associations 19, 20, 21, 101
Territorial Force (TF) 7, 8, 13, 19–22, 24, 39, 40, 42, 49, 55, 62, 65, 67, 77, 95, 107, 117, 120, 122, 142, 153, 154, 179, 181, 182, 189, 205
Thiepval 119, 174, 187, 189, 190, 191, 197, 204
Tickler, Thomas MP 198
'Tower Bridge' 182
Training 8, 21, 37, 42, 45 46, 47, 52, 58, 59, 63, 74, 77–91, 119, 121, 122, 133, 162, 163, 169, 170, 203, 204
Trench warfare 164–75, 202, 204
Tunstill, Captain Harry Gilbert 50–2
Tunstill's Men 50–3, 88, 94, 165, 166, 205
Tyneside 131–7, 192, 193, 194, 196

'Ulster Covenant' 146
Ulster Tower 192
Ulster Volunteer Force (UVF) 148–52
University and Public Schools Brigade (UPS) 59, 79, 122–5

Verdun, Battle of 186
Vermelles 182
Volunteer Battalions 13, 19

Wallace, Edgar 24, 26, 33, 35, 36, 83, 94
War Office 8, 9, 12, 13, 24, 39, 55, 81, 87, 91, 101, 105, 121, 127, 128, 132, 133, 136, 137, 138, 139, 142, 146, 153, 154, 157, 179, 180, 200
Welsh Army Corps 65, 66, 152–61
Welsh Army Corps National Executive Committee (WNEC) 154
West Ham FC 128
'White feather' 55, 56, 110, 111, 131, 152
'Wonderwork' (Wundt-werk) 190

YMCA 80, 81
Ypres Salient 52, 171, 173, 181